POLYARCHY

POLYARCHY

Participation and Opposition

by Robert A. Dahl

New Haven and London, Yale University Press

Library of Congress catalog card number: 70–140524
ISBN: 0–300–01391–4 (cloth);
0–300–01565–8 (paper)

Designed by Sally Hargrove Sullivan
and set in Times Roman type.
Printed in the United States of America by
LithoCrafters, Inc., Chelsea, Michigan.

Published in Great Britain, Europe, Africa, and
Asia (except Japan) by Yale University Press,
Ltd., London. Distributed in Australia and
New Zealand by Book & Film Services, Artarmon,
N.S.W., Australia; and in Japan by Harper & Row,
Publishers, Tokyo Office.

To the memory of
Mary
and her hopes

CONTENTS

ACKNOWLEDGMENTS

I wish to express my appreciation to the Rockefeller Foundation for financial support that has helped to make possible this volume and others I have undertaken on the subject of governments and oppositions. I am also indebted to the Concilium of Yale University for financial assistance from the Henry L. Stimson Fund for Research in World Affairs and to Yale University for a Senior Faculty Fellowship that enabled me to complete the manuscript.

The comments of a number of colleagues who have read various drafts in whole or in part have been particularly helpful. These include Frederick Barghoorn, Robert Dix, William Foltz, Michael Leiserson, Rajni Kothari, Juan Linz, and Gordon Skilling, all of whom are coauthors of a companion volume, *Regimes and Oppositions,* and also Hans Daalder, Joseph LaPalombara, Val Lorwin, Nelson Polsby, and Stein Rokkan. I wish to thank students in my graduate and undergraduate courses for allowing themselves to be subjected to a draft of the manuscript and providing reactions that were often extremely useful.

For the patience, skill, and speed with which they transformed my drafts into readable typescript, I wish to express both my thanks and my admiration to Mrs. Betty Mauceri, Mrs. Miriam Swanson, and Mrs. Nancy Hoskins. And once again I have increased my debt to Mrs. Marian Ash for her editorial supervision at the Yale University Press.

R.A.D.

1. DEMOCRATIZATION
AND PUBLIC OPPOSITION

Given a regime in which the opponents of the government cannot openly and legally organize into political parties in order to oppose the government in free and fair elections, what conditions favor or impede a transformation into a regime in which they can? That is the question with which this book is concerned.

Concepts

Since the development of a political system that allows for opposition, rivalry, or competition between a government and its opponents is an important aspect of democratization, this book is necessarily about one aspect of democratization. But the two processes—democratization and the development of public opposition—are not, in my view, identical. A full description of the differences could lead us into a tedious exploration of a semantic bog. To avoid this detour, I hope I may be allowed to indicate rather summarily some of my assumptions without much in the way of defense or elaboration.

I assume that a key characteristic of a democracy is the continuing responsiveness of the government to the preferences of its citizens, considered as political equals. What other characteristics might be required for a system to be strictly democratic, I do not intend to consider here. In this book I should like to reserve the term "democracy" for a political system one of the characteristics of which is the quality of being completely or almost completely responsive to all its citizens. Whether such a system actually exists, has existed, or can exist need not concern us for the moment. Surely one can conceive a hypothetical system of this kind; such a conception has served as an ideal, or part of an ideal, for many people. As a hypothetical system, one end of a scale, or a limiting state of affairs, it can (like a perfect vacuum) serve as a basis for estimating the degree to which various systems approach this theoretical limit.

I assume further that in order for a government to continue over a period of time to be responsive to the preferences of its citizens, considered as political equals, all full citizens must have unimpaired opportunities:

1. To formulate their preferences
2. To signify their preferences to their fellow citizens and the government by individual and collective action
3. To have their preferences weighed equally in the conduct of the government, that is, weighted with no discrimination because of the content or source of the preference

These, then, appear to me to be three necessary conditions for a democracy, though they are probably not sufficient. Next, I assume that for these three opportunities to exist among a large number of people, such as the number of people who comprise most nation-states at the present time, the institutions of the society must provide at least eight guarantees. These are indicated in table 1.1.

I am going to make the further assumption that the connections between the guarantees and the three fundamental opportunities are sufficiently evident to need no further elaboration here.[1]

Table 1.1. Some Requirements for a Democracy
among a Large Number of People

For the opportunity to:	The following institutional guarantees are required:
I. Formulate preferences	1. Freedom to form and join organizations 2. Freedom of expression 3. Right to vote 4. Right of political leaders to compete for support 5. Alternative sources of information
II. Signify preferences	1. Freedom to form and join organizations 2. Freedom of expression 3. Right to vote 4. Eligibility for public office 5. Right of political leaders to compete for support 6. Alternative sources of information 7. Free and fair elections
III. Have preferences weighted equally in conduct of government	1. Freedom to form and join organizations 2. Freedom of expression 3. Right to vote 4. Eligibility for public office 5. Right of political leaders to compete for support 5a. Right of political leaders to compete for votes 6. Alternative sources of information 7. Free and fair elections 8. Institutions for making government policies depend on votes and other expressions of preference

Now from examination of the list of eight institutional guarantees, it appears that they might provide us with a theoretical scale along which it would be possible to order

1. Some of the relationships are discussed in my *A Preface to Democratic Theory* (Chicago: University of Chicago Press, 1956), pp. 63–81, and in Robert A. Dahl and Charles E. Lindblom, *Politics, Economics and Welfare* (New York: Harper, 1953), chaps. 10 and 11.

different political systems. Upon closer examination, however, it appears that the eight guarantees might be fruitfully interpreted as constituting two somewhat different theoretical dimensions of democratization.

1. Both historically and at the present time, regimes vary enormously in the extent to which the eight institutional conditions are openly available, publicly employed, and fully guaranteed to at least some members of the political system who wish to contest the conduct of the government. Thus a scale reflecting these eight conditions would enable us to compare different regimes according to the extent of permissible opposition, public contestation, or political competition.[2] However, since a regime might permit opposition to a very small or a very large proportion of the population, clearly we need a second dimension.

2. Both historically and contemporaneously, regimes also vary in the proportion of the population entitled to participate on a more or less equal plane in controlling and contesting the conduct of the government: to participate, so to speak, in the system of public contestation. A scale reflecting the breadth of the right to participate in public contestation would enable us to compare different regimes according to their inclusiveness.

The right to vote in free and fair elections, for example, partakes of both dimensions. When a regime grants this right to some of its citizens, it moves toward greater public contestation. But the larger the proportion of citizens who enjoy the right, the more inclusive the regime.

Public contestation and inclusiveness vary somewhat independently. Britain had a highly developed system of public contestation by the end of the eighteenth century, but only a miniscule fraction of the population was fully included in

2. Throughout this book the terms liberalization, political competition, competitive politics, public contestation, and public opposition are used interchangeably to refer to this dimension, and regimes relatively high on this dimension are frequently referred to as competitive regimes.

it until after the expansion of the suffrage in 1867 and 1884. Switzerland has one of the most fully developed systems of public contestation in the world. Probably few people would challenge the view that the Swiss regime is highly "democratic." Yet the feminine half of the Swiss population is still excluded from national elections. By contrast, the USSR still has almost no system of public contestation, though it does have universal suffrage. In fact one of the most striking changes during this century has been the virtual disappearance of an outright denial of the legitimacy of popular participation in government. Only a handful of countries have failed to grant at least a ritualistic vote to their citizens and to hold at least nominal elections; even the most repressive dictators usually pay some lip service today to the legitimate right of the people to participate in the government, that is, to participate in "governing" though not in public contestation.

Needless to say, in the absence of the right to oppose the right to "participate" is stripped of a very large part of the significance it has in a country where public contestation exists. A country with universal suffrage and a completely repressive government would provide fewer opportunities for oppositions, surely, than a country with a narrow suffrage but a highly tolerant government. Consequently, when countries are ranked solely according to their inclusiveness, not taking into account the surrounding circumstances, the results are anomalous. Nonetheless, as long as we keep clearly in mind the fact that the extent of the "suffrage" or, more generally, the right to participate indicates only *one* characteristic of systems, a characteristic that cannot be interpreted except in the context of other characteristics, it is useful to distinguish between regimes according to their inclusiveness.

Suppose, then, that we think of democratization as made up of at least two dimensions: public contestation and the right to participate. (Figure 1.1) Doubtless most readers believe that democratization involves more than these two di-

mensions; in a moment I shall discuss a third dimension. But
I propose to limit the discussion here to these two. For the
point has already emerged, I think: developing a system of
public contestation is not necessarily equivalent to full democratization.

To display the relationship between public contestation
and democratization more clearly, let us now lay out the

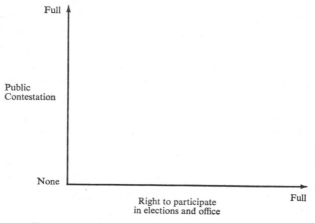

FIGURE 1.1 Two Theoretical Dimensions
of Democratization

two dimensions as in figure 1.2.[3] Since a regime may be
located, theoretically, anywhere in the space bounded by the
two dimensions, it is at once obvious that our terminology
for regimes is almost hopelessly inadequate, for it is a terminology invariably based upon classifying rather than ranking. The space enclosed by our two dimensions could of
course be cut up into any number of cells, each of which
might be given a name. But the purposes of this book make
an elaborate typology redundant. Let me instead provide a
small vocabulary—a reasonable one, I hope—that will en-

3. An array of 114 countries along these two dimensions will be
found in appendix A, table A-1.

able me to speak precisely enough about the kinds of changes in regimes that I want to discuss.
    Let me call a regime near the lower left corner of figure 1.2 a closed hegemony. If a hegemonic regime shifts upward, as along path I, then it is moving toward greater public contestation. Without stretching language too far, one could say that a change in this direction involves the liberalization

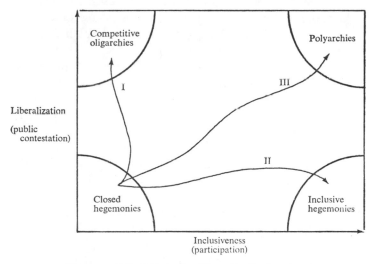

FIGURE 1.2 Liberalization, Inclusiveness, and Democratization

of a regime; alternatively one might say that the regime becomes more competitive. If a regime changes to provide greater participation, as along path II, it might be said to change toward greater popularization, or that it is becoming inclusive. A regime might change along one dimension and not the other. If we call a regime near the upper left corner a competitive oligarchy, then path I represents a change from a closed hegemony to a competitive oligarchy. But a closed hegemony might also become more inclusive without liberalizing, i.e., without increasing the opportunities for public contestation, as along path II. In this case the regime changes from a closed to an inclusive hegemony. Democracy might be conceived of as lying at the upper right corner. But since democracy may involve more dimensions than the two in figure 1.2, and since (in my view) no large system in the real world is fully democratized, I prefer to call real world systems that are closest to the upper right corner polyarchies. Any change in a regime that moves it upward and to the right, for example along path III, may be said to represent some degree of democratization. Polyarchies, then, may be thought of as relatively (but incompletely) democratized regimes, or, to put it in another way, polyarchies are regimes that have been substantially popularized and liberalized, that is, highly inclusive and extensively open to public contestation.

You will notice that although I have given names to regimes lying near the four corners, the large space in the middle of the figure is not named, nor is it subdivided. The absence of names partly reflects the historic tendency to classify regimes in terms of extreme types; it also reflects my own desire to avoid redundant terminology. The lack of nomenclature does not mean a lack of regimes; in fact, perhaps the preponderant number of national regimes in the world today would fall into the mid-area. Many significant changes in regimes, then, involve shifts within, into, or out of this important central area, as these regimes become more (or less) inclusive and increase (or reduce) opportunities for public contestation. In order to refer to regimes in this large middle area, I shall sometimes resort to the terms near or nearly: a nearly hegemonic regime has somewhat more opportunities for public contestation than a hegemonic regime; a near-polyarchy could be quite inclusive but would have more severe restrictions on public contestation than a full polyarchy, or it might provide opportunities for public contestation comparable to those of a full polyarchy and yet be somewhat less inclusive.[4]

The need to use terms like these later on in this book testifies to the utility of classification; the arbitrariness of the boundaries between "full" and "near" testifies to the inadequacy of any classification. So long as we keep firmly in mind that the terms are useful but rather arbitrary ways of dividing up the space in figure 1.2, the concepts will serve their purpose.

4. The problem of terminology is formidable, since it seems impossible to find terms already in use that do not carry with them a large freight of ambiguity and surplus meaning. The reader should remind himself that the terms used here are employed throughout the book, to the best of my ability, only with the meanings indicated in the preceding paragraphs. Some readers will doubtless resist the term polyarchy as an alternative to the word democracy, but it is important to maintain the distinction between democracy as an ideal system and the institutional arrangements that have come to be regarded as a kind of imperfect approximation of an ideal, and experience shows, I believe, that when the same term is used for both, needless confusion and essentially irrelevant semantic arguments get in the way of the analysis. At the opposite corner, hegemony is not altogether satisfactory; yet given the meaning I have indicated, the term hegemonic seems to me more appropriate than hierarchical, monocratic, absolutist, autocratic, despotic, authoritarian, totalitarian, etc. My use of the term "contestation" in "public contestation" is well within normal (if infrequent) English usage; in English contestation means to contest, which means to make something the subject of dispute, contention, or litigation, and its most immediate synonyms are to dispute, challenge, or vie. The utility of the term was, however, first suggested to me by Bertrand de Jouvenel's "The Means of Contestation," *Government and Opposition* 1 (January 1966): 155–74. Jouvenel's usage is similar to my own, as is the identical French term he used in the original, meaning: *débat, objection, conflit, opposition.* In the same issue of this journal, however, Ghita Ionescu ("Control and Contestation in Some One-Party States" pp. 240–50) uses the term in its narrower but currently quite common meaning as "the anti-system, basic and permanent postulates of any opposition on the grounds of fundamental, dichotomic differences of opinion and ideologies" (p. 241). Clearly this is a more restricted definition of the concept than the one I use here and that, I believe, Jouvenel uses in his essay.

The Question Restated

The question with which this chapter opens can now be restated as follows:

1. What conditions increase or decrease the chances of democratizing a hegemonic or nearly hegemonic regime?
2. More specifically, what factors increase or decrease the chances of public contestation?
3. Even more specifically, what factors increase or decrease the chances of public contestation in a highly inclusive regime, that is, a polyarchy?

Qualifications

This book, then, is about the conditions under which systems of public contestation are likely to develop and exist. Because public contestation is an aspect of democratization, this book is necessarily to some extent about democratization, as I noted at the beginning of this chapter. But it is important to keep in mind that the focus here excludes a number of important matters that would be considered in an analysis of democratization.

It is convenient to think of democratization as consisting of several broad historical transformations. One is the transformation of hegemonies and competitive oligarchies into near-polyarchies. This was, in essence, the process at work in the Western world during the nineteenth century. A second is the transformation of near-polyarchies into full polyarchies. This was what occurred in Europe in the three decades or so that spanned the end of the last century and the First World War. A third is the further democratization of full polyarchies. This historical process can perhaps be dated to the rapid development of the democratic welfare state after the onset of the Great Depression; interrupted by the Second World War, the process seems to have renewed itself in the late 1960s in the form of rapidly rising demands, notably among young people, for the democratization of a variety of social institutions.

This book is concerned with the first and second of these transformations but not the third.[5] Whether it prospers or fails, the third wave of democratization will surely prove as important as the others. Since it will take place only in the most "advanced" countries and will help to shape the character of life in the "advanced" countries in the twenty-first century, to many people in these countries the third wave may well seem more important than the others. Yet most of the world still lies beyond the possibility of this particular transformation. Of the 140 nominally independent countries existing in 1969, about two dozen were highly inclusive and had highly developed systems of public contestation: they were, in short, inclusive polyarchies. Perhaps another dozen or fewer were near-polyarchies within reasonable reach of full polyarchy. It is in these three dozen countries that the third wave must occur. Whether some nonpolyarchies can overleap the institutions of polyarchy and arrive somehow at a fuller democratization than now exists in the polyarchies, as ideologues sometimes promise, seems remote, in the light of the analysis that follows. For most countries, then, the first and second stages of democratization—not the third—will be the most relevant.

The focus of this book is, in fact, even narrower than an analysis of the first two stages of democratization. I have referred to "regimes" and "systems of public contestation." But so far I have not specified the level of the polity at which regimes and public contestation may be effective. Let me then emphasize at once that the analysis here deals with national regimes, that is, regimes taken at the level of the

5. I have dealt with some aspects of the third in *After the Revolution? Authority in a Good Society* (New Haven: Yale University Press, 1970).

country, or, if you will, the legally independent state, or, to use less appropriate terms, the nation or the nation-state. Doubtless some of the analysis could be applied to subordinate levels of political and social organization, such as municipalities, provinces, trade unions, firms, churches, and the like; perhaps some of it might even be relevant to the polities that are emerging at more inclusive levels—international organizations of various kinds. But the argument is specifically developed only with respect to national regimes.

Again, this would be a grave omission in a book about democratization. Even from the perspective of public contestation, the omission is important. For casual observation suggests that countries differ in the extent to which they furnish opportunities for contestation and participation in the processes not only of the national government but of various subordinate governmental and social organizations as well. Now to the extent that gross differences in the general characteristics of subnational units appear to be associated with differences in the nature of the national regime (for example, whether it is a polyarchy or not), I shall try to take these into account in the analysis.

Yet it might seem reasonable to insist that the analysis ought to go a good deal further. A full description of the opportunities available for participation and contestation within a country surely requires one to say something about the opportunities available within subnational units. The extraordinary attempt in Yugoslavia to grant a large measure of self-government in subnational units means that the opportunities for participation and contestation are greater in that country, despite the one-party regime, than, let us say, in Argentina or Brazil. An inclusive view of the matter, then, would require one to pay attention to all the possibilities suggested in figure 1.3. Indeed a number of recent critics of incomplete democratization in polyarchies contend that while polyarchies may be competitive at the national level a great many of the subnational organizations, particularly private associations, are hegemonic or oligarchic.[6]

Important as the task is of moving beyond the description of the national regime to the subnational units, at present the attempt to examine a fairly large number of countries would I think require an analysis so complex and would encounter problems of data so overwhelming as to make the

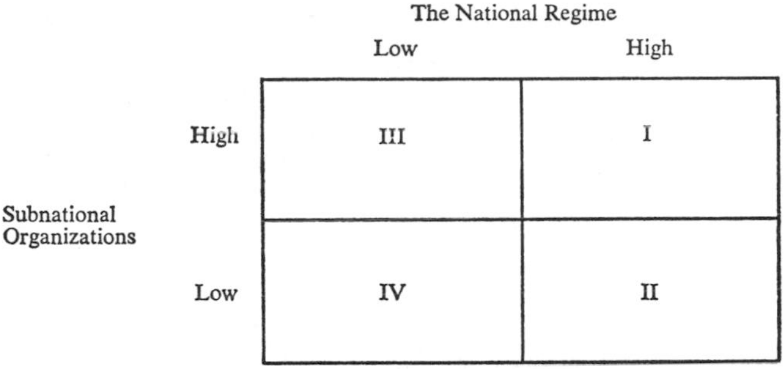

The National Regime

		Low	High
High		III	I
Subnational Organizations			
Low		IV	II

I. Fully "liberalized" or "competitive" regimes
II. Competitive at the national level, hegemonic within subnational organizations
III. Competitive within subnational organizations, hegemonic at the national level
IV. Fully hegemonic polities

FIGURE 1.3 A Hypothetical Ordering of Countries According to the Opportunities Available for Contestation

enterprise highly unsatisfactory. In principle, to be sure, subnational orgnizations could be located along the two dimensions illustrated in figures 1.1 and 1.2. Yet the problem is not simply to locate countries in the hypothetical space suggested by figure 1.3. For one thing, that space has to do with only one of the two main dimensions: contestation. Ob-

6. Cf. in particular Grant McConnell, *Private Power and American Democracy* (New York: Knopf, 1966); Henry S. Kariel, *The Decline of American Pluralism* (Stanford: Stanford University Press, 1961); and to some extent also Robert Paul Wolff, *The Poverty of Liberalism* (Boston: Beacon Press, 1968).

viously a similar procedure would be required for the other
main dimension: participation. What is more, even within
a country, subnational units often vary in the opportunities
they provide for contestation and participation. For example,
in many modern countries these opportunities are much
greater in municipal governments than in trade unions, and
greater in trade unions than in business firms. Consequently,
one would have to break subnational units into a number of
categories: business firms, trade unions, municipal governments, churches, educational institutions, etc.[7] At this stage,
these requirements are, unfortunately, little short of utopian,
and it is for this reason—pragmatic rather than theoretical
—that I have decided to restrict my attention to the national level.

Assumptions

When hegemonic regimes and competitive oligarchies
move toward polyarchy they increase the opportunities for
effective participation and contestation and hence the number of individuals, groups, and interests whose preferences
have to be considered in policy making.

From the perspective of the incumbents who currently
govern, such a transformation carries with it new possibilities
of conflict as a result of which their goals (and they themselves) may be displaced by spokesmen for the newly incorporated individuals, groups, or interests.

The problem of their opponents is the mirror image of
the problem of the incumbents. Any transformation that
provides opponents of the government with greater opportunities to translate their goals into policies enforced by the

7. The already classic study by Seymour Martin Lipset, Martin A.
Trow, and James S. Coleman, *Union Democracy* (Glencoe: The
Free Press, 1956), concentrates on the deviant case of a trade union
in which contestation and participation are high. To describe and
explain that deviant case within the context of a single country was
a very sizable undertaking.

state carries with it the possibility of conflict with spokesmen for the individuals, groups, or interests they displace in the government.

Thus the greater the conflict between government and opposition, the more likely that each will seek to deny opportunities to the other to participate effectively in policy making. To put it another way, the greater the conflict between a government and its opponents, the more costly it is for each to tolerate the other. Since the opposition must gain control of the state in order to suppress the incumbents (at which point opposition and government have changed roles), we can formulate the general proposition as an axiom about governments tolerating their opponents:

> AXIOM 1. *The likelihood that a government will tolerate an opposition increases as the expected costs of toleration decrease.*

However, a government must also consider how costly it would be to suppress an opposition; for even if toleration is costly, suppression might be very much more costly and hence obviously foolish. Therefore:

> AXIOM 2. *The likelihood that a government will tolerate an opposition increases as the expected costs of suppression increase.*

Thus the chances that a more competitive political system will emerge, or endure, may be thought of as depending on these two sets of costs:

> AXIOM 3. *The more the costs of suppression exceed the costs of toleration, the greater the chance for a competitive regime.*

Axiom 3 can be illustrated graphically as in figure 1.4.

The lower the costs of toleration, the greater the security of the government. The greater the costs of suppression, the

---

greater the security of the opposition. Hence conditions that provide a high degree of mutual security for government and oppositions would tend to generate and to preserve wider opportunities for oppositions to contest the conduct of the government.

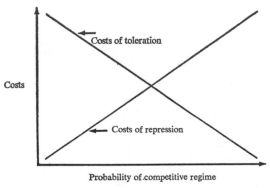

Probability of competitive regime

FIGURE 1.4

The question posed a moment ago can therefore be restated:

> What circumstances significantly increase the mutual security of government and oppositions and thereby increase the chances of public contestation and polyarchy?

But before I try to answer that question, let me first consider a prior one: does polyarchy matter?

2. DOES POLYARCHY MATTER?

Some readers might be inclined to think that differences in national regimes do not matter much. For example, one might share the view of those like Gaetano Mosca who argue that every regime is, after all, dominated by a ruling minority. As an astringent challenge to the belief that portentous consequences for the people of a country must necessarily follow a transformation of the regime, Mosca's skepticism has a good deal to be said for it. Moreover, what appear superficially to be changes of regime are sometimes not really changes in regime at all, but simply changes in personnel, rhetoric, and empty constitutional prescriptions.

Yet few people seem able to adhere consistently to the view that differences in regimes—for example, differences between polyarchy and inclusive hegemony—are at base negligible. In fact, I have the impression that this view is most often espoused by intellectuals who are, at heart, liberal or radical democrats disappointed by the transparent failures of polyarchies or near-polyarchies; and that, conversely, intellectuals who have actually experienced life under severely repressive hegemonic regimes rarely argue that differences in regime are trivial. Perhaps the most telling examples are furnished by Italian intellectuals like Mosca and Croce who spent their lives attacking the sorry and patently defective parliamentary regime that existed in Italy before Fascism.

17

Although during the seventy years between unification and Fascism the Italian polity traversed the classic path from competitive oligarchy to inclusive polyarchy, the defects of *trasformismo* in political affairs and the general *incivismo* of Italians in public life were too glaring to enable the parliamentary regime to win much support. Yet even this highly defective regime was, Mosca saw, different in important essentials from Fascism—and what is more, unworthy though it may have been, better than Fascism. In his last speech to the Italian Senate in 1925, Mosca confessed that he spoke

> with a certain emotion because, let us be frank, we take part in the funeral rites of a form of government. I should not have thought it possible that I would be the one to deliver the funeral oration on the parliamentary regime . . . I, who have always taken a harsh attitude toward it, I am today obliged to lament its departure . . . One may say in all sincerity: the parliamentary regime was better.

But he was not permitted to drink the bitter potion in one grand gesture of regret, for he lived until 1941 and thus witnessed all but the final disintegration of that wretched new order. As for Croce, who first welcomed Fascism, he was finally to admit that all during the time he had been pouring out his contempt for the parliamentary regime,

> it had never seemed to him even remotely possible that Italy could let herself be robbed of the liberty that had cost her so much and that his generation had considered a permanent acquisition.

And by 1945, Gaetano Salvemini, who as an intellectual of radical persuasion had been a fierce critic of Giolitti's Italy, had no doubt that for all its defects the parliamentary regime was far better in actuality and in potential than what came later. "As for the results of the Fascist dictatorship in contrast with those of Italian democracy in the making," he concluded, "they are here before our very eyes. Let us hope that the Italians will not be the only ones to learn from that frightful experience." [1]

Although eyewitness testimony of this kind does not prove the point, it cautions against accepting the easy notion that changes of political regime do not matter very much. To analyze in a responsible way the extent to which, and the conditions under which, changes of regimes "matter" would, I fear, require a book, and I intend to forgo that effort in this one. Moreover, if theory and data are far from satis-

1. The quotation from Mosca is in James Meisel, *The Myth of the Ruling Class* (Ann Arbor: University of Michigan Press, 1958), pp. 225–26. That from Croce is in Giovanni Sartori, *Democratic Theory* (Detroit: Wayne State University Press, 1962), p. 37; Croce's early acceptance of fascism is discussed in Sartori, *Croce Etico-Politico e Filosofo della Liberta* (Florence: Universita degli Studi, n.d.), pp. 191 ff. Salvemini's statement is from the introductory essay to A. William Salamone, *Italy in the Giolittian Era: Italian Democracy in the Making, 1900–1914* (Philadelphia: University of Pennsylvania Press, 1945, 1960). Salvemini's brief essay in effect argues that representative government as it was emerging in Italy compared not too unfavorably with England and the United States. His judgment is summed up by his statement that "Italian democracy would have needed still another generation of trial and error before becoming not a 'perfect democracy' but a 'less imperfect democracy.' The crisis that followed the First World War, however, was fatal to the democratic process." (p. xx) Salvemini goes on to say:

Looking back at the work of the crusader after thirty years, I find that I have nothing to regret. I must acknowledge, however, that I would have been wiser had I been more moderate in my criticism of the Giolittian system. My knowledge of the men who came after Giolitti in Italy as well as of countries in which I have lived during the last twenty years has convinced me that if Giolitti was not better, neither was he worse than many non-Italian politicians who followed him. For while we Italian crusaders attacked him from the Left accusing him of being—and he was—a corrupter of Italian democracy in the making, others assailed him from the Right because he was even too democratic for their taste. Our criticism thus did not help to direct the evolution of Italian public life toward less imperfect forms of democracy, but rather toward the victory of those militarist, nationalist, and reactionary groups who had found even Giolitti's democracy too perfect.

factory for determining the conditions most favorable to the development of different regimes, they are in an even more deplorable state with respect to the differences in the consequences (in the recent argot of political science, "outputs") of different regimes. Nonetheless, there are good reasons for thinking that a transformation of a regime from a hegemony into a more competitive regime or a competitive oligarchy into a polyarchy does have significant results.

1. To begin with, there are the classic liberal freedoms that are a part of the definition of public contestation and participation: opportunities to oppose the government, form political organizations, express oneself on political matters without fear of governmental reprisals, read and hear alternative points of view, vote by secret ballot in elections in which candidates of different parties compete for votes and after which the losing candidates peacefully yield their claim to office to the winners, etc. In the well-established polyarchies, these freedoms have long since lost the attraction of a new cause, let alone any revolutionary appeal. Familiar, imperfectly achieved, clearly insufficient to insure a good society, trivialized over many generations by rhetorical overkill, they are easily taken for granted as an inheritance of quite modest significance. Their value no doubt appears greater to those who have lost them or have never had them. It was liberties of this kind that critics of the pre-Fascist parliamentary regime in Italy like Mosca, Croce, and Salvemini took so much for granted that they failed to foresee how oppressive Italy would become under a new regime. It was largely to expand freedoms of this kind that the liberalizing forces were moving in Czechoslovakia before their revolution was halted and reversed by the Soviets. To gain liberties like these for Spain is the one goal that many of the oppositions to Franco's dictatorship have shared.

2. Broadened participation combined with political competition brings about a change in the composition of the po-

litical leadership, particularly among those who gain office by means of elections—mainly, then, members of parliament. As new groups are granted the suffrage, candidates closer in their social characteristics to the newly incorporated strata win a greater share of elective offices. Thus when the narrow suffrage of a competitive oligarchy has been extended to the middle classes, the number of party leaders and members of parliament drawn from the middle classes has increased. Something of the same kind has occurred when the working classes have been enfranchised, particularly in countries where labor or socialist parties have acquired a large share of working-class votes.[2] When Reconstruction provided southern Negroes with the suffrage after the American Civil War, black Southerners for the first time began to hold office; when Reconstruction came to an end, blacks dis-

2. There is a wealth of evidence about these changes, but so far as I am aware no comparative analysis. Systematic, long-range studies include Mattei Dogan, "Political Ascent in a Class Society: French Deputies 1870–1958," in Dwaine Marvick, ed., *Political Decision-Makers: Recruitment and Performance* (Glencoe: The Free Press, 1961), pp. 57–90; and W. L. Guttsman, *The British Political Elite* (London, MacGibbon and Key, 1963). For the changes brought about in Britain after 1832, the evidence is ample but apparently unsystematic. However, compare Sir Lewis Namier's data on members of Parliament from the boroughs in 1761 in *The Structure of Politics at the Accession of George III*, 2d ed. (London: Macmillan, 1961), pp. 84 ff., with W. Ivor Jennings, *Parliament* (Cambridge: Cambridge University Press, 1939), table II, p. 38, and with Guttsman, *The British Political Elite*. For changes in the occupational and social class composition of the Italian parliament from 1909 to 1963 (universal suffrage was introduced in 1913 and proportional representation in 1919), see S. Somogyi, L. Lotti, A. Predieri, and G. Sartori, *Il Parlamento Italiano, 1946–1963* (Naples: Edizioni Scientifiche Italiane, 1963), pp. 160–62, 168–69, and 197–200.

For differences in Argentina between the socioeconomic levels of parliamentarians from the conservative parties that had dominated parliament before universal suffrage in 1911, and from the Radical and Socialist parties that had a majority of seats after the elections of 1916, see Darío Canton, "Universal suffrage as an Agent of Mobilization" (paper presented to the VIth World Congress of Sociology, Evian, France, September 1966), p. 24.

appeared from public life. When they began to regain the suffrage after the passage of the Civil Rights Act of 1964, they once again began to win public offices.[3]

This is not to say that political leadership and parliaments ever become a representative sample of the various socio-economic strata, occupations, or other groupings in a society. They never do. In contemporary legislative bodies, middle-class and professional occupations are numerically over-represented; blue collar occupations are numerically under-represented (even among representatives of labor, socialist, and communist parties) as are many other categories—farmers and housewives, for example.[4] Even if the "political

---

3. Negro suffrage and its results under Reconstruction are discussed in C. Vann Woodward, *The Burden of Southern History* (New York: Vintage Books, 1960), pp. 98–103. For the recent period, data from the Voter Education Project, Southern Regional Council, show that by the summer of 1968 the percentages of Negroes registered to vote had enormously increased. The percentages, with corresponding percentages of whites registered shown in parentheses, were: Alabama, 56.7 (82.5); Arkansas, 67.5 (75.2); Florida, 62.1 (83.8); Georgia, 56.1 (84.7); Louisiana, 59.3 (87.9); Mississippi, 59.4 (92.4); North Carolina, 55.3 (78.7); South Carolina, 50.8 (65.6); Tennessee, 72.6 (81.3); Texas, 83.1 (72.3); Virginia, 58.4 (67.0). For these states as a whole the totals were 62.0 (78.1). Southern Regional Council, Voter Education Project, "Voter Registration in the South, Summer, 1968" (Atlanta: Southern Regional Council, 1968). By the summer of 1969, some 473 black officials had been elected in southern states, including 17 mayors and 200 city councilmen. "Black Elected Officials in the Southern States," a memorandum to selected members of the American Political Science Association, August 12, 1969, from Emory F. Via, Director, Labor Program, Southern Regional Council, Inc.
4. On Britain, see W. L. Guttsman, "Changes in British Labour Leadership," in *Political Decision-Makers;* pp. 91–137. For data on candidates for and members of the House of Commons in the 1950s and 1960s, see J. Blondel, *Voters, Parties, and Leaders* (Baltimore: Penguin, 1963), pp. 135–45, and Peter G. J. Pulzer, *Political Representation and Elections, Parties and Voting in Great Britain* (New York: Praeger, 1967), pp. 67 ff.
For the postwar Italian parliament, see Sartori et al., *Il Parlaimento Italiano,* pp. 93–97. For Belgian members of parliament in 1964, see F. Debuyst, *La Fonction Parlementaire en Belgique: Mecanismes d'Access et Images* (Brussels: CRISP, 1966), pp. 90–

class" is never a fair sample of a country's social and economic categories—and many advocates of representative democracy would argue that it need not and should not be[5] —a broadening of the suffrage together with political competition does nonetheless make parliaments in particular and political leadership in general considerably less unrepresentative in the purely statistical sense.

3. As a system becomes more competitive or more inclusive, politicians seek the support of groups that can now participate more easily in political life. The response of politicians to the existence of new opportunities for participation and public contestation are manifold and have far-reaching effects. I have just described one of these: to offer candidates whom the voters feel are in some sense "closer" to themselves. Another is to adapt rhetoric, program, policy, and ideology to what are thought to be the desires or interests of the groups, segments, or strata not hitherto represented. Thus the rise of socialist and labor parties in Western Europe is intimately tied to the grant of the suffrage to urban and rural working strata. When, as was true in many countries that are now polyarchies, political parties were relatively free to organize before the suffrage had been broadened, among the first demands of socialist and labor parties was universal suffrage. Once the working classes had the vote, naturally these parties initially directed most of their efforts to mobilizing these strata.

Competition and inclusiveness bring about changes in the party system itself. The most drastic and visible changes occur, of course, when a one-party hegemonic regime is rapidly replaced by a polyarchy: the hegemony of the single

---

109. Debuyst also has tables comparing the professional backgrounds of members of the national legislatures in Belgium, France, Britain, Italy, and the U.S. (Senate) (p. 110), and the percentages in various European socialist and communist parties of M.P.'s from lower middle or working-class occupations or party functionaries (p. 113).
5. E.g., Hanna Fenichel Pitkin, *The Concept of Representation* (Berkeley: University of California Press, 1967), chap. 4, pp. 60–91.

party suddenly gives way to two or more competing parties, as in Italy, Germany, and Japan at the end of World War II. Countries in which opportunities for participation and contestation expand over a lengthier period of time display somewhat similar developments in slow motion. When the suffrage moves beyond the notables and their clients, the old parties and factions based mainly on the social connections among the notables—on ties of family, class, residence, life style, and tradition—are displaced or supplemented by parties more effective in appealing to the middle classes. The process is repeated again when the working classes are granted the suffrage. In Britain, the old Whigs gave way to the Liberals after the Reform Act of 1832; the Reform Acts of 1867 and 1884 facilitated the formation and growth of the Labor party. In Norway, the struggle over the mobilization of the peasantry in the 1860s and 1870s led to the development of electoral and parliamentary coalitions of the Left and the Right. The struggle over manhood suffrage and its achievement in 1900 produced new parties. While the old Right became the Conservative party, the old Left alliance fragmented into its main components of Liberals, rural Christian fundamentalists, and farmers, while the Labor party acquired a large share of the working classes.[6] Although the details vary from country to country, a similar pattern seems to emerge wherever polyarchy has evolved over a considerable period of time.

The parties also change in structure and organization. As has often been pointed out, the need to mobilize a bigger electorate triggers off the development of "modern" party organizations. For as the electorate grows, the traditional, mainly informal arrangements that worked well enough with a tiny group of voters (many of whom were in any case

6. Cf. Stein Rokkan, "Norway: Numerical Democracy and Corporate Pluralism" in Robert A. Dahl, ed., *Political Oppositions in Western Democracies* (New Haven: Yale University Press, 1966), pp. 70–115, esp. pp. 75–81.

under the thumb of the notables) are simply inadequate. If a party is to survive in the new competition, it must reach out to its members, followers, and potential voters with organizations at the level of ward, section, cell, and the like. Many of these now familiar forms of party organization were initially developed in the country where mass suffrage was first established—the United States—but they rapidly appear wherever political competition takes place in the midst of a broad suffrage. In Britain, for example, the formation of local Conservative and Liberal associations, and the famous Birmingham Caucus followed hard on the heels of the broad suffrage created in 1867 and the introduction of the secret ballot in 1872.[7]

The change in the organization of parties and their increasing penetration of urban and rural areas trips off still further changes in political life. Political competition and participation are both heightened. As the nationally organized parties reach out to mobilize their voters, the number of uncontested or nonpartisan elections declines. And the competition for members, adherents, and voters increases the politicization of the electorate, at least in the initial stages; participation in elections, for example, is likely to be higher in constituencies where there are competing parties.[8]

7. See, for example, Pulzer, *Political Representation.* On the origin of the Conservative party's "handmaid," the National Union, as an organization for wooing the newly enfranchised urban workers, see R. T. McKenzie, *British Political Parties* (London: Heinemann, 1955), pp. 146 ff. On the Liberal associations and the Birmingham Caucus, see Sir Ivor Jennings, *Party Politics,* vol. 2, *The Growth of Parties* (Cambridge: Cambridge University Press, 1961), pp. 134 ff.
8. Again, comparative cross-national data are lacking. In Britain, the number of constituencies without a contest in parliamentary elections was 57% in 1835, 43% in 1868, and 23% in 1880. Pulzer, *Political Representation,* pp. 61–62. In Norway, as the Labor party established units to mobilize voters at the local level (communes), opponents found it necessary to do likewise; thus from 1900 onward the number of rural communes with nonpartisan plurality elections declined (from 78% in 1901 to 2% in 1959), while the number with two or more competing party lists increased. Turnout at elections was markedly lower in communes with nonpartisan plurality elec-

4. In any given country, the greater the opportunities for
expressing, organizing, and representing political preferences,
the greater the number and variety of preferences and interests that are likely to be represented in policy making.
In a given country at a given time, therefore, the number and
variety of preferences and interests represented in policy
making are likely to be greater if the political regime is a
polyarchy than if it is a mixed regime, and greater under
a mixed regime than under a hegemony. Hence in any given
country the transformation of a hegemony into a mixed regime or a polyarchy, or a mixed regime into a polyarchy,
would be likely to increase the number and variety of preferences and interests represented in policy making.[9]

5. The consequences for government policies of lower
thresholds for participation and public contestation are, unfortunately, obscure. Cross-national studies confront extraordinary difficulties in this area. Even studies of variations
among the fifty American states in policies, politics, and
socioeconomic variables have not so far produced unambiguous findings on the extent to which variations in policies
are related to variations in political competition and participation—though of course the range of variation on all
these variables must be markedly narrower than among
countries.[10] Because of the powerful impact on govern-

tions than with proportional representation and party lists. Cf. Stein
Rokkan and Henry Valen, "The Mobilization of the Periphery: Data
on Turnout, Party Membership and Candidate Recruitment in Norway," in Stein Rokkan, ed., *Approaches to the Study of Political
Participation* (Bergen: The Chr. Michelsen Institute, 1962), pp. 111–
58, esp. tables 2, 2.1, and 2.2, pp. 144–45. See also Torstein Hjellum,
"The Politicization of Local Government: Rates of Change, Con-
ditioning Factors, Effects on Political Culture," *Scandinavian Political
Studies* 2 (1968): 69–93, tables 1 and 2, pp. 73–74.
9. I have developed this point at greater length in the introduction
to *Regimes and Oppositions* (New Haven: Yale University Press,
forthcoming 1971).
10. The first statistical analyses found that political variables like
voter participation and party competition had little relation to state
policies; the most powerful explanatory factor was the level of
socioeconomic development as indicated, for example, by per capita

mental policies of such factors as a country's level of socio-economic development, the characteristics of its social and economic systems, and its traditions, it may well be that the character of the regime has little independent effect on most governmental policies.

We probably need to look elsewhere to find the impact of regime on policy, in particular, on the extent to which the government adopts policies that involve severe physical coercion for relatively large numbers of people. The lower the barriers to public contestation and the greater the proportion of the population included in the political system, the more difficult it is for the government of a country to adopt and enforce policies that require the application of extreme sanctions against more than a small percentage of the population; the less likely, too, that the government will attempt to do so.

The evidence on this point is impressionistic. However, so far as I know, no polyarchy has ever undertaken policies involving anything like the degree and extent of coercion used during the forced collectivization of farming in the USSR in 1931–32, when millions of people were deported to Siberian labor camps or died from execution or starvation. Stalin's purges in the thirties sent many more millions to prison, torture, and death.[11] Hitler's policy of extermination

income. Thomas R. Dye, *Politics, Economics and the Public* (Chicago: Rand McNally, 1966), and Richard E. Dawson and James A. Robinson, "Inter-party Competition, Economic Variables and Welfare Policies in the American States," *Journal of Politics* 25 (1963): 265–89. See also Ira Sharkansky, *The Politics of Taxing and Spending* (Indianapolis: Bobbs-Merrill, 1969), pp. 121–45. More recent analysis indicates, however, that political variables do have effects. Charles F. Cnudde and Donald J. McCrone, "Party Competition and Welfare Policies in the American States," *American Political Science Review* 53 (September 1969): 858–66; Ira Sharkansky and Richard I. Hofferbert, "Dimensions of State Politics, Economics, and Public Policy," ibid., pp. 867–78; and Brian R. Fry and Richard F. Winters, "The Politics of Redistribution," ibid., 54 (June 1970): 508–22.
11. We shall probably never have reliable data on these matters. In his famous letter, the Russian physicist Andrei D. Sakharov indicates the figure of up to 15 million deaths attributable to Stalin is accepted

of Jews and all political opponents is too well known to
need emphasis. Changes of leadership and basic policies in
hegemonic regimes frequently entail considerable bloodshed.
When Indonesia shifted from a procommunist to an anti-
communist dictatorship in October 1965, it is estimated that
at least a quarter of a million people lost their lives over the
space of a few months.[12] In late 1969, some 116,000 persons suspected of communist sympathies had been incar-
cerated.[13]

I do not mean to argue that such massive coercion inevitably occurs in hegemonies nor, certainly, in mixed regimes, but only that the risk is significant, whereas it does
not incur in polyarchies. The seeming exception that most
readily comes to mind actually supports the point. In chapter
6 I shall argue that in order for the white people to coerce
Negroes in the American South, the South had to develop
a dual system, a kind of polyarchy for whites and hegemony
for blacks. It is important to keep the distinction in mind,.
not for the sake of logic chopping, definitional purity, or
"saving" polyarchy at all costs, but precisely because of the

by many Russian intellectuals. *New York Times,* July 22, 1968, p. 15.
In his meticulously detailed but hostile account, Robert Conquest
estimates that collectivization produced "about 5½ million deaths
from hunger and from the diseases of hunger," while "some three
million seem to have ended up in the newly expanding labour camp
system." Conquest cites "the most careful estimates" of the labor
camp population as "mainly at the 5 million level" in 1933–35, and
at 6 million in 1935–37; he accepts "a figure of about 8 million
purgees in the camps in 1938." Of those in the camps in 1936–38,
he estimates that "about 3 million" died. *The Great Terror, Stalin's
Purge of the Thirties* (New York: Macmillan, 1968), pp. 23–24,
333, 335–36.
12. Donald Hindley, who conducted interviews in Indonesia from
May to December 1967, states that, "In all, perhaps 250,000 persons
were killed, an equal number herded into prisons and hastily constructed concentration camps." In a footnote, however, he states that
"informed foreign observers have estimated the number of dead as
high as one million." "Dilemmas of Consensus and Division: Indonesia's Search for a Political Format," *Government and Opposition*
4 (Winter 1969): 79.
13. *New York Times,* June 22, 1970, p. 8.

empirical generalization that it reinforces: if the freed Negroes had been allowed to participate in the system of public contestation in the South, they could not have been subjected to systematic repression by coercion and terror, I believe, for they were much too large a minority. It was only by excluding them forcibly from the polyarchy that the system of coercion and terror could be maintained in the South. And precisely to the extent that black people were excluded, polyarchy in the United States was not fully inclusive.[14] It was, in fact, less inclusive than most other polyarchies after the First World War, for following the general adoption of universal suffrage no other country with a polyarchal regime (with the exceptions of Switzerland and the transitory polyarchy in Argentina) contained an excluded group of comparable size. (It would not be entirely unreasonable to define polyarchy as requiring a degree of inclusiveness greater than that met by the United States, in which case this country would have to be classified as a near polyarchy.)

The example of the United States suggests a final point about the consequences of regimes for policy. I do not believe that polyarchies are more considerate than other regimes toward people who are effectively excluded from the rights of citizens. Among these excluded groups were (and to some extent still are) black people living in the American South, but for every polyarchy foreigners living outside the boundaries of the particular country are excluded. Though there is no reason to think they are worse, countries with polyarchal regimes are probably no better than other countries in responding to the interests of people beyond their boundaries.

6. One could speculate about other possible consequences of differences in regimes. It is possible, for example, that

14. Southern Negroes were 10.3% of the total population of the United States in 1900, 8.4% in 1920, and 6.8% in 1950. U.S. Bureau of the Census, *Historical Statistics of the United States, Colonial Times to 1957* (Washington, D.C.: Government Printing Office, 1961), pp. 7 and 12.

over long periods of time differences in regime may have
effects on beliefs, attitudes, culture, and personalities. As we
shall see in chapter 8, these are usually treated as intervening
or independent variables affecting regimes. But it is also
reasonable to suppose that there is a reciprocal interaction
between factors of this kind and the character of a regime:
if these factors affect the chances of a particular type of
regime, over time the nature of the regime influences beliefs,
attitudes, culture, and perhaps even personalities that are
likely to develop in a country. There are fascinating and important possibilities along these lines, but so many alternative
hypotheses are plausible and yet impossible to appraise in
the light of satisfactory evidence that I shall not take the
matter any further in this book.

The thrust of the argument is, however, clear enough. It
seems reasonably evident that different regimes do have different consequences. Although some people may deny the
importance of these consequences, at least the advocates of
polyarchy and their opponents both agree that the consequences are significantly different and important. If the consequences of polyarchy were no different from those of nonpolyarchy, or if the consequences were unimportant, there
would be no reason to advocate a polyarchy rather than a
one-party dictatorship—or the converse. Probably most readers will also agree that the consequences—particularly the
first—are important.

The source of the controversy over the relative value of
polyarchy versus hegemonic or mixed regimes may not be
so much in the results to be expected from public contestation and inclusion discussed above as in the consequences for
other values. For example, it has been argued that one-party
regimes are desirable in most African countries because a
one-party regime expresses a natural consensus or solidarity
or is necessary to achieve economic development, to build
a nation out of the country's diverse subcultures, or to secure
political stability. As S. E. Finer has convincingly shown,

some of these arguments are self contradictory—one cannot logically defend the single party as an expression of "natural" consensus and also argue that it is required in order to build national solidarity out of tribal diversity and disharmony; all the alleged advantages of one-party regimes seem to be belied by the facts.[15]

But it is not my purpose here to make a case for polyarchy. It is enough if I have shown that important consequences will follow from reducing the obstacles to public contestation and increasing the share of the population entitled to participate. A great many people will agree, I think, not only that these consequences are important but that they are also desirable, that the benefits often (if not always) outweigh the adverse consequences, and that the net gain in such cases is well worth striving for.

The conceptual scheme I employ in this book reflects a commitment (or as others might see it, a bias) in favor of polyarchy as against less democratized regimes. (What may not be apparent, since it is less relevant to the subject of this book, is a bias also in favor of greater democratization of polyarchies.) Nonetheless, I do not assume that a shift from hegemony toward polyarchy is invariably desirable. Let me make clear at once my conviction that a shift from hegemony toward polyarchy *is* frequently desirable; my belief furnishes one of the motives for examining the subject of this book and for formulating the central questions and the concepts as I do. Strictly speaking, however, one could deal with the questions posed in this book and employ the concepts set out here with no assumptions at all as to the desirability of any particular direction of change. In fact, even one who held the extreme position that a shift from hegemony toward polyarchy is *never* desirable would want to understand, I should think, the conditions required to prevent such a change. In this sense, the analysis is intended

15. S. E. Finer, "The One-Party Regimes in Africa: Reconsiderations," *Government and Opposition* 2 (July–October 1967): 491–508.

to be independent of my commitments or biases in favor of polyarchy—though given the difficulties of data analysis at this stage I may not have wholly succeeded.

Finally, I want to make clear that I make no assumption that a shift from hegemony toward polyarchy is historically inevitable. Just as the outcome of the third wave of democratization remains in doubt and could even lead to a regressive narrowing of the opportunities for public contestation now available in polyarchies, so it would be absurd to suppose that some sort of historical law of development imposes on societies an inevitable transition away from political hegemony to public contestation—or, for that matter, in the opposite direction. Since modern nation-states have displayed movements in both directions, a few well-known cases are enough to falsify any simple law of unidirectional development. One might reflect, for example, on the histories of Argentina, Brazil, Germany, Italy, Russia, Czechoslovakia, and Japan. One of the implications of the analysis in this book is, as we shall see, that the conditions most favorable for polyarchy are comparatively uncommon and not easily created.

Returning now to the question posed at the end of the last chapter—what conditions significantly increase the chances of public contestation and polyarchy?—I shall explore in the chapters that follow the consequences of seven sets of conditions: historical sequences, the degree of concentration in the socioeconomic order, level of socioeconomic development, inequality, subcultural cleavages, foreign control, and the beliefs of political activists.

3. HISTORICAL SEQUENCES

One can conceive of historical processes as having two aspects relevant to our central question: the specific path or sequence of transformations of a regime and the way in which a new regime is inaugurated.

The Path to Polyarchy

Does the sequence matter? [1] Are some sequences more likely than others to lead to mutual security and thus to facilitate the shift toward a more polyarchal regime? The two figures introduced in the last chapter to represent the two dimensions of democratization with which we are concerned allow, of course, for an infinite number of paths. History has traced out some of these. But even if one were to limit his imagination by history and common sense, he would surely discover and invent more paths than anyone could deal with. A modest concern for a reasonably parsimonious and manageable theory impels me to try for a narrower

1. This is also the central question in Barrington Moore, Jr., *Social Origins of Dictatorship and Democracy: Lord and Peasant in the Making of the Modern World* (Boston: Beacon Press, 1966). However, as the subtitle suggests, Moore is concerned with different variables and longer historical sequences. Moreover, he chooses to ignore the experience of smaller countries on grounds I find unpersuasive (p. xiii).

focus. Let me begin, then, by considering only three possible
paths to polyarchy:

I. Liberalization precedes inclusiveness:

    A. A closed hegemony increases opportunities for pub-
lic contestation and thus is transformed into a competitive
oligarchy.

    B. The competitive oligarchy is then transformed into
a polyarchy by increasing the inclusiveness of the regime.

II. Inclusiveness precedes liberalization:

    A. A closed hegemony becomes inclusive.

    B. The inclusive hegemony is then transformed into a
polyarchy by increasing opportunities for public contestation.

III. Shortcut: A closed hegemony is abruptly transformed
into a polyarchy by a sudden grant of universal suffrage and
rights of public contestation.

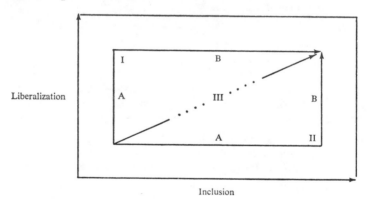

FIGURE 3.1 Some Paths to Polyarchy

These three paths are represented in figure 3.1. The first
is a fair approximation of the paths taken by England and
by Sweden.[2] The second is roughly the path taken by Germany from the Empire to Weimar. The third is roughly the

2. Their paths were of course not nearly as schematic as the diagram
suggests. For example, until the effects on the suffrage of the Reform
Act of 1832 began to be felt, in many constituencies the candidates

path taken in France from 1789 to 1792 (although given various restrictions on voting and the freedom to organize the terminus would perhaps be more accurately described as near-polyarchy).[3]

put forward by the notables won without being contested in the election. "Of the 22 towns with over 1000 voters, eleven went to the poll in 1761; of the 22 towns with 500–1000 voters, twelve; while of the remaining 201 English constituencies only 18: i.e., more than half of the larger boroughs were contested, and about one in ten of all the other constituencies." Sir Lewis Namier, *The Structure of Politics at the Accession of George III* (London: MacMillan, 1961), p. 83. As late as 1830, elections in the counties usually went uncontested: "In the forty counties of England and Wales there were in 1830 only nine contests, the same number as in 1820; and in 1831 there were eleven, one more than in 1826. In most counties the great landowners nominated the candidates, very often by agreement among themselves so as to avoid the expense of a contested election and the disturbance of the peace of the county." Sir Ivor Jennings, *Party Politics* (Cambridge: Cambridge University Press, 1961), p. 81. Even in 1833, when the first election under the Reform Act occurred, there were no contests in nearly one third of the constituencies. Ibid., p. 84, n. 1.

3. About 60% of the adult males had the right to vote under the electoral law of 1789. Under a system of indirect election these "active citizens" chose delegates who in turn elected the deputies. Although the figure is in dispute, probably not more than 45% of the adult males could qualify as delegates. Cf. R. R. Palmer, *The Age of the Democratic Revolution: The Challenge* (Princeton: Princeton University Press, 1959), appendix V, pp. 522 ff., and Peter Campbell, *French Electoral Systems and Elections, 1789–1957* (London: Faber and Faber, 1958), pp. 50–57. The electoral law of 1792, under which the Convention was elected, introduced manhood suffrage, though it retained indirect elections; the Constitution of 1793 provided for universal manhood suffrage, but that constitution was never applied. "At all elections in this period large numbers of electors did not vote. In 1792 only 700,000 of the national electorate of 7,000,000 voted. In the referenda on the successive constitutions between one-third and five-sixths of the electorate abstained. Under the Republic corruption, fraud, intimidation, and violence were practised by the candidates of all factions and their supporters . . . electors with the wrong views were prevented from voting; citizens who might have the wrong views were disfranchised." Campbell, p. 57. Moreover, the Le Chapelier Law prohibited economic organizations of workers (and also in principle if not in practice, of entrepreneurs and merchants). Val R. Lorwin, *The French Labor Movement* (Cambridge: Harvard University Press, 1954), p. 4.

Probably the commonest sequence among the older and more stable polyarchies has been some approximation of the first path, that is, competitive politics preceded expansion in participation.[4] As a result, the rules, the practices, and the culture of competitive politics developed first among a small elite, and the critical transition from nonparty politics to party competition also occurred initially within the restricted group. Although this transition was rarely an easy one, and party conflict was often harsh and bitter, the severity of conflict was restrained by ties of friendship, family, interest, class, and ideology that pervaded the restricted group of notables who dominated the political life of the country. Later, as additional social strata were admitted into politics they were more easily socialized into the norms and practices of competitive politics already developed among the elites, and generally they accepted many if not all of the mutual guarantees evolved over many generations. As a consequence neither the newer strata nor the incumbents who were threatened with displacement felt that the costs of toleration were so high as to outweigh the costs of repression, particularly since repression would entail the destruction of a well-developed system of mutual security.

The other two paths are more dangerous, and for the same reason: to arrive at a viable system of mutual security is a

4. Obviously this capsule description ignores variations that in another context would be vital for explaining differences in contemporary European systems—the party systems, for example. The most extensive analysis of which I am aware of the different historical paths of European countries and their political consequences is to be found in the work of Stein Rokkan. Cf. his "The Comparative Study of Political Participation," in A. Ranney, ed., *Essays on the Behavioral Study of Politics* (Urbana: University of Illinois Press, 1962), pp. 45–90; "Mass Suffrage, Secret Voting, and Political Participation," *Arch. Eur. Sociol.* 2 (1961): 132–52; "Cleavage Structures, Party Systems, and Voter Alignments" (with S. M. Lipset), in Stein Rokkan and Seymour Martin Lipset, eds., *Party Systems and Voter Alignments* (New York: The Free Press, 1967), pp. 1–64; and "The Structuring of Mass Politics in the Smaller European Democracies: A Developmental Typology" (Paper presented to the International Political Science Association, Brussels, September 1967).

difficult matter at best; the greater the number of people and the variety and disparity of interests involved, the more difficult the task and the greater the time required. Tolerance and mutual security are more likely to develop among a small elite sharing similar perspectives than among a large and heterogeneous collection of leaders representing social strata with widely varying goals, interests, and outlooks. This is why the first path is more likely than the other two to produce stable transformations away from hegemony toward polyarchy. The third path drastically shortens the time for learning complex skills and understandings and for arriving at what may be an extremely subtle system of mutual security. The second path requires that the system of mutual security be worked out, not within a small and relatively homogeneous elite, but among spokesmen who reflect the whole spectrum of social strata and political perspectives in the society, or at least in a broad part.

There seem to be few if any unambiguous cases in which the shortcut has been successfully taken.[5] To be sure, in

5. The case of Denmark seems to be somewhat anomalous, though I know too little about it to make a valid appraisal. Under the constitution of 1665, the power of the monarch was absolute, and during the next two centuries the country was ruled by a highly centralized administration under the king. The July revolution of 1830 in France persuaded the king to establish four provincial assemblies for consultative purposes. Under the stimulus of the revolution of 1848, the monarch proclaimed a constitution that entrusted the legislative power to the Rigsdag. Suffrage was granted to all men 30 years of age or older, except those working as servants and farm helpers not having their own household, and those receiving or having received poor relief. In this sense, Denmark did indeed take a shortcut. However, voting for the lower house was in public, by show of hands; that for the upper house was indirect, and under the constitution of 1866 the landowners and highly taxed citizens were given preponderant influence in the upper chamber. Moreover, the monarch refused to accept the principle that his ministers were responsible to Parliament; after 1901 responsibility existed de facto and after 1915 de jure. The constitution of 1915 also established universal suffrage for men and women 29 years of age and over, and abolished the privileged suffrage for the upper chamber. Thus Denmark took a shortcut in 1849 to a broad suffrage and a considerable increase in opportunities for public contestation but delayed for half a century

Italy, Germany, and Japan an existing hegemony was destroyed by military conquest in the Second World War, and the hegemonic regime was replaced during the occupation that followed defeat by an inclusive polyarchy. But these are highly ambiguous cases. For in all three countries, a transition to competitive politics had already been made before the dictatorial seizure of power, and some of the older traditions of competitive politics reappeared after the destruction of the dictatorship. In Japan, the preservation of the monarchy also helped to convey some traditional legitimacy to the new regime of competitive politics. Moreover, in each case the dictatorship was not destroyed from within but from outside by overwhelming military defeat; the occupying forces at least temporarily banned the spokesmen of the old dictatorship from public life, and for a few years they decided all the crucial questions. For all these reasons, and doubtless others, the new regimes were not beset by fatal conflicts over legitimacy arising out of counterclaims set forth by spokesmen for the old regime. Nonetheless, these three cases do show that under certain highly unusual conditions an abrupt shift from hegemony to polyarchy may result in tolerably stable regimes. The conditions may, however, prove to be historically unique.

The second path is also risky. When the suffrage is extended *before* the arts of competitive politics have been mastered and accepted as legitimate among the elites, the search for a system of mutual guarantees is likely to be complex and time consuming. During the transition, when conflict erupts neither side can be entirely confident that it will be safe to tolerate the other. Because the rules of the political game are ambiguous, and the legitimacy of competitive politics is weak, the costs of suppression may not be in-

---

the final transition to the eighth institutional guarantee listed in table 1.1. The Danish political experience has been subjected to so little systematic analysis that I am unclear as to how it bears on the argument of this section.

ordinately high. The danger is, then, that before a system of mutual security can be worked out among the contestants, the emerging but precarious competitive regime will be displaced by a hegemony ruled by one of the contestants.

Although the first path seems to be the safest of the three, it is not likely to be followed in the future, for as we have already seen most countries with hegemonic regimes are already inclusive. Only a rather small minority of countries deny the suffrage to more than 10 percent of their male citizens, and probably no more than a half dozen traditional monarchies or dictatorships have refused to grant the suffrage at all. Moreover, the suffrage seems to be more easily expanded than contracted; historically the process has typically been in one direction: once granted, it is rarely taken away. In this respect, the oscillations in France from 1789 to 1848 between a wide or universal manhood suffrage and a restricted electorate seem to be unusual. Even the few regimes now existing that have not yet granted their citizens the suffrage will probably not pursue the first path. For if demands for inclusion and liberalization begin to threaten the regime, the leadership will doubtless be tempted to make the cheapest concession possible: by granting the suffrage they can clothe the hegemony with the symbols and some of the legitimacy of "democracy"—at little cost, initially, to the leaders.

The argument thus far can then be summarized in four propositions:

1. The first path is more likely than the others to produce the degree of mutual security required for a stable regime of public contestation.

2. But the first path is no longer open to most countries with hegemonic regimes.

3. Hence the liberalization of near-hegemonies will run a serious risk of failure because of the difficulty, under conditions of universal suffrage and mass politics, of working out a system of mutual security.

4. The risks of failure can be reduced, however, if steps toward liberalization are accompanied by a dedicated and enlightened search for a viable system of mutual guarantees.

Inaugurating the Competitive Regime

Does it matter how a competitive regime is inaugurated? By inauguration I mean the application of power, influence, or authority to introduce and to legitimize a regime—in this case a competitive regime. In this sense inauguration emphasizes transitional processes that are, conceptually speaking, somewhere between the paths to polyarchy that we have just been concerned with and the maintenance of the regime after it has been inaugurated. Although the distinctions between paths, inauguration, and maintenance blur at the edges, the concept of inauguration[6] helps us to focus on an important element in the development of competitive regimes.

One way of deciding whether inauguration matters is to consider some of the important ways in which polyarchies or near-polyarchies have been inaugurated in the past. The chief forms seem to be:

I. Within an already independent nation-state
   A. The old regime is transformed by evolutionary processes: the new regime is inaugurated by incumbent leaders, who yield peacefully (more or less) to demands for changes and participate in the inauguration of polyarchy or near-polyarchy.
   B. The old regime is transformed by revolution: the new regime is inaugurated by revolutionary leaders, who overthrow the old regime and install a polyarchy or near-polyarchy.

6. I am indebted to my colleague, Juan Linz for his insistence on the relevance of the way in which a competitive regime is inaugurated.

C. The old regime is transformed by military conquest: after a military defeat, victorious occupying forces help inaugurate a polyarchy or near-polyarchy.

II. In a hitherto dependent country subject to another state

D. The old regime is transformed by evolutionary processes: the new regime is fostered among the local population, whose leaders inaugurate polyarchy or near-polyarchy without a national independence movement or serious struggle against the colonial power.

E. The old regime is transformed as a part of the struggle for national independence, in the course of a "revolution" against the colonial power: the new regime is inaugurated by leaders of a national independence movement, who install polyarchy or near-polyarchy during or after a succesful struggle for national independence.

Examples of the inauguration of polyarchies are given in table 3.1.

Although the examples in table 3.1 show that there has been no uniform process of inaugurating polyarchies, they also suggest that the various alternatives may not be equally auspicious. A disproportionately large number of the stable high-consensus polyarchies seem to have come about in the first way, by peaceful evolution within an already independent nation-state, or the fourth, by peaceful evolution within a dependent country. The reason is probably that peaceful evolution is most likely to result in a polyarchy supported by a widespread sense of legitimacy. As the incumbents yield peacefully (on the whole) and participate in the changes, their consent is won, the legitimacy attached to the previous regime is transferred unbroken to the new regime, and the

Table 3.1. Processes of Inaugurating Polyarchies

I. Within an already independent nation-state

A. By evolutionary processes
   Britain
   Belgium
   Chile
   Costa Rica
   Denmark
   Japan (Meiji Restoration to the 1930s)
   Netherlands
   Norway
   Sweden
   Switzerland
   Uruguay

B. By collapse or revolutionary displacement of old regime
   France (1789–92, 1848, 1870)
   Germany (1919)
   Austria, First Republic (1918)
   Spain (1931)

C. By military conquest (all following World War II)
   Austria, Second Republic
   German Federal Republic
   Italy
   Japan

II. Within a subject state

D. By evolutionary processes
   Australia
   Canada
   Iceland
   New Zealand
   Philippines

E. By a national independence struggle
   Finland
   India
   Ireland
   Israel
   United States

process of peaceful change, so important to polyarchy, gains in legitimacy.

By comparison with the first process, the second—inauguration after the abrupt collapse or revolutionary overthrow of the old regime—is infrequent: in the three most notable cases—the French Revolution, Weimar Germany, and the Spanish Republic—revolution or collapse was followed by an unstable regime that soon regressed to hegemony. Was this reversal accidental? Probably not, for where peaceful evolution cannot or does not take place and revolution occurs, the legitimacy of the new regime is more likely to be contested. A sudden collapse of the old regime leaves the new without a legacy of legitimacy; a revolutionary inaugural by the new legitimates the use of revolution against itself. The most critical years, then, are likely to be the early ones, when the legitimacy of the new regime is still in question, and loyalties to the old regime are still alive.

The third process has proved so far to lead to surprisingly stable polyarchies in the only four countries where inauguration of polyarchy by conquest has occurred in recent times. Some possible reasons for the stability of the polyarchies inaugurated under the Allies after World War II have already been suggested; I also suggested that these may be historically unique cases.

The fifth process is the one with which Americans are most familiar and, at least rhetorically, most sympathetic. As in the United States, so too in Finland, Ireland, Israel, and India the independence movement blended nationalism with the ideology of representative government and political liberalism. Thus the ideology of democracy was reinforced by the ideology of nationalism: to attack representative democracy was to attack the nation. The success of the movement for national independence largely liquidated the principal contenders for the legitimacy of the old regime. Mainly agents of the colonial power, they either returned to the home country or permanently exiled themselves from the new nation, as in the case of the Tories who moved to Canada after the American Revolution. Or, as with Ireland and Ulster, those who would have constituted a disaffected minority in the new country remained a part of the old.

In the future, however, stable polyarchies are unlikely to

be inaugurated by the fifth process. For one thing, in many of the new states where the sense of nationhood is weak, the leaders of nationalist movements, who during the struggle for independence proclaimed the goal of democracy, later on as leaders of the new and fragile nation see organized opposition as a threat to the integrity of the country. In the new states, then, nationalism does not so much encourage toleration of dissent and oppositions as it provides a ready and acceptable justification for intolerance and repression.[7] (It is worth keeping in mind that in the United States throughout our national history fears about nationhood and loyalty have resulted in attempts—sometimes successful—to repress dissent. The relationship between nationalism, loyalty, and fear of dissent in the United States is nicely symbolized by the original name of the official organization that has most fully displayed hostility to dissent: the Un-American Activities Committee of the U.S. House of Representatives.)

What may be an even more important limitation on the fifth strategy is that world developments have made it obsolescent. With the disappearance of colonial empires, most of the world now consists of nominally sovereign states. In a world of independent states there are no longer many opportunities for movements of national independence to inaugurate more competitive regimes.

In fact, the options seem to be even more narrowly restricted. The disappearance of colonial empires also reduces the opportunities for the fourth process of inauguration. If it is true that the third process—via military conquest—is unlikely, then the most likely alternatives are reduced to the first two: in existing hegemonic regimes a more competitive system will have to be inaugurated either by evolution or by revolution. Simply because the revolutionary process carries a high risk of failure does not mean that it will not be tried,

7. Edward Shils, "Opposition in the New States of Asia and Africa," and Hans Daalder, "Government and Opposition in the New States," *Government and Opposition* 1 (January 1966): 175–226.

but revolutions will probably saddle new regimes with serious conflicts over legitimacy and hence create from the start a high probability of regression toward hegemonic rule.

In the future as in the past, then, stable polyarchies and near-polyarchies are more likely to result from rather slow evolutionary processes than from the revolutionary overthrow of existing hegemonies.[8]

If this interpretation seems unduly restrictive, it is worth recalling that among most of the well-established polyarchies today, where there exists a high tolerance for oppositions of all kinds, the transformation was exceedingly slow. In Britain a "formed" opposition was still illegal and illegitimate at the end of the seventeenth century. A century later the idea of a more or less organized but "loyal" opposition in Parliament to His Majesty's government had gained a considerable legitimacy.[9] But still another century elapsed before Britain evolved its present system of highly organized parties competing for the support of a broad electorate. Elsewhere, as in France, attempts to short-circuit this slow evolutionary process by revolution sometimes produced lasting oppositions to the new regime. It is also worth recalling that in 1968 the USSR celebrated the 50th anniversary of the Bolshevik Revolution. While the extreme hegemony of the Stalinist period has been replaced, the USSR has not yet been transformed into a near-hegemony, and the inauguration of a near-polyarchy appears even to optimistic observers to be considerably more than a generation away.

That polyarchies and one-party hegemonies have de-

8. Moore's emphasis on the vital importance of the violent revolution as a stage along the road to democracy is, I believe, misleading, particularly if it is applied to the process of inauguration. Moore stresses heavily the English Civil War, the French Revolution, and— a very doubtful case—the American Civil War. *Social Origins of Dictatorship and Democracy,* passim. His argument here is, I think, weakened by his belief that the experience of the smaller countries is somehow irrelevant. The question is: irrelevant to what?

9. See Archibald Foord, *His Majesty's Opposition* (Oxford: Oxford University Press, 1964).

veloped in the twentieth century means that neither evolution
nor revolution can occur in complete isolation from existing
models that were quite unknown and would have been in-
comprehensible in the eighteenth century. A loyal opposition,
a two-party system, a one-party dictatorship do not have to
be reinvented as if there were no models to copy. No country needs to grope through centuries of experience with no
clear idea of the elementary institutions required for a highly
liberalized regime: competitive parties and uncoerced elections are not merely a goal, but a fact. Likewise when a near-
polyarchy collapses, antidemocratic leaders do not have to
fumble for the one-party formula.

The consequences of this for the inaugural process are
unclear. An evolutionary process leading to polyarchy in the
future need not, and probably cannot, consume the centuries
it took in Britain, Sweden, and elsewhere. Already "tested"
models are now available that offer modern societies such
radically different regimes as a unified hegemony in its most
totalitarian form or an inclusive polyarchy with an extraordinary tolerance for oppositions of all kinds. The availability of these "tested" models, which do not have to be
reinvented, may sometimes facilitate rapid transformation of
regimes and even oscillations from one extreme to the other
within a very short historical period: witness Italy, Germany,
and Japan from, say, 1919 to 1950.

The argument of this section can be summed up in the
following propositions:

1. The process of inauguration most auspicious for a
   polyarchy is one that transforms previously legitimate
   hegemonic forms and structures into the forms and
   structures suitable for political competition and thus
   produces no lasting cleavages or widespread doubts
   about the legitimacy of the new regime.
2. The inaugural process most likely to lead to this result is peaceful evolution within an independent

nation-state or within a quasi-independent nation that is granted independence without a national independence movement.

3. The process of inauguration least auspicious for a polyarchy is one that leaves a large segment of the citizen body opposed to the legitimacy of competitive politics.

4. This result is likely when a polyarchy is inaugurated by a civil war or revolution in which a large segment of the people who uphold the legitimacy of the old regime or deny the legitimacy of the new are defeated but nonetheless incorporated as citizens in the new regime.

5. The decline of colonial empires and the unlikely repetition of the circumstances facilitating the introduction of polyarchy in the defeated countries by the Allies at the end of World War II mean that in the future the main options available are evolution or revolution within an already independent nation-state.

6. The presence in the world of functioning models of polyarchy and one-party hegemony probably has an impact on the process of inaugurating regimes, but the effects are uncertain. At a minimum, their presence probably raises expectations that regimes can be rapidly trasformed in either direction.

7. Yet in countries without a recent legacy of experience in the operation of competitive politics, the transformation of hegemonic regimes into polyarchies is likely to remain a slow process, measured in generations.

8. The length of the process can probably be reduced and the prospects of a stable transformation increased if inaugural processes are accompanied by a search for an internal system of mutual security.

4. THE SOCIOECONOMIC ORDER: CONCENTRATION OR DISPERSION?

What difference does the social and economic order make? Are the chances that a hegemonic regime will be transformed into a more competitive regime higher under some socioeconomic orders than others? Are the chances that a polyarchy will be maintained dependent on the socioeconomic order?

Assumptions

In the first chapter I introduced a more or less self-evident axiom which asserted that a government is more likely to tolerate an opposition as the expected costs of suppression increase and as the expected costs of toleration decrease. Since the costs of toleration or suppression are in turn dependent on the relative resources available to the government and to the opposition, it is obvious that:

> AXIOM 4: *The likelihood that a government will tolerate an opposition increases as the resources available to the government for suppression decline relative to the resources of an opposition.*

Now the key resources that governments use to suppress oppositions are of two broad types: violent means of coercion, persuasion, and inducement, typically wielded by military and police forces; and nonviolent means of coercion, persuasion, and inducement, or, as they will be called here, socioeconomic sanctions, chiefly in the form of control over economic resources, means of communication, and processes of education and political socialization. Hence

> AXIOM 5: *The likelihood that a government will tolerate an opposition increases with a reduction in the capacity of the government to use violence or socioeconomic sanctions to suppress an opposition.*

Two very general kinds of circumstances can reduce the capacity of a government to use violence or socioeconomic sanctions against an opposition. First, these factors sometimes cease to be available as political resources. This possibility is particularly relevant to violence against opponents of the government by police or military forces, for the police and military may actually be very small, or, what amounts to very nearly the same thing, they may become so depoliticized that they can no longer be used by political leaders for internal political purposes. Second, these (and other) political resources may be so widely dispersed that no unified group, including the government (or a unified group of leaders in the government) has a monopoly over them.

Thus, in the eighteenth century, the "professional" military and police forces of Britain, other than the Navy, were not only dispersed throughout the counties, where they were subject to control by the local gentry, but they were in fact very nearly nonexistent. Britain's greatest instrument of organized violence was the Navy, over which the government enjoyed a monopoly control, but it was not an effective instrument for domestic coercion. The United States developed into a polyarchy without a standing army or a national police force and with a very wide distribution of firearms among its citizens. Even if the police in American communities were sometimes involved in politics, control over the police was widely dispersed among innumerable local governments throughout the country. In Switzerland, providing for the defense of the country by universal military service has made for a microscopic professional standing army.

Where the military is relatively large, centralized, and hierarchical, as it is in most countries today, polyarchy is of course impossible unless the military is sufficiently depoliticized to permit civilian rule. Why highly organized military forces intervene in politics in some countries but not others has been the subject of an enormous amount of inquiry, controversy, and puzzlement. The crucial intervening factor, clearly, is one of beliefs. But why beliefs in political neutrality, constitutionalism, and obedience to civil authority are developed and sustained among military forces only in certain countries (not all of which are polyarchies), raises problems of so vast a scope that I cannot examine them here, crucial though they may be. The point to be made here is simple and obvious: the chances for polyarchy today are directly dependent on the strength of certain beliefs not only among civilians but among all ranks of the military. Thus polyarchy has been possible in Chile, where the military has traditionally been reluctant to intrude into the political arena; while in neighboring Argentina, polyarchy is impossible so long as the military responds to the belief that its leaders have a right and duty to set aside the results of elections whenever the outcome, in their view, bodes ill for the country.

Although it is obvious that when a government has a monopoly over violence and socioeconomic sanctions and is free to use these resources to suppress oppositions the chances for competitive politics are practically nonexistent, it does not follow that the mere absence of a governmental monopoly over these key resources necessarily favors competitive politics. For in some circumstances the lack of these key resources may produce only a weak and unstable competitive regime. Table 4.1 will help to clarify the point.

The circumstances most favorable for competitive politics exist when access to violence and socioeconomic sanctions is either dispersed or denied both to oppositions[1] and to government. The least favorable circumstances exist when violence and socioeconomic sanctions are exclusively available to the government and denied to the oppositions. But what of the remaining case when these key resources are a

Table 4.1. Relative Access to Violence and Socioeconomic Sanctions: Government and Opposition

Available to government?

		Yes	No
Available to opposition?	Yes	Dispersed	Monopolized by opposition; access denied to government
	No	Monopolized by government; access denied to opposition	Neutralized: access denied to both

monopoly of the opposition? The pure case would hardly exist, since under these conditions a "government" would lack the definitional characteristics of a government. However, the situation may exist temporarily in a country where economic resources are monopolized by a small group of local or foreign owners and managers or where the military forces are politically committed to the defense of specific social strata or ideologies. Confronted by situations of this kind, a government is bound to be weak and unstable, for whenever its conduct displeases the opposition, the government can easily be overthrown.

A number of Latin American countries provide a rough approximation to the circumstances I have in mind, not so much because socioeconomic sanctions are monopolized but

1. To simplify the theory and exposition at this point, I treat "government" and "opposition" each as single, unified actors. Clearly this is rarely the case.

because cf a tradition of military intervention. Where the military forces are prone to intervene in political life in defense of special interests or their own conception of the country's interest, then any government that pursues policies of which they disapprove is likely to be short-lived, as in Argentina.

It would be misleading to conclude, however, that violence and socioeconomic sanctions are necessarily distributed in the same way. Consider table 4.2.

Table 4.2. Distribution of Violence and Socioeconomic Sanctions

		Access to violence is:	
		Dispersed or neutralized	Monopolized
Access to socioeconomic sanctions is:	Dispersed or neutralized	A	B
	Monopolized	C	D

Clearly the most favorable situation for competitive politics is A, which I shall call a pluralistic social order.

It is equally obvious that the situation least favorable for competitive politics and most favorable for hegemony is D, which I shall call a centrally dominated social order.

The other two situations are more ambiguous. Both are less favorable to political competition than is a pluralistic social order, but both are less favorable to a hegemonic regime than is a centrally dominated social order. Contemporary Spain, Portugal, and Argentina roughly approximate B, which might be called a quasi-pluralistic social order with repressive violence. The remaining possibility, C, which might be called a quasi-dominated social order without repressive violence seems to be rare, perhaps because a governing elite with such great resources for dominance would have no incentives for allowing all the major instruments of violence to be dispersed or politically neutralized and would probably possess enough resources (for example, legal authority, promotions, pay, and wealth) to prevent it.

Agrarian Societies

Since so many countries in the world today are still predominantly agrarian or barely emerging into the industrial stage, the tendencies of agrarian societies have more than purely historical interest. Historically, agrarian societies seem to have fallen roughly into two extreme types, with of course, many variations. The most prevalent type, which might be called the traditional peasant society, has a very high propensity for inequality, hierarchy, and political hegemony.[2]

The other, which I shall call a free farmer society, is considerably more egalitarian and democratic. Although the free farmer society is often ignored in discussion of agrarian societies, it furnishes too many important historical examples to pass it by: Switzerland, the United States,[3] Canada, New Zealand, and Norway, to take the leading cases.[4]

It would be a large and fascinating enterprise to try to unravel the causes leading to one or the other. Tocqueville is an obvious point of departure for the ambitious theorist. But that effort is beyond the scope of this essay, and I shall do little more here than provide a descriptive summary.

Three underlying conditions seem to be particularly rele-

2. Gerhard Lenski, *Power and Privilege* (New York: McGraw-Hill, 1966), chaps. 8 and 9; Kaare Svalastoga, *Social Differentiation* (New York: David McKay, 1965), chap. 3.
3. The absence of a feudal past has strongly been emphasized by Louis Hartz as an explanation for the development of a liberal democracy in the United States. See his *The Liberal Tradition in America* (New York: Harcourt Brace, 1955).
4. There are other relevant examples, though these would require greater qualification: e.g. Australia, Chile (nineteenth and early twentieth centuries), Ireland (twentieth century), and, provided one is prepared to ignore the existence of slavery, Athens in the fifth and fourth centuries B.C. Historically, Sweden was perhaps at the margin between the two types. Costa Rica is perhaps the closest approximation in Latin America.

vant and will help to give our description a bit of dynamics.
Tocqueville was perhaps the first to point out how difficult
it is to explain the political development of the United States
(as compared, let us say, with other countries to the south)
unless one gives considerable weight to the independent
effects of beliefs, including naturally beliefs about "equality." [5]
For a second explanatory factor one might look, as Tocqueville did, to the degree of equality in distribution of land.
Because in an agrarian society the possession of land or a
right to the produce of the land is the main source of status,
income, and wealth, inequality in land is equivalent to inequality in the distribution of political resources. To put it
differently, in an agrarian society inequalities will be cumulative, not dispersed, and (as Harrington, the seventeenth-cen-
tury English philosopher, argued) power will be highly correlated with landed property. A third factor, one to which
Tocqueville paid less attention, is the state of military technology, that is, the bearing of technology on the capacity of
individuals to employ coercion. During some periods, military
technology reinforces inequalities by facilitating a monopoly
over instruments of coercion among a small minority, as in
the familiar case of the expensively armed and mounted
knight before whom the unarmed or lightly armed medieval
peasant was relatively ineffectual. Or to offer another example,
the initial monopoly over horses and muskets held by the
Conquistadores allowed a handful of Spaniards to conquer
and subjugate the advanced Indian civilizations of Mexico
and Peru. In other periods, military technology reinforces
equality by dispersing the most effective instruments of
coercion widely over the population, as in the case of the

5. This masterly demonstration, which superbly exhibits his capacity
for comparative analysis, will be found in *Democracy in America*
(New York: Vintage Books, 1955), vol. 1, chap. 17, "Principal
Causes Which Tend to Maintain the Democratic Republic in the
United States," pp. 298 ff. The main references to Latin America are
on pp. 331–33. He uses Latin America as a kind of "control" for his
mental experiment on pp. 331–33.

relatively cheap but efficient musket and rifle in eighteenth-
and nineteenth-century America.

In the traditional peasant society, these three factors all
operate in the same direction. Cumulative inequalities of
status, wealth, income, and means of coercion mean a marked
inequality in political resources, an inequality that is reinforced by prevailing beliefs. A small minority with superior
resources develops and maintains a hegemonic political system (often headed by a single dominant ruler) through which
it can also enforce its domination over the social order and
hence strengthen the initial inequalities even more. Limits on
this potentially run-away cycle of ever-increasing inequalities
are set by dangers of mass starvation, passive resistance, and
even sporadic uprisings among the peasants, a decline in
agricultural output, and, because of wide disaffection, vulner-
ability to foreign invasions. But for the great bulk of the population life is one of hardship, deprivation, dependence, re-
pressed dissent, and comparative ignorance,[6] while a tiny
minority enjoy exceptional power, wealth, and social esteem.[7]
The dynamics of the traditional peasant society might then
be represented crudely as in figure 4.1.

In the contrasting society of free farmers, land is more
equally distributed, even though it is always a far cry from
perfect equality. If the norms are egalitarian and democratic,

6. Mehmet Beqiraj, *Peasantry in Revolution* (Ithaca, N.Y.: Center
for International Studies, Cornell University, 1966), passim.
7. "For example, recent research indicates that in nineteenth century
China, the gentry or degree holders, who formed the governing
class, totaled about 1.3 per cent of the population in the first half of
the century and about 1.9 per cent toward the end. In mid-nineteenth
century Russia the nobility constituted 1.25 per cent of that nation's
population. In France, on the eve of the Revolution, the nobility of
all ranks and grades constituted only 0.6 per cent, despite the recent
influx of many wealthy mercantile families. During the last days of
the Roman Republic, the governing class is estimated to have included about 1 per cent of the capital's population. Finally, in
seventeenth century England, peers, baronets, knights, and esquires
combined constituted roughly 1 per cent of the total population."
Lenski, *Power and Privilege,* p. 219.

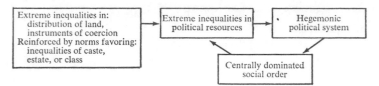

FIGURE 4.1 Dynamics of the Peasant Society

as Tocqueville insisted they were in the United States, then the one reinforces the other. Finally, in a number of cases both of these tendencies toward equality (or toward a lower limit on inequality) are strengthened by certain aspects of military

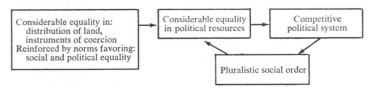

FIGURE 4.2 Dynamics of the Free Farmer Society

technology. In the United States, the musket and later the rifle helped to provide a kind of equality in coercion for over a century. In Switzerland the mountains, in Norway and New Zealand the mountains and fjords, the continental proportions and the enormous length of Chile—all reduced the prospects for a successful monopoly of violence by any one stratum of the population.[8] The way these factors interact in a society of free farmers is represented by figure 4.2.

8. Nor should one underestimate the effects on the use of violent coercion of beliefs and norms toward law, order, and individual violence. Of the two English-speaking countries in North America, Canada has traditionally been the more law-abiding and the less violent. See, for example, Seymour Martin Lipset, *Revolution and Counterrevolution* (New York: Basic Books, 1968), pp. 37–39. A Canadian writer has argued that these two cultures even displayed themselves during the Gold Rush:

> Canadian and U.S. mining camps grew up with varying legal customs, which to a considerable extent point up the very real difference between the Canadian and the U.S. character. The

Commercial and Industrial Societies

Historically, commercial and industrial societies have been more hospitable than agrarian societies to competitive politics. Orthodox liberal doctrine explained this by establishing a connection between a pluralistic social order and a privately owned competitive economy: competitive politics requires a competitive economy. In effect classic liberal doctrine set forth the following equation:

$$\text{Competitive politics} \Rightarrow \text{a pluralistic social order}$$

$$\Rightarrow \text{a competitive economy} \Rightarrow \text{private ownership}^9$$

American, freed by his own will of what he considered colonial bondage, has always insisted on running his own affairs from the ground up—especially on the frontier. The Canadian, who never knew the blood bath of revolution, has more often preferred to have law and order imposed from above rather than have it spring from the grass roots.

In the three British Columbia gold rushes, constabulary and courts of justice enforced a single set of laws in the British colonial tradition. Mining law was the same everywhere, and the gold commissioner in charge had such absolute power that the lawlessness so familiar to American mining history was unknown in the B.C. camps.

But in the Rocky Mountain camps of the U.S.A., and later in Alaska, each community had its own customs and its own rules made on the spot. Authority was vested in the miners themselves, who held town meetings in the New England manner to redress wrongs or dispense justice . . . On Alaskan territory, during the hectic days of 1897–98, there was no organized machinery of government, to speak of: rule was by local committee, sometimes wise, sometimes capricious, always summary. On the Canadian side there was, if anything, too much government, as the graft in Dawson City was to demonstrate; but there were also, at every bend in the river, the uniformed and strangely comforting figures of the Mounted Police.

Pierre Berton, *The Klondike Fever* (New York: Knopf, 1958), pp. 23–24.

9. The double arrow can be read as "implies" or "requires." Reading in the reverse direction from right to left, the symbol means "is a necessary condition for."

For, it was argued, just as toleration of oppositions and the existence of a competitive representative government require a pluralistic social order, so a pluralistic social order in turn requires a competitive capitalist economy. At the same time, classical liberal thought argued that in order for a socialist economy to exist—and socialism was understood to be the only modern alternative to capitalism—there would have to be a completely centralized social order with access to social, economic, and physical sanctions concentrated in the hands of central authorities; obviously such a social order would require (and make possible) a hegemonic regime. The twin equation, then, was:

A socialist economy $\Rightarrow$ a centrally dominated social order

$\Rightarrow$ a hegemonic regime

Thus classic liberalism rigidly premised the existence of competitive politics and later of polyarchy on competitive capitalism: it said, in effect, that you cannot logically choose to have the freedoms associated with competitive politics unless you also choose to have a competitive capitalist economy; if you choose to have a socialist economy, logically you are also opting for a hegemonic regime and the destruction of political liberties. After the Bolshevik Revolution, the Soviet Union could be cited as proof of these two equations, for there a highly hegemonic political system maintained a centrally dominated social order, a key element of which was its completely centralized socialist economy.

This analysis, though superficially persuasive, did not really demonstrate, however, that the equations were correct, and other historical developments have revealed their inadequacy.

Classical liberal economists like Adam Smith knew from the history of mercantilism that private ownership is not a *sufficient* condition for economic competition; the first equation only specifies that it is a *necessary* condition. Further experience with numerous dictatorships—in Italy, Germany, Japan, Spain, and elsewhere—has shown that private ownership is indeed no guarantee of a competitive economy or a political order that permits public contestation, much less polyarchy. The extreme cases—as in Italy, Germany, and Japan—demonstrated that a kind of private ownership[10] could coexist even with a centrally dominated social order.

Since the equations speak of necessary and not sufficient conditions, strictly speaking these developments left the argument intact. But other developments have actually falsified the equations. One is the persistence of inclusive polyarchy in countries with mixed (not strictly competitive-capitalist) economies that employ an endless variety of techniques and controls which, in combination, preserve and may even strengthen a pluralistic social order. One thinks of Sweden as the archetype. In 1959 expenditures of government, social security, and public enterprises were 53 percent of Sweden's GNP.[11] But practically all industrialized countries with polyarchal regimes have displaced pure competitive capitalism with mixed systems, and in the process they have managed to maintain pluralistic social orders.

Where the equations of classic liberalism went wrong was in supposing that any alternative to competitive capitalism necessarily required a centrally directed economy, whereas in fact competition among privately owned firms is by no means the unique method of decentralizing an economy.

10. Of course, this kind of ownership might not be equivalent to some definitions of "private" ownership. The term might be defined so that a centrally dominated social order would *by definition* exclude the existence of private ownership of the means of production and distribution.
11. Other figures were: U.K. 45%; Austria (with not all public enterprises included), 44%; and New Zealand, 43%. Russett et al., *World Handbook of Political and Social Indicators* (New Haven: Yale University Press, 1964), table 15, p. 63. It has been estimated that in Austria "75% of the total corporate capital is directly or indirectly in the public domain." Alexander Vodopivec, *Wer Regiert in Oster-reich?* 2d ed. (Vienna: Verlag für Geschichte und Politik, 1962), p. 255, cited in Frederick C. Englemann, "Austria: The Pooling of Opposition," in Robert A. Dahl, ed., *Political Oppositions in Western Democracies* (New Haven: Yale University Press, 1966), p. 270.

Indeed, in recent years some of the communist regimes of
Eastern Europe have been moving away from central direction; among these, Yugoslavia has gone farthest in decentralizing controls over economic enterprises. If decentralized
socialist economies prove capable of handling major economic
problems with a fair degree of success, then there is no
inherent reason why socialism cannot produce and sustain
a highly pluralistic social order, and hence competitive
politics.

The correct equations, in short, seem to be:

$$\text{Competitive politics} \Rightarrow \text{pluralistic social order}$$

$$\Rightarrow \text{decentralized economy}$$

$$\text{Highly centralized economy} \Rightarrow \text{centrally dominated social order}$$

$$\Rightarrow \text{hegemonic regime}$$

The argument of this chapter can thus be summed up as
follows:

1. A competitive political regime, and therefore a polyarchy, is unlikely to be maintained without a pluralistic social
order. A centrally dominated social order is more favorable
to a hegemonic than to a competitive regime (and therefore
to a polyarchy).

2. A competitive regime cannot be maintained in a country
where the military or police forces are accustomed to intervening in politics, even if the social order is otherwise pluralistic and not centrally dominated.

3. Agrarian societies seem to approach two extreme types,
the traditional peasant society characteristically associated
with a hegemonic political regime and the society of free
farmers characteristically associated with a competitive regime and evolution toward an inclusive polyarchy. The main
factors determining the direction an agrarian society takes

seem to be: norms about equality, the distribution of land, and military techniques.

4. Private ownership is neither a necessary nor a sufficient condition for a pluralistic social order and hence for public contestation and polyarchy.

5. A pluralistic social order, and hence public contestation and polyarchy, can exist in a country with a decentralized economy, no matter what the form of ownership.

6. But public contestation, and hence polyarchy, is unlikely to exist in a country with highly centralized direction of the economy, no matter what the form of ownership.

5. THE SOCIOECONOMIC ORDER: LEVEL OF DEVELOPMENT

It is widely assumed that a high level of socioeconomic development not only favors the transformation of a hegemonic regime into a polyarchy but also helps to maintain—may even be necessary to maintain—a polyarchy. To what extent is this assumption correct?

Earlier answers that leaned heavily on impressionistic interpretations and a case study or two have recently given way to more ambitious efforts to exploit a rapidly increasing supply of cross-national data and easy access to suitable computer programs for handling these data. Even if the data, the measures used, and the interpretations do not yield unambiguous or unchallenged answers, recent studies[1] do give impressive support to several propositions.

1. Seymour Martin Lipset, "Economic Development and Democracy," in his *Political Man* (New York: Doubleday, 1960), pp. 45–76; Phillips Cutright, "National Political Development, Its Measurement and Social Correlates," in Nelson W. Polsby, Robert A. Dentler, and Paul A. Smith, *Politics and Social Life* (Boston: Houghton Mifflin, 1963), pp. 569–81; Everett E. Hagen, "A Framework for Analyzing Economic and Political Changes," in *Development of the Emerging Countries: An Agenda for Research* (Washington, D.C.: The Brookings Institution, 1962), chap. 1; Irma Adelman and Cynthia Taft Morris, *Society, Politics and Economic Development: A Quantitative Approach* (Baltimore: The Johns Hopkins Press, 1967); Deane E. Neubauer, "Some Conditions of Democracy," *American*

Some Settled Questions

First, various measures of socioeconomic level are all highly intercorrelated. Thus Russett writes that

> In a study of over 100 countries and colonies there was found to be a high correlation between G.N.P. per capita and such other indicators of economic and social development as the percentage of the population in cities of over 20,000 (r = .71), the percentage of adults literate (.80), the proportion of the population enrolled in higher education (.58), the number of radios per 1000 population (.85), and the number of hospital beds per inhabitant (.77). These variables, along with others like the percentage of the labor force employed in agriculture, the percentage of wage and salary earners in the population, and other indices of health and mass communications, form a cluster that tends to vary according to the level of economic development.[2]

If a country is relatively poor or relatively rich, then, its poverty or affluence shows up in all sorts of ways in addition to per capita income. The commonsense notion that different countries are at different "stages" of economic and social development is amply confirmed by the data.[3]

Second, there is unquestionably a significant association between socioeconomic level and "political development."

Political Science Review 61 (December 1967): 1002–09; Bruce M. Russett, et al., *World Handbook of Political and Social Indicators* (New Haven, Yale University Press, 1964), pp. 293–303.

2. Bruce M. Russett, *Trends in World Politics* (New York: Macmillan, 1965), pp. 125–26.

3. For example, nine indicators applied to 107 countries yield five "stages" of economic and political development in Russett, *Trends in World Politics,* p. 127. Factor scores used as indicators yield three levels of socioeconomic development for 74 "less developed countries" ranging from Niger with a 1961 per capita GNP of $40 to Israel with a 1951 per capita GNP of $814 in Adelman and Morris, *Society, Politics and Economic Development,* p. 170.

Expressed in terms of the questions raised in this essay, there
can no longer be any doubt that competitive politics and
socioeconomic level do tend to run together. The data show
rather conclusively that:

> The higher the socioeconomic level of a country, the
> more likely it is to have a competitive political regime.

> The more competitive a country's political regime, the
> more likely the country is at a relatively high level of
> socioeconomic development.

Thus Russett finds that among countries in the two most
"advanced" stages of economic development (which he calls
Industrial Revolution Societies and High Mass Consumption
Societies) the proportion of "competitive" and "semi-com-
petitive" systems is much higher than among the countries in
the three less advanced stages, where "authoritarian" regimes
predominate. (Table 5.1)[4]

4. Adelman and Morris in their factor analysis of 74 "less developed" countries find that per capita GNP is correlated with both a
social factor and a political factor (table IV, p. 151). The political
factor is essentially the extent and strength of competitive political
institutions. "An increase in this factor may be interpreted to represent a movement along a scale that ranges from centralized authoritarian political forms to specialized political mechanisms capable of
representing the varied group interests of a society and aggregating
these interests through participant national political organs . . . Thus
a positive change in Factor II is composed of (1) increases in the
effectiveness of democratic institutions, freedom of political opposition and press, competitiveness of political parties, and strength of
the labor movement; (2) a movement from political parties emphasizing considerations of national unity toward those stressing
ideological platforms; and (3) decreases in the strength of the military and in the extent of centralization" (pp. 155–56). Additional
evidence is also provided by Arthur S. Banks and Robert B. Textor,
A Cross-Polity Survey (Cambridge: M.I.T. Press, 1963): see, for
example, the characteristics of "polities where the electoral system
is competitive, rather than non-competitive" versus "polities where
the electoral system is non-competitive, rather than competitive" (FC
104). See also FC 101, FC 107, FC 139. And see also Cutright,
"National Political Development: Its Measurement and Social Correlates," table 1, p. 577.

A relationship between socioeconomic development and inclusive or nearly inclusive polyarchy shows up perhaps even

Table 5.1. Economic Development and Political System

Political system	"Stage" of development				
	I	II	III	IV	V
Competitive	13%	33%	12%	57%	100%
Semicompetitive	25	17	20	13	0
Authoritarian	63	50	68	30	0
N	(8)	(12)	(25)	(30)	(14)

Source: Bruce M. Russett, *Trends in World Politics* (New York: Macmillan, 1965), table 8.2., p. 140.
Note: Percentages do not always add to 100% because of rounding.

more sharply in the data. (Tables 5.2 and 5.3) As with competitive regimes, so with polyarchy:

The higher the socioeconomic level of a country, the more likely that its regime is an inclusive or near-polyarchy.

If a regime is a polyarchy, it is more likely to exist in a country at a relatively high level of socioeconomic development than at a lower level.

The major propositions advanced so far are, on the evidence, pretty much beyond dispute: it makes sense to speak of "levels" or "stages," for all the major socioeconomic indicators are highly interrelated and tend to change together. And not only competitive politics in general but polyarchy in particular are significantly associated with relatively high levels of socioeconomic development. The answer to the question posed at the beginning of this section is, then, reasonably clear: The chances for political competition do indeed depend on the socioeconomic level of the society.

Yet even though the argument up to this point is well supported by all the evidence now available, it does not take us

Table 5.2. Distribution of 29 Polyarchies
by Levels of Socioeconomic Development

	Total N	GNP per capita Range	Mean	Polyarchies Percent of countries at same socioeconomic level N	Polyarchies Percent of countries at same socioeconomic level	Percent of all polyarchies
"Traditional primitive" societies	11	$45–64	$56	0[a]	0	0
"Traditional civilizations"	15	70–105	87	1[b]	6.7%	3.5%
"Transitional societies"	31	108–239	173	1[c]	3.6	3.5
"Industrial Revolution" societies	36	262–794	445	13	36.0	45.0
"High mass consumption" societies	14	836–2577	1330	14	100.0%	48.0
Totals	107			29		100.0%

Note: Polyarchies classified by the author; see appendix table A-3. The six near-polyarchies in table A.3 are excluded from the polyarchies above. Levels of socioeconomic development are from Bruce M. Russett et al., *World Handbook of Political and Social Indicators* (New Haven: Yale University Press, 1964), p. 294. The number of countries in this table is slightly larger than in table 5.1, which is from Russett's *Trends in World Politics*. Russett's five stages use six socioeconomic indicators and three political indicators (percent voting, percent military personnel, and expenditures of the central government). While relationships among the six socioeconomic indicators are strong, their relation to these particular "political" variables is quite weak, and the location of a country among the five "stages" seems to be independent of the three political indicators. Consequently, in spite of the slight contamination of "percent voting" with our measure of polyarchy, the relationship between polyarchy and the five "stages" given by Russett does not appear to be spurious.

[a] Somalia, which had maintained an inclusive polyarchy from independence in 1960 to 1969, was not included by Russett et al. in this classification. Somalia's per capita GNP is given as $57 (ibid, p. 157). In October 1969, the Somali Army seized power, arrested all government ministers, and dissolved the National Assembly.

[b] India.

[c] The Philippines.

very far. In fact, it leaves a number of crucial questions unanswered about the nature and strength of the very general relation between competitive politics and socioeconomic "level."

Table 5.3. Polyarchy and Socioeconomic Development

Socioeconomic indicator	All countries		Polyarchies and near-polyarchies	
	N	Mean	N	Mean
Population in localities over 20,000	120	23%	31	38%
GNP per capita, 1957	122	$377	32	$822
Wage and salary earners	79	35%	31	42%
Labor force in agriculture	98	50%	27	19%
Nonagricultural employment as % of working-age pop.	77	36%	31	46%
Employment in industry as % of working pop.	78	15%	31	20%
Enrollment in higher education per 100,000 pop.	105	281	33	499
Enrollment in primary and secondary education as % of pop. aged 5–19	125	43%	33	62%
Literate, 15 years and over	118	52%	33	82%

Note: Figures for all countries are from Russett et al., *World Handbook*. Figures for polyarchies and near-polyarchies are computed from data supplied by Yale Political Data Program. Variations in number of countries occur because of missing data. Classification of polyarchies by the author; see appendix table A-3.

Some Unsettled Questions

Are there "thresholds"?

One such question is whether there are "thresholds" below or above which the chances for competitive politics or polyarchy do not change enough to matter. To pose the problem in a different way, is the relationship linear or curvilinear?

An inspection of the evidence (for example, in tables 5.2 and 5.3) strongly suggests that the relationship is not linear, and instead that:

There exists an upper threshold, perhaps in the range of about $700–800 GNP per capita (1957 U.S. dollars), above which the chances of polyarchy (and hence of competitive politics) are so high that any further increases in per capita GNP (and variables associated with such an increase) cannot affect the outcome in any significant way.

There exists a lower threshold, perhaps in the range of about $100–200 GNP per capita, below which the chances for polyarchy (although not necessarily other forms of competitive politics) are so slight that differences in per capita GNP or variables associated with it do not really matter.

What about the deviant cases?

Yet even if we accept the idea of "thresholds," it is definitely not true that competitive regimes or even polyarchies exist only in countries at a high level of socioeconomic development. Nor is it true that all countries at a high level of socioeconomic development have polyarchies, or even competitive regimes. Any ranking of a considerable number of countries along the dimensions of economic or socioeconomic development and political competition or polyarchy invariably displays a fair number of deviant cases.[5] Discrepancies and deviant cases are furnished, for example, by India, a

5. For examples see Hagen's "Classification of Asian and African Countries by Type of Political Structure and Rank in Economic Development" and also his similar classification of Latin American countries in "A Framework for Analyzing," Tables 1.1, 1.2, pp. 2, 4; and figure 1, "Relationship of Political Development to Communications Development: 71 nations," in Cutright, "National Political Development, Its Measurement and Social Correlates," pp. 572–73. See also James S. Coleman's "Composite Rank Order of Latin American Countries on Eleven Indices of Economic Development" and the similar rank ordering of Asian and African countries in Gabriel A. Almond and James S. Coleman, *The Politics of the Developing Areas* (Princeton: Princeton University Press, 1960), pp. 541–42. Also Adelman and Morris, "Scatter Diagram Relating per capita GNP and Country Scores on Factor Representing the Extent of Democracy," *Society, Politics, and Economic Development,* p. 262.

competitive regime—indeed a polyarchy—in a country with a 1957 GNP per capita of about $73; by the USSR and East Germany, both hegemonic regimes at high socioeconomic levels (1957 GNP: $600); by the puzzling political contrasts among four Latin American countries at comparatively high levels of socioeconomic development—Argentina ($490), Chile ($379), Cuba ($431), and Uruguay ($478); among "transitional" societies by the existence of competitive regimes in the Philippines ($220), Turkey ($220), and Ceylon ($128) but not in Paraguay ($114), Indonesia ($131), Egypt ($142), and Portugal ($224).

If the contemporary world furnishes a large supply of discrepant examples, history also provides its share. How do we account for the early appearance of an inclusive polyarchy in the United States? Goldsmith has estimated that at about the time Tocqueville wrote *Democracy in America,* American GNP per capita was around $350–400.[6] But competitive politics was established in the United States well before Tocqueville's visit. The country already had created an inclusive polyarchy (for whites) by 1800, when per capita GNP would have been considerably lower than in 1840. What is more, according to the usual indicators of socioeconomic level, the United States in 1800 was definitely agricultural, premodern and nonindustrial. By 1820, there were only five cities larger than 50,000. Only about 3 percent of the total population lived in cities over 25,000. As much as 93 percent of the population lived in strictly rural territory. Of the total working force, some 70 percent were

6. In 1957 prices. Raymond Goldsmith, "Long Period Growth in Income and Product, 1939–1960" in Ralph Andreano, ed., *New Views on American Economic Development* (Cambridge, Mass.: Schenkman, 1965), chart II, p. 357. Goldsmith calculated GNP in 1929 prices. I have converted to 1957 prices using U.S., Department of Commerce, *U.S. Income and Output* (Washington, D.C.: Government Printing Office, 1958), table VII-2, "Implicit Price Deflators for Gross National Product or Expenditure 1929–1957," pp. 220–21.

engaged in agriculture.[7] And of course no families had telephones, radios, or automobiles. A social scientist armed only with the data examined so far—and the theories often used to explain these data—might justifiably conclude that in the early nineteenth century there was scarcely a chance for the development of democracy in America, yet I suspect that most of us continue to find Tocqueville's interpretation more convincing.

What holds for the United States holds not only for Australia, New Zealand, and Canada, but in some degree for Britain, Norway, Sweden, and a number of other European countries where competitive politics (though not inclusive polyarchy) existed in the nineteenth century. By the indicators applied to the contemporary world, these countries were then at low levels of socioeconomic development.

That competitive politics is undoubtedly associated in some way with socioeconomic development is not, it seems, a very satisfactory—nor perhaps even a very interesting—conclusion. What is more tantalizing is the fact that the association is weak, that the conclusion ignores a number of critical deviant cases, and that the relationship of one to the other is unexplained. Among other mysteries in the relationship is the direction of causation.

What about the causal direction?

Do high levels of socioeconomic organization and productivity "cause" competitive politics? Does competitive politics, conversely, induce socioeconomic development? Do competitive politics and socioeconomic development interact and reinforce one another? Or, finally, are both caused by something else?

As the authors of the studies cited earlier frequently warn, to demonstrate that a relationship exists tells nothing about

7. The data are from U.S., Bureau of the Census, *Historical Statistics of the United States, Colonial Times to 1957* (Washington, D.C.: Government Printing Office, 1960), pp. 14 and 72.

causes.[8] Causes can be teased out of data only with the aid of theory.

One thing seems clear, however: whatever the causal relationships may be, they are not simple and one-directional.

Causal theory that could account for both the general tendency and the deviant cases would have to be complex. For the evidence simply does not sustain the hypothesis that a high level of socioeconomic development is either a necessary or a sufficient condition for competitive politics nor the converse hypothesis that competitive politics is either a necessary or a sufficient condition for a high level of socioeconomic development.[9]

I do not believe it is possible at this time to advance acceptable causal theory that will account for all the cases. All I hope to de here is to offer some explanations that will help us to understand both the general tendency and the deviant cases. I do not offer what follows as in any sense a complete theory.

Are preindustrial societies inherently unsuitable for competitive politics?

The relation between competitive politics and preindustrial societies poses a paradox. In the nineteenth century, in certain preindustrial societies, competitive politics and in some cases even polyarchy flourished: the United States, Australia, New Zealand, Canada, Norway, Sweden, to name a few. But in the contemporary world, few countries in the preindustrial stages have polyarchal regimes; in fact they are much more likely to have hegemonic or authoritarian regimes.

8. See, for example, the disclaimer of Adelman and Morris, *Society, Politics, and Economic Development,* p. 148.
9. For a similar critique, see Dankwart A. Rustow, "Democracy, Consensus, and the New States," presented to the International Political Science Association, Brussels, September 1967; and his "Transitions to Democracy: Toward a Dynamic Model," *Comparative Politics* 2 (April 1970): 337–64.

The solution to this paradox is to be found in the fact that the European and English-speaking preindustrial, agrarian societies of the nineteenth century (not to mention the Athens of Pericles) were in many respects very different from the preindustrial societies of the modern world. Doubtless preindustrial United States would contrast most sharply with a contemporary preindustrial society, which is ordinarily marked by widespread illiteracy, a tradition-bound, preliterate, prescientific culture, weak or fragmented systems of communication, severe inequalities of wealth, status, and power, a tiny or nonexistent independent middle class, and frequently a tradition of autocratic or authoritarian rulership. One has only to read Tocqueville to see how radically different on each of these characteristics was the America he saw.[10]

Added to all these structural differences there is frequently an important difference in the role assigned to the state in socioeconomic development. To be sure, the state was never a negligible force in the complex processes of transforming agricultural societies into urbanized industrial societies in

10. Even making due allowance for exaggeration by Tocqueville, it is obvious that no contemporary would describe a preindustrial society today in these terms: "The social condition of the Americans is eminently democratic; this was its character at the foundation of the colonies, and it is still more strongly marked at the present day . . . Even the germs of aristocracy were never planted in [New England] . . . But wealth circulates with inconceivable rapidity, and experience shows that it is rare to find two succeeding generations in the full enjoyment of it . . . I do not believe that there is a country in the world where, in proportion to the population, there are so few ignorant and at the same time so few learned individuals. Primary instruction is within the reach of everybody; superior instruction is scarcely to be obtained by any . . . In America there are but few wealthy persons . . . In America most of the rich men were formerly poor . . . In America the aristocratic element has always been feeble from its birth . . . We can scarcely assign to it any degree of influence on the course of affairs . . . Men are there seen on a greater equality in point of fortune and intellect, or, in other words, more equal in strength, than in any other country of the world, or in any age of which history has preserved the remembrance." *Democracy in America* (New York: Vintage Books, 1955), 1: 48–55.

the nineteenth and twentieth centuries; governments, even in the United States, generally played a key part. But ordinarily they did not have a commanding role; economic development was more "autonomous" than "induced." [11] By contrast, in many preindustrial countries today political leaders are committed to using all the means of inducement and coercion available to the state in order to transform or displace the traditional and often stubbornly resistant institutions of the older society.

Thus wherever competitive politics was highly developed in preindustrial societies during the nineteenth century, political leaders were essentially commited to an outlook and strategy that left most of the initiative for development to nongovernmental groups. Among preindustrial societies today, the leadership is much more prone to the outlook and strategy of *dirigisme*. The first perspective helped to produce a considerable measure of autonomy and decentralization in the social order. In the perspective more characteristic of today's world, autonomy and decentralization merely perpetuate the traditional society and impede the transformations needed for economic growth. Hence the strategies of change employed by leaders in contemporary preindustrial societies are more likely to emphasize a compelling need for centralization and hegemony.

If some deviant cases in this century make perfectly clear that industrialization and urbanization are not sufficient conditions for competitive politics (for example, the USSR or Germany in the 1930s), the historical deviant cases demonstrate that industrialization and urbanization are not even necessary conditions for competitive politics.[12] Preindustrial,

11. Bert F. Hoselitz, *Sociological Aspects of Economic Growth* (Glencoe: The Free Press, 1960), pp. 74 and 97 ff.
12. Ignoring the historically important deviant cases in which competitive politics did develop in a preindustrial setting leads, I think, to an exaggerated emphasis on the importance of urbanization in the development of democratic systems. For an example, see Donald J. McCrone and Charles F. Cnudde, "Towards A Communications

rural, agrarian societies are definitely not inherently unsuitable for competitive politics or even for polyarchy. For some preindustrial, rural, agrarian societies have had competitive political systems—have sometimes, indeed, provided a marvelous foundation for an inclusive polyarchy.

If a preindustrial society is a poor setting for competitive politics or polyarchy in the modern world, surely this is a consequence of social characteristics such as illiteracy, poverty, a weak middle class, and an authoritarian political culture. Today these characteristics are associated with a weak industrial and urban base. But they are not—or at any rate were not—inherent features of preindustrial societies.

Explaining the Relationship

Assuming, now, that there is a relationship between public contestation (and polyarchy) and level of socioeconomic development, that there are important exceptions, and that there may be thresholds below and above which the chances for polyarchy or public contestation do not change significantly—how can we account for all this?

A very general hypothesis will help, I think, to establish the connection between political system and socioeconomic level:

> The chances that a country will develop and maintain a competitive political regime (and, even more so, a polyarchy) depend up on the extent to which the country's society and economy
>> (a) provide literacy, education, and communication,
>> (b) create a pluralistic rather than a centrally dominated social order,
>> (c) and prevent extreme inequalities
> among the politically relevant strata of the country.

Theory of Democratic Political Development: A Causal Model," *American Political Science Review* 61 (March 1967): 72–79.

I shall examine briefly the first two conditions in this chapter. Because of its importance and complexity, the next chapter is devoted entirely to the third.

Literacy, education and communication

It is surely unnecessary to argue here that whenever the citizen body is large the chances for extensive participation and a high degree of public contestation depend to some degree on the spread of reading, writing, literacy, education, and newspapers or their equivalents. I do not propose to explore the exact nature of this dependence and the possibilities of compensating for illiteracy in various ways, as in India or Turkey. The relevant point is that the extent of literacy, education, newspapers, and other forms of communication is—as we saw earlier—related to urbanization and industrialization. The development of cities, commerce, industry, and the professions not only requires but also fosters these elemental requirements.

However, a moderately educated people with a generous supply of newspapers (or, today, access to radios and television sets) does not require a highly industrialized or urbanized society. After all, as Tocqueville pointed out, most white Americans were literate in the early nineteenth century; opportunities for a modest education were fairly widespread (though perhaps less than Tocqueville thought), newspapers were generally available, and political communication seems to have been moderately efficient despite the great area over which Americans were spread. In other countries, too, widespread literacy and education have preceded extensive industrialization, the growth of cities, and high average per capita incomes: New Zealand, Australia, Canada, Norway, Iceland, and Finland are all examples. For the costs of providing a general access to education and news media are not so high that they cannot be borne by moderately prosperous agrarian societies.

It seems reasonable, then, to conclude that:

> The hypothetical lower threshold for competitive politics could be accounted for, in part, by the difficulty countries below this level have in mobilizing the resources required for widespread literacy, education, and news media.

> Nonetheless, these minimal needs for competitive politics, and particularly for polyarchy, can be met by countries above this lower threshold, even though these countries are predominantly agricultural, rural, and unindustrialized.

> Thus the need to meet these minimal requirements helps to account for the lower threshold but does not account for the general relationship.

A pluralistic social order

Consider now what a relatively "advanced economy" both makes possible *by* its performance and requires *for* its performance. An advanced economy not only can afford but also requires the reduction of illiteracy, the spread of universal education, widespread opportunities for higher education, and a proliferation of means of communication. Not only can it afford to produce an educated labor force, but it needs one: workers able to read and write, skilled workers who can read blueprints and respond to written directions, engineers, technicians, scientists, accountants, lawyers, managers of all kinds. Not only does it produce but it must have speedy and reliable systems of communication, including systems that transmit a vast amount of public or quasi-public information. It not only makes possible but at the same time requires a multiplicity of durable and highly specialized organizations manned by strongly motivated staffs who are loyal to the goals of the organization: factories, banks, stores, schools, universities, hospitals, mass transit systems, and thousands upon thousands of other types of organizations.

Because of its inherent requirements, an advanced economy and its supporting social structures automatically distribute political resources and political skills to a vast variety of individuals, groups, and organizations. Among these skills and resources are knowledge; income, status, and esteem among specialized groups; skill in organizing and communicating; and access to organizations, experts, and elites. These skills and resources can be used to negotiate for advantages —for oneself, for a group, for an organization. Groups and organizations develop a thrust toward autonomy, internal and parochial loyalties, complex patterns of cohesion and cleavage. When conflicts arise, as they inevitably do, access to political resources helps individuals and groups to prevent the settlement of the conflict by compulsion and coercion and to insist, instead, upon some degree of negotiation and bargaining—explicit, implicit, legal, a-legal, illegal. Thus systems of bargaining and negotiation grow up within, parallel to, or in opposition to hierarchical arrangements; and these systems help to foster a political subculture with norms that legitimate negotiating, bargaining, logrolling, give and take, the gaining of consent as against unilateral power or coercion.

Even within ostensibly hierarchical organizations, leaders learn that compulsion and coercion are often damaging to incentives. In an advanced economy, long-run performance under threat or coercion is less productive at all levels than a more willing performance based upon voluntary compliance. Thus the fear of punishment for bad performance is not merely supplemented but in many respects displaced by the expectation of rewards for successful performance. Just as slave labor is in general less efficient than free labor, so badly paid, discontented workers are less productive in the long run than highly paid, contented workers. For technicians, executives, scientists, and intellectuals the need for a measure of willing performance, based on their "consent,"

is even greater. And a large measure of autonomy and dis-
cretion is also found to produce better results than rigid,
overcentralized supervision.

Thus an advanced economy automatically generates many
of the conditions required for a pluralistic social order. And
as a pluralistic social order evolves, at least in an elementary
form, some of its members make demands for participating
in decisions by means more appropriate to a competitive
than to a hegemonic political system.

If we use a single arrow with a C to suggest the direction
of causation, the argument might be represented as follows:

Advanced economy −C→ pluralistic social order −C→
     demands for a competitive political system

The argument as it stands is, to be sure, oversimple. It
requires at least three qualifications:

First, even if an advanced economy creates *some* of the
conditions required for a pluralistic social order, it does not
create *all* the conditions required: witness the USSR and
East Germany, which combine rather advanced economies
with centrally dominated social orders.

As we have already observed, the fit between economic
"level" and political system is loose; yet just as the fit is
better at very low levels (polyarchies rare), so it is better
at very high levels (hegemonic systems rare). Our argument
implies—rightly, I think—that as countries with hegemonic
systems move to high levels of economic development (for
example, the USSR and the Eastern European countries) a
centrally dominated social order is increasingly difficult to
maintain. For if our argument is correct, economic development itself generates the conditions of a pluralistic social
order. The monopoly over socioeconomic sanctions enjoyed
by the hegemonic leaders is therefore undermined by the
very success of their economy: the more they succeed in
transforming the economy (and with it, inevitably, the society) the more they are threatened with political failure.

If they allow their monopoly over socioeconomic sanctions to fragment and yet seek to retain their political hegemony by exploiting their monopoly over violence—a transformation from a centrally dominated social order to what was called earlier a quasi-pluralistic social order with repressive violence—then they confront the enormous limitations, costs, and inefficiencies of violence, coercion, and compulsion in managing an advanced society where incentives and complex behavior are needed that cannot be manipulated by threats of violence.[13]

The tensions within a hegemonic regime in a society at a high level of development might be indicated as follows, where the jagged, double-ended arrows represent conflict.

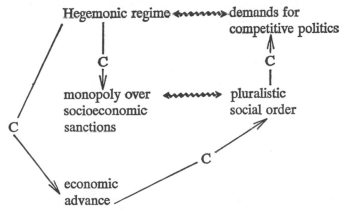

13. For a similar view see Alexander Eckstein, "Economic Development and Political Change in Communist Systems," *World Politics* 22 (1970): 475–95. George Fisher argues that the Soviet authorities may be able to contain pressures for social pluralism and liberalization without imparing economic incentives. If I understand his argument correctly, he foresees a "limited monism" in which "autonomy from state control" is denied to "major social groups in the society" but permitted "in professional and personal life, in technical activities (including the economy), and in some parts of law and public affairs." *The Soviet System and Modern Society* (New York: Atherton, 1968), pp. 14–18, 142–53. However, I am unable to see how the evidence in his book on the emergence of "dual executives" in the USSR supports his argument.

Second, while economic "success" may threaten hegemonies by generating demands for political liberalization, economic success has not threatened polyarchies, but economic failure has. For economic difficulties, particularly when they take the form of severe unemployment or rapid inflation, generate demands for a hegemonic regime and a centrally dominated social order.

Third, it may be that the sharpness of this difference is already being blunted, for it is now becoming evident that affluent societies generate their own frustrations and discontents. Although affluence may increase the pressures for competitive politics in countries now ruled by hegemonic regimes, it is far from clear that affluence will continue to strengthen allegiance to democracy in countries that already have inclusive polyarchies.

6. EQUALITIES AND INEQUALITIES

Ever since Aristotle, and probably since the pre-Socratic philosophers, it has been commonly held among political theorists that extreme inequalities help to produce hegemonic regimes and that nonhegemonic systems of a more egalitarian sort must contain a preponderant middling group of citizens more or less equal and therefore must avoid extreme differences (among citizens) in status, income, and wealth. Advanced industrial societies harbor powerful tendencies toward extreme inequalities, and yet—a phenomenon the Greeks could not foresee—inclusive polyarchies have flourished most in advanced industrial countries. This seeming contradiction has given rise to many explanations. Some seek to solve the puzzle by explaining away the inequalities in these countries, while others solve it by explaining away the "democracy": their outwardly "democratic" regimes are really hegemonies in disguise.

The bearing of the social order and the economic level on equality has already been touched on at a number of points in our discussion, but it is time now to bring certain inconclusive matters into sharper focus.

Equalities and inequalities in a society seem to affect the chances for hegemony or political competition by way of at least two different sets of intervening variables: the distribution of political resources and skills and the creation of resentments and frustrations.

The Distribution of Political Resources and Skills

In allocating income, wealth, status, knowledge, occupation, organizational position, popularity, and a variety of other values, every society also allocates resources with which an actor can influence the behavior of other actors in at least some circumstances. These resources then become political resources. Who receives what and how much political resources is not, however, simply an inert output of socioeconomic institutions. Actors who influence or control the state may use the various powers of the state to rearrange the initial distribution of political resources that results from the processes of the socioeconomic institutions: by income taxes, for example, or by imposing limits on campaign contributions; or they may actually create and allocate new political resources, such as the suffrage.

Extreme inequalities in the distribution of such key values as income, wealth, status, knowledge, and military prowess are equivalent to extreme inequalities in political resources. Obviously a country with extreme inequalities in political resources stands a very high chance of having extreme inequalities in the exercise of power, and hence a hegemonic regime. So much for the axiomatics.

In agrarian societies, I suggested earlier, such key values as knowledge, wealth, income, status, and power are strongly intercorrelated: the well-off are well-off in all these respects while the badly-off—who are the bulk of the population in many agrarian societies—are badly-off in all respects. Political resources then, are strongly cumulative: if actor A outranks actor B with respect to one political resource, say wealth or income, then A also outranks B with respect to all other political resources, knowledge, say, or status. Yet as we have seen there are two major variants of the agrarian society. To put it simply: in the traditional peasant society there is extreme inequality in the distribution of values, hence in political resources, and consequently in the exercise of power. But in the free farmer society there is a considerably greater degree of equality in the distribution of values, hence in political resources, and so in the exercise of power. If the relatively greater condition of equality in a free farmer society is also associated with a larger measure of political equality allocated through suffrage, competitive parties, elections, and responsive leaders, then the accumulation of inequalities is even further inhibited. By accumulating popularity, followers, and votes, leaders may offset some of the potential effects of differences in wealth and status, and use the regulatory powers of the state to curtail these differences or their consequences for political life.

Some interesting evidence on this point is furnished in a study by Russett on the relationship between regime and inequality in the distribution of land in 47 countries around 1960. Inclusive polyarchies are more common among countries with the greatest equality in land distribution. Conversely, countries with the greatest inequality tend to be nonpolyarchies. (Tables 6.1 and 6.2) Of the 23 countries with greater than median equality in land, 17 are inclusive polyarchies. To look at the data in another way, of the 24 inclusive polyarchies, 17 are above the median. Of the 24 countries with median equality or less, only 7 are inclusive polyarchies and 15 are nonpolyarchies. Because polyarchal countries are more developed economically on the average, in these countries less of the labor force is employed in agriculture; hence equalities and inequalities in land distribution have a smaller impact on political life. For example, among the 7 inclusive polyarchies with median equality or less, 5 have less than a third of their labor force in agriculture. By contrast, among the hegemonies, which have a relatively high proportion of their labor force in agriculture, the consequences of land inequality for political life are enhanced.

Table 6.1. Polyarchies, Near-Polyarchies, and Nonpolyarchies,
by Degree of Inequality in Land Distribution,
47 Countries, circa 1960

Gini index of inequality[a]	Inclusive polyarchies[b]	Near-polyarchies[b]	Nonpolyarchies[b]
43.7			Yugoslavia
45.0			Poland
45.8	Denmark		
47.0	Japan		
49.7	Canada		
49.8	Switzerland		
52.2	India		
56.4	Philippines		
57.7	Sweden		
58.3	France		
58.7	Belgium		
59.8	Ireland		
59.9	Finland		
60.5	Netherlands		
63.8	Luxembourg		
65.2			Taiwan
66.9	Norway		
67.1			South Vietnam
67.4	West Germany		
70.0			Libya
70.5	United States		
71.0	United Kingdom		
73.7		Panama[d]	
74.0	Austria		
74.0			Egypt
74.7			Greece
75.7			Honduras
75.7			Nicaragua
77.3	New Zealand		
78.0			Spain
79.2			Cuba
79.5			Dominican Republic
80.3	Italy		
81.7	Uruguay		
82.8			El Salvador
83.7			Brazil
84.9		Colombia	
86.0			Guatemala
86.3			Argentina
86.4			Ecuador
87.5			Peru
88.1			Iraq

EQUALITIES AND INEQUALITIES

85

Table 6.1 (*continued*)

Gini index of inequality[a]	Inclusive polyarchies[b]	Near-polyarchies[b]	Nonpolyarchies
89.1	Costa Rica		
90.9		Venezuela	
92.9	Australia		
93.8	Chile[c]		
93.8			Bolivia

Data Source: Bruce M. Russett, "Inequality and Instability: The Relation of Land Tenure to Politics, *World Politics* 16 (April 1964): 442–54, table 2.
[a] The Gini index is a generally accepted measure of inequality. See, e.g., Hayward Alker, Jr., and Bruce M. Russett, "Indices for Comparing Inequality," in Richard L. Merritt and Stein Rokkan, eds., *Comparing Nations: The Use of Quantitative Data in Cross-National Research* (New Haven: Yale University Press, 1966), pp. 349–82.
[b] The classification here differs from Russett's, who classifies the countries as stable democracies, unstable democracies, and dictatorships. For the classification used here, see appendix table A-3.
[c] Because of suffrage limitations based on literacy, in 1960 Chile was much less inclusive than the others, though high on the dimension of public contestation.
[d] Subsequently a nonpolyarchy.

Among the hegemonies with median equality or less, all except Argentina have more than a third of their labor force in agriculture; many in fact have more than half in agriculture.

Table 6.2. Polyarchy and Inequality in Land

	Greater than median equality (N)	Median equality or less (N)	Total
Inclusive polyarchies	17	7[a]	24
Near-polyarchies	1	2	3
Nonpolyarchies	5	15	30
Total N	23	24	57

Data Source: Russett, "Inequality and Instability."
[a] Includes Chile.

As an agrarian society becomes industrialized a profound change takes place in the nature of the equalities and inequalities among the citizens or subjects. Industrialization reallocates rewards and privileges in a drastic way. To be

sure, these new allocations are often highly unequal. Yet as
I suggested earlier the needs of an advanced industrial society
and the aspirations it helps to create and to satisfy, disperse
many political resources that in traditional peasant societies
are the monopoly of tiny elites—literacy, education, technical
knowledge, organizational skills, access to leaders, and the
like. If industrial societies do not eliminate inequalities they
significantly reduce many of them.[1] As average income rises
with advancing technology and growing productivity, more
and more advantages hitherto arrogated to small elites come
within reach of an expanding proportion of the population.
Even inequality in incomes (before taxes) probably decreases.

Some interesting evidence on this point is provided by a
study of income and inequality in the United States in 1959–
60. Among the 51 political units consisting of the 50 states
and the District of Columbia, there is a rather strong negative
correlation ($-.78$) between the median income of each unit
and the degree of inequality in the distribution of income
in the unit. As might be expected, the more unequal the distribution of incomes in a state, the more unequal also the
distribution of housing and education.[2] (Table 6.3)

In loose language, then, one might say that as a country
approaches high levels of industrialization, extreme inequalities in important political resources decline; while this
process does not produce equality it does produce greater
parity in the distribution of political resources.

1. See Lenski's conclusion (Gerhard Lenski, *Power and Privilege*
[New York: McGraw-Hill, 1966]), p. 437.
2. David I. Verway, "A Ranking of States by Inequality Using Census
and Tax Data," *Review of Economics and Statistics* 48, no. 3 (August 1966): 314–21. In Verway's study (p. 320) the Gini index of
inequality in incomes correlates as follows with other standard
measures:

       Share of top 20% 0.98
       Share of top 10% 0.88
       Share of top 5 % 0.72

Moreover, industrial societies, I suggested earlier, change
the pattern of inequalities in still another way: although they
do not wholly prevent the accumulation of values—particularly wealth, income, and status—in comparison with a traditional peasant society they drastically reduce the accumulation of *political* resources and create instead a system of
dispersed inequalities under which actors badly off with respect to one kind of political resource stand a good chance

Table 6.3. Income and Inequality for the United States,
by States and the District of Columbia, 1959–60:
Coefficients of Correlation

	Gini index of inequality in incomes
Median income	−.78
Gini index of inequality	
Housing	
Owner-occupied	0.65
Renter-occupied	0.73
Education	0.76
Use of servants: percentage	
employed in households	0.77

Source: David I. Verway, "A Ranking of States by Inequality Using Census
and Tax Data," *Review of Economics and Statistics* 48, no. 3 (August
1966): 319–20.

of having access to some other and partly offsetting political
resource. If the political regime itself is a polyarchy, then
the system of dispersed inequalities is strengthened even
more.

Whether the development of an industrial society increases
or decreases equality depends, then, on the type of agrarian
society within which industrialization takes place. Introduced
into a traditional peasant society, industrialization is, sooner
or later, an equalizing force: it transforms a system of cumulative inequalities into a system of greater parity with
respect to some key resources, and with respect to political
resources in general it disperses (but does not eradicate)
inequalities. Introduced into a free farmer society, however,

industrialization may actually increase inequalities in political resources, even though these inequalities are dispersed rather than cumulative.[3]

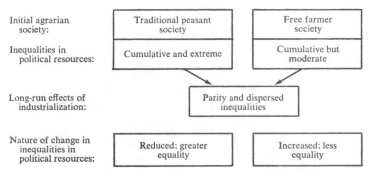

FIGURE 6.1 Industrial Society and Inequality

The argument of this section is summarized schematically in Figure 6.1.

The Creation of Resentments and Frustrations

If inequalities foster resentments, then resentments over inequality must exist even in industrial societies, for although inequalities may be less extreme and more dispersed in an industrial society than in a traditional peasant society, the

3. In *Who Governs* (New Haven: Yale University Press, 1961), I interpreted historical evidence drawn from New Haven (which would be typical in this respect, I think, of most old cities of the Eastern seaboard) as indicating a shift between the eighteenth and twentieth centuries from cumulative to dispersed inequalities. This is not inconsistent with the view that in agrarian America, as distinct from these few old urban centers, the shift from the early eighteenth to the twentieth century was from relative equality to dispersed inequalities. Michael Zuckerman's arresting interpretation of town life in colonial Massachusetts as highly consensual and relatively egalitarian would lend support to this view. See his *Peaceable Kingdoms: New England Towns in the Eighteenth Century* (New York: Knopf, 1970).

remaining inequalities are very far from negligible. Do they not then weaken the allegiance to the regime among the less well-off strata? If so, how can we explain the fact that most polyarchies, presumably the very regimes most endangered by inequality, actually developed in the midst of severe and widespread inequalities? What is more, many polyarchal regimes exist even now in societies with enormous inequalities of some kinds, for example, with respect to incomes, wealth, or the chances for higher education. How, in these circumstances, can polyarchy endure?

I hope that every reader will understand that in trying to explain these things, as I am about to do, I do not wish to justify them. That polyarchies have tolerated a good deal of inequality does not imply that they should. Yet the fact that considerable inequality in the distribution of incomes, wealth, education, and other values can persist in polyarchies without stimulating enough opposition to bring about a change either in the governmental policies that permit these inequalities or in the regime itself is a matter that needs explaining.

The explanation is, I think, in two parts:

> When demands for greater equality arise, a regime may gain allegiance among the deprived group by responding to some part of the demands, though not necessarily all of them.

> But a great deal of inequality does not generate among the disadvantaged group political demands for greater equality.

Responses by governments

A situation of objective inequality may give rise to a demand that its causes be removed, but it may not. If demands do arise, they may or may not be directed to the government. The inequality may be reduced or eliminated as a result of actions taken by the government, but unequal conditions may also be reduced even if the government takes no positive action—or in some cases even in spite of wrongly directed actions of the government. In some cases, even though the government's actions are misdirected, they may reduce further demands simply because these actions symbolize to the disadvantaged group that the government is concerned. Indeed, it seems at least theoretically possible that sometimes a government's wrong-headed but seemingly well-intentioned policies may completely fail to reduce inequalities, yet the very fact that the government demonstrates its concern may be enough to hold, perhaps even to win over, the allegiance of the deprived group.

Among the various possibilities, however, two seem particularly relevant to the questions of this chapter. One moderately familiar path leads from an inequality to government responses that reduce the inequality (or the sense of inequality) and hence strengthen the allegiance of the deprived group to the regime. Here one thinks of the successful efforts of the Swedish government to reduce unemployment in the 1930s, or, during the same decade, various actions taken by the government of Franklin Roosevelt to provide more economic security in the United States.

In fact, in a number of European and English-speaking countries that now have inclusive and seemingly quite stable polyarchies, liberalized regimes responded in the last century and this to demands for a reduction in inequalities. Typically, these demands at first emphasized and resulted in the extension of political rights to strata who were excluded from legal participation in the political system; this process was substantially completed in these countries by about 1920. Then these democratic regimes became more responsive to demands, which had been made earlier, for an expansion of "social rights" to security, welfare, education, and the like. This process is still under way, though in a number of countries it has slowed down as a result of extensive reforms already carried out. By responding to these demands for greater political and social equality, a number of countries seem to have won the long battle for the allegiance of hitherto disadvantaged groups, particularly, of course, the working classes. This is illustrated by the path on the left in figure 6.2. Because this process has been adequately analyzed elsewhere, I do not think it is necessary

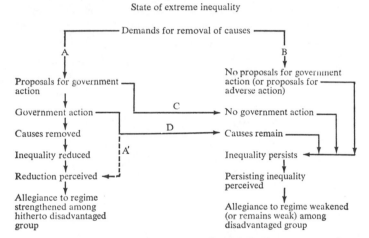

FIGURE 6.2 Some Possible Effects of Inequality on Allegiance to a Regime

to discuss it further here.[4] Path A′ represents the case of a government which is *perceived* among a disadvantaged group as having reduced inequalities, even though its actions have failed to get at the causes and the inequalities remain more

4. See, among others, T. H. Marshall, *Citizenship and Social Class* (Cambridge: Cambridge University Press, 1950) and Robert A. Dahl, ed., *Political Oppositions in Western Democracies* (New Haven: Yale University Press, 1966), pp. 359–67. Though it is still too early to judge, it is possible that a new phase began in the late 1960s that will emphasize the democratization of a variety of social, economic, and political organizations in which authority has been predominantly hierarchical.

or less unchanged. In time, of course, the fact that the government has not succeeded in reducing the inequalities may, and indeed probably will, become apparent. Yet it is quite possible that by the time this happens, the government may have acquired a considerable reserve of allegiance.

A second possibility, however, is that by its acts of commission or omission the government maintains the inequality and becomes the target for the hostilities of the disadvantaged group. Perhaps no proposals for government action arise, or at least are not vigorously pressed in public. Or, for whatever reasons, the government fails to act despite the demands made on it. Or, if it acts, its policies are misdirected. Or it may even be that policies deliberately chosen by the government are perceived as a principle cause of deprivation (for example, racial discrimination imposed by state governments). These possibilities are represented in figure 6.2 by paths B, C, and D. If, as a result, the inequality persists, then the allegiance of the disadvantaged group to the particular regime is likely to be weakened.

Because any type of regime is endangered by widespread alienation and disaffection, an extreme state of inequality resented by a large segment of the people of a country presents a threat to any regime, no matter whether hegemonic or competitive. Yet there is reason for thinking that hegemonic regimes can tolerate "more" inequality than competitive systems, particularly polyarchies. For hegemonic regimes, especially those with centrally dominated social orders, have at their disposal much more comprehensive means of coercion which they can employ to suppress the expression of discontent; the frustrations and aggressions of the disadvantaged can thus be contained and perhaps even turned inward on themselves or deflected into despair, apathy, and hopelessness. Competitive political systems have fewer resources at their disposal for coercing their people, because the essential conditions for a competitive regime, and particularly for a polyarchy, include a more or less pluralistic social order and a variety of effective legal and constitutional constraints on governmental coercion.

The difference is, I believe, a real one, and vital. But it should not be exaggerated. Athenian and American democracy each furnish us with an example of a competitive system that was inclusive with respect to one part of the population but hegemonic with respect to another (slaves, and in the United States also ex-slaves).

The American case is not only too salient to be ignored, but it helps to clarify the complex relationships between inequality and regime. As everyone knows, a competitive polyarchy in the United States enforced a state of extreme inequality on its black population both during slavery and after. In the North, for almost a century a rather inclusive polyarchy was not threatened in any significant way by the inequalities imposed on the Negroes in its midst, probably because until the end of the Second World War Negroes were a comparatively small minority, impoverished in political resources and lacking in militancy. In the South, on the other hand, Negroes were a much larger minority, and in two states even a majority.[5] To enforce a long-standing condition of extreme deprivation upon the black people of the South, southern whites (like the free Athenians) had to develop two political systems, one superimposed on the other: a more or less competitive polyarchy in which most whites were included and a hegemonic system to which Negroes were subject and to which southern whites were overwhelmingly allegiant. To maintain its dual system, the South developed repressive violence within a quasi-pluralistic social order: violence and terror were directed at Negroes in

5. In 1860, the percentage of slaves in the total population among the leading slave states was: South Carolina, 57%; Mississippi, 55%; Louisiana, 47%; Alabama, 45%; Georgia, 43%; Virginia, 40%; and North Carolina, 33%. Richard B. Morris, *Encyclopedia of American History* (New York: Harper, 1953), p. 516; U.S., Bureau of the Census, *Historical Statistics of the United States, Colonial Times to 1957* (Washington, D.C.: Government Printing Office, 1960), p. 13.

general and at the handful of deviant whites who from time
to time openly opposed the hegemonic system. The stability
of the South's dual system depended not only on the effects
of past, present, and threatened coercion in creating and
reinforcing a mood of resignation and hopelessness among
Negroes (and as the "Uncle Tom" image suggests, even a
sense that white supremacy was legitimate), but also on the
strength of an understanding with the main political strata
of the North not to interfere with the southern system. By
mid-twentieth century both of these conditions began to decay, and as each weakened, its decay reinforced the destruction of the other. While the older hegemony is by no means
totally displaced, for the past decade it has visibly been in
profound crisis. By the end of the 1960s the entry of southern Negroes into the competitive political system was well
on its way.[6] And the political hegemony based on coercive
violence was disintegrating.

Does the case of Negroes in the United States challenge
the hypothesis that competitive regimes can sustain less
relative deprivation than hegemonic regimes? The example,
I believe, argues quite the contrary: to inflict severe relative
deprivation on a large segment of the population is likely to
require, *as it did in the South,* a hegemonic political system
and a social order—whether quasi-pluralistic or centrally
dominated—with repressive violence.

Yet the example does suggest two important qualifications:
even an inclusive polyarchy can impose a relatively high
state of deprivation on a small minority if that minority, like
Negroes in the North until after World War II, is, for whatever reasons, weak not only in numbers but in all political
resources, skills, and demands. And as Athens and the American South both illustrate, historically it has been possible
to develop and even to sustain over a very long period a
dual system that is competitive with respect to the dominant
group and hegemonic with respect to a deprived minority.

6. For some data, see footnote 3, chap. 2, above.

Responses by the disadvantaged

Between a condition of objective inequality and the response of a disadvantaged person lie the perceptions, evaluations, expectations—in short, the psyche—of the individual. To the dismay and astonishment of activists who struggle to rouse a disadvantaged group to oppose its lot, the human psyche does not invariably impel those who are deprived of equality to seek it, or sometimes even to want

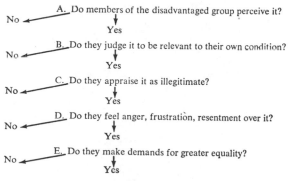

FIGURE 6.3. A Hypothetical Path from Objective Inequality to Demands for Greater Equality

it.[7] This phenomenon deserves a fuller—and better—treatment than it can have here, for I must limit myself to a few aspects of it.

Consider, then, a hypothetical path leading from objective inequality to demands for greater equality among the disadvantaged group. (Figure 6.3) To complete the circuit, "Yes" answers are required to all the questions. Yet several of the linkages are prone to failure, to "No" responses.

To be sure, it is utterly fatuous to think that the connec-

7. Robert E. Lane, "The Fear of Equality," *American Political Science Review* 53 (March 1959): 35–51.

tion between objective reality and subjective awareness breaks down so completely that the disadvantaged are unaware of their lot. If the myth of the happy poor (and the unhappy rich) still needs puncturing, Hadley Cantril provides some solid evidence that the gap between condition and aspirations decreases all over the world as one's objective situation improves. In a 14-nation survey respondents were asked to locate themselves on a hypothetical ten-step ladder between "the best possible life for you . . . and the worst possible life for you." They were also asked to locate their country on a comparable ladder. Cantril found that the higher the socioeconomic level of a country, the higher on the average its people locate their present and past positions on the "ladder" of satisfaction, as well as their country's present and past positions. He found further that people who are objectively better off with respect to education, income, or occupational status expressed more satisfaction with their condition, on the average, than did those who had low education, low incomes, or lower status occupations.[8]

Nonetheless, even if they are relatively more disatisfied with their condition, the members of a disadvantaged group may not complete all the connections along our hypothetical path. For example, at A, perceptions of inequality are sometimes clouded by changes in the conditions of one's "own" group. Thus Runciman concludes that in Britain "after the Second War, relative deprivation was damped down by the achievement of some gradual amelioration of the class situation of manual workers and the conviction that a greater distribution was taking place than in fact did occur."[9]

8. Hadley Cantril, *The Pattern of Human Concerns* (New Brunswick: Rutgers University Press, 1965), pp. 194, 258–59. The countries, by rank on Cantril's socioeconomic index, were the United States, West Germany, Israel, Japan, Poland, Cuba, Panama, Yugoslavia, Philippines, Dominican Republic, Brazil, Egypt, Nigeria, and India.
9. W. G. Runciman, *Relative Deprivation and Social Justice* (Berkeley: University of California Press, 1966), p. 94.

The connection at B often breaks down because people who are objectively disadvantaged generally do not compare themselves with the most advantaged groups, whose good fortune they simply do not consider to be relevant to their own condition, but substitute other comparisons instead. For one thing, a person in a disadvantaged group almost certainly will compare the present situation of his group with its own past (or its myths about the past); if the group believes that it is now better off than it was in the past, that belief may be far more salient and relevant than the fact that certain other groups are currently very much better off. Then, too, many people identify themselves some of the time with large collectivities like the nation or country; hence for the particular individual or group, past and present inequalities may be attenuated by the thought that the collectivity as a whole—the country, for example—is moving toward a richer or more just condition. Finally, when a person does compare himself or his "own" specific group with other individuals or groups, he is likely to make the comparison with others who are, socially speaking, not distant but quite close or adjacent to him. To the skilled worker, for example, the income and privileges of the company president are likely to be less relevant than those of semi-skilled workers just "below" him or his foreman just "above" him, or skilled workers in other plants.

Because of these various comparisons, in a society with extensive inequalities an individual may have a relatively favorable judgment of his own position even though, objectively speaking, he is seriously disadvantaged in comparison with the elites.

Some evidence directly bearing on the last possibility is provided by Runciman from his survey of some 1400 respondents in Britain. Runciman distinguished between a "comparative reference group," whose situation or attributes a person contrasts with his own, and a "membership reference group," which is "the starting-line for the inequality with the comparative reference group by which a feeling of *relative deprivtion* is engendered." [10] He found that the sense of "relative deprivation" engendered by inequalities in Britain was greatly attenuated, among other things by the tendency to compare oneself with groups socially rather close to one's own. Moreover, as I indicated above, he ascribed the rather low level of sense of relative deprivation among manual workers to recent improvements in their situation and perhaps an exaggerated notion of just how greatly the old inequalities had actually been reduced. Conversely, middle-class people were likely to harbor resentments not about the very wealthy but about the rapid gains among the working classes. Runciman also found that:

> There is a wide discrepancy between objective inequality and a subjective sense of relative deprivation.

> Irrespective of whether or not they feel their position is worsening, middle-class people are more likely to feel the prosperity of others a grievance.

> Those at the top of the manual stratum are least likely of all to think of any other sorts of people as doing better than they.

> Manual workers and their wives who have reached the top level of incomes for manual occupations are likely not to feel relatively deprived because in terms of comparisons natural to them they have done well.

> A fair proportion of the respondents give a figure as a desired income that is little or no higher than their actual income, and an even higher proportion say that they are satisfied with what they are getting.

> Within each one-third of the overall income distribution, manual ("working class") respondents are considerably more likely than nonmanual ("middle-class")

10. Ibid., p. 12. Italics mine.

respondents to give a figure as a "proper" income that is more or less equivalent to what they say they can earn at present.

Not only are comparative reference groups not chosen in accordance with the facts of inequality but such a correspondence with the facts is least likely of all among those who are in fact most unequally placed.[11]

Cantril's cross-national survey also provides some interesting, although more tangential, evidence on the connection at B. His results support the view that people often judge their own situation by what they perceive to be the direction of change for a larger collectivity with which they identify, in this case the country. He found that:

How highly people rated their own present condition— where they stood on the "ladder"—was significantly related to how highly they rated the condition of their own country, i.e., where their country stood on the "ladder."

The extent to which people felt that their condition had improved over the previous five years was significantly related to the extent they felt their country had improved.

If people expected that their personal standing would rise over the next five years, they were likely to expect that their country would also improve.[12]

These correlations do not, of course, tell us anything about the direction of cause, which doubtless flows both ways. But some comparisons of how people in specific countries rated themselves are at least suggestive. For example, in rating their present condition the two highest groups were a sample of members in 10 kibbutzim in Israel—where ob-

11. Ibid., pp. 197–210.
12. Cantril, *The Pattern of Human Concerns,* pp. 184–94.

jective equality is exceptionally high—and a sample of adults
in the United States, where the average income is exceptionally high but inequalities in income distribution are also
great. The country with the third highest ratings by its people of their personal situation was Cuba, which had undergone a revolution that greatly reduced (but by no means
eliminated) previous inequalities (probably at some cost to
average incomes) and Egypt, which had also undergone a
revolution but still suffered from extraordinary poverty and
inequalities. The highest personal expectations for the *future*
were held (in decreasing order) by the people surveyed in
Cuba, Egypt, the kibbutzim, the United States, Nigeria,
Brazil, and Panama.[13] The country that led all the rest in
the size of the change in personal ratings from past to future
(that is, in expectations of improvement) was Nigeria, one
of the poorest countries in the world and one destined, at
the time of the survey, for a catastrophic civil war. Nigeria
was followed by Cuba, the Dominican Republic, Egypt,
Brazil, and Panama.[14] Thus hopes for the future seemed to
be so much influenced by the immediacy of revolutions,
national independence, or other dramatic political changes
that there was virtually no relationship between the socioeconomic level of a country and the expectations its citizens
expressed either for their own future or that of their country.[15]

The effectiveness of the connection at C depends on the
prevailing ideas in the culture or subculture into which an
individual is socialized. A deprived group may well believe
that its present inferior condition is an inherent part of the
order of things, justified by religion and cosmology (as Hinduism gave legitimacy to caste), subject only to change
through some ultimate and perhaps apocalyptic redemption.
A world-view justifying and "rationalizing" inequality does

13. Ibid., table IX:4, p. 187.
14. Ibid., table IX:6, p. 188.
15. See the rank order correlations in ibid., p. 194.

not persist only because it is to the advantage of the elites who benefit from the status quo. Among the disadvantaged groups themselves, such a self-denying world-view may help to make a miserable and often humiliating existence more bearable and understandable. A group confronted over a long period of time by seemingly ineradicable inequalities may learn to keep its demands low and thus bring them more into line with the harsh limits of the possible.[16]

The cross-national survey by Cantril furnishes some interesting illustrative evidence on this process of "attenuation." By means of a rather open-ended but carefully designed set of questions, people were asked to talk about their hopes and fears. One might suppose that people in the more highly developed countries would express a larger number of hopes than people in poorer countries, but fewer fears. Cantril did in fact find a "positive but modest" relationship between a country's level of socioeconomic development and the volume of hopes expressed by its people, both for the self and for the nation. But contrary to what one might expect, he also found an even stronger positive corre-

16. Thus over against "the complex of ideas of ascendance which always stress the rights of the individual" in peasant societies, Mahmet Bequiraj describes the ideas of "attenuation" that

> support the existing design of the system . . . It is reasoned that persisting social problems are not so much caused by existing forms of social organization as by the faults of man; man is the reason why the presumably faultless design of social organization fails . . . The ideas of ascendance . . . endanger the balance by suggesting new wants. In contrast the ideas of attenuation supply the individual with the strength to delay gratifications and thus permit the minimization of needs . . . Given the low level of knowledge, the ideas of attenuation are functionally more significant than the ideas of ascendance. . . . They become "ends" in themselves. As virtues, they aim to solidify the existing forms of social organization . . . Detached from the influence of the ideas of ascendance and hardened into virtues, the ideas of attenuation block further development or advance in knowledge for the system.

Peasantry in Revolution (Ithaca: Center for International Studies, Cornell University, 1966), pp. 31–33.

lation between the socioeconomic level of the country and the volume of fears expressed by its people: in short, the better off the country, the more hopes *and* fears both. The two countries in which people expressed the fewest fears for both self and nation were India and Brazil. Improbable as it may seem, the country with the *lowest* volume of references to health—whether hopes or fears—was India, "where health conditions are worse than in any of the other countries studied." [17] There, the process of "attenuation," supported by Hinduism, has been carried to exhausting lengths.

The connections at the end of the path (at D and E) may also break down. Frustration, resentments, and anger may not stimulate demands for greater equality but instead may turn into resignation, apathy, despair, hopelessness, self-denigration, fantasy, millenial dreams, pious acceptance, fatalism, the mentality of the "Uncle Tom," etc. Terms like these are used, in fact, to describe the psyche of the peasant in the acutely deprivational peasant society.[18]

17. Cantril, *The Pattern of Human Concerns,* p. 164. The rank order correlations (p. 199) between volume of "concerns" (hopes and fears) and the socioeconomic index for the country was:

> Personal hopes 0.24
> National hopes 0.25
> Personal fears 0.46
> National fears 0.51

In reporting the volume of concerns, Japan and Poland are omitted. For total concerns, see p. 155.
18. See, for example, Bequiraj's remarkable portrait of the peasant, *Peasantry in Revolution,* especially pp. 1–43. For example:

> Both the pessimistic philosophy and the trend toward piety are universal among peasant groups . . . Even in his own eyes the peasant is the "dolt," the "brute," and sometimes the "villain." He has learned to live with this self-abasement with the help of a pessimistic philosophy based on an assumption of his group's inadequacies, which he uses to explain personal failures. This explanation . . . enables him to adjust to a social world which he correctly recognizes as being unjust, intemperate, and cruel. [pp. 11–12] . . . Fastening upon the utopian ethical precepts of the mores, the peasant sustains himself against the effect of the constant failures which make up his performances. His faith

The argument of this chapter can be summarized in the following propositions:

> In a country with a hegemonic regime, extreme inequalities in the distribution of key values reduce the chances that a stable system of public contestation will develop.
>
> In a society that already has a regime with public contestation, extreme inequalities increase the chances that competitive politics will be displaced by a hegemony.
>
> Polyarchies are particularly vulnerable to the effects of extreme inequalities.
>
> Extreme inequalities in the distribution of key values are unfavorable to competitive politics and to polyarchy because this state of affairs:
>
>> is equivalent to extreme inequality in the distribution of key political resources and is likely to generate resentments and frustrations which weaken allegiance to the regime.

However, systems of competitive politics and even polyarchies manage to survive a considerable measure of inequality because:

---

in the eventual advent of the "good order" induces in him reverence for the good and sacred, directing him in this way to piety. The projection of his place in this "good order" sustains his belief in his own worth, counterbalancing the debasement he experiences daily. [p. 19]

Of course it would be wrong to assume that peasants always and everywhere adhere to these views, and as Bequiraj points out, they may also stimulate insurrection and revolution if his faith in the good order is destroyed. Peasant insurrections have been, in fact, fairly common, as can be seen from the sizable number of peasant insurrections in Sorokin's list of 173 disturbances in France from the year 531 to 1908. Pitirim A. Sorokin, *Social and Cultural Dynamics* (New York: American Book Co., 1937), vol. 3, appendix. See also George Rude, *The Crowd in History, 1730–1848* (New York: Wiley, 1964), chap. 1, "The French Rural Riot of the Eighteenth Century

A great deal of inequality does not generate among the disadvantaged group political demands for greater equality or a change in the regime.

When demands for greater equality do arise, a regime may gain allegiance among the deprived groups by responding to some part of the demands, though not necessarily all of them, or by responses that do not reduce the objective inequalities but do reduce feelings of relative deprivation.

7. SUBCULTURES, CLEAVAGE PATTERNS, AND GOVERNMENTAL EFFECTIVENESS

Obviously any system is in peril if it becomes polarized into several highly antagonistic groups. Confronted by severe polarization, competitive regimes are prone to collapse, to a coup d'etat, to civil war: for example, Italy from 1919 to 1923, the first Austrian Republic virtually throughout its brief existence, the Weimar Republic from about 1929 to its demise, the Spanish Republic from 1934 to 1936, and the United States in the decade preceding our Civil War.

In the United States the victors were committed to a more or less inclusive polyarchy, a commitment that for a decade after the end of that war included even the freed slaves. But in other cases, victory went to antidemocratic movements that successfully introduced a hegemonic regime into the country.

There are conflicts, then, that a competitive political system does not manage easily and perhaps cannot handle at all. Any dispute in which a large section of the population of a country feels that its way of life or its highest values are severely menaced by another segment of the population creates a crisis in a competitive system. Whatever the eventual outcome may be, the historical record argues that the system is very likely to dissolve into civil war or to be displaced by a hegemony or both.

Thus any difference within a society that is likely to polarize people into severely antagonistic camps is a cleavage of exceptional importance. Are some countries, then, less likely than others to have competitive regimes and more likely to have hegemonic regimes because, for whatever reason, they are unusually subject to cleavages that are particularly favorable to acute polarization?

Answers to this question are, unfortunately, obscured by the massive impact on social thought of certain dramatic aspects of Marxist thought. For over a century, reflections about polarization and civil war have been dominated, even among non-Marxists, by Marx's conception of polarization around the node of economic classes—working class and bourgeoisie. Yet in the 120 years since the Communist Manifesto was published, no country has developed according to the Marxist model of conflict, nor has any regime, whether hegemonic or competitive, fallen or been transformed because of a clear-cut polarization of working class and bourgeoisie.

A preoccupation with class conflict and often an unarticulated assumption even among sophisticated social theorists that classes are somehow the "real" basis of differences in an industrial society, to which all others are "ultimately" reducible, has tended to deflect attention from other differences that give rise to durable subcultures into which individuals are socialized: these are differences in religion, language, race, or ethnic group, and region.[1]

1. Subcultures may of course be formed around economic or social "classes" or "statuses" (as these are variously defined) or around occupations, educational levels, or other characteristics that need not be strictly related to ethnic, religious, or regional characteristics. As used here, however, the term subcultural pluralism refers to the presence of ethnic, religious, or regional subcultures. One can think of subcultural pluralism as a hypothetical dimension for which a measure can be constructed in order to compare the relative "amount" of subcultural pluralism in different societies.

One might protest that it is redundant to include the term "ethnic group" in the list of characteristics on which an ethnic subculture can

Differences along these axes, differences that frequently reinforce one another, have obvious, important, and persistent consequences for political life in a great many countries —indeed, it is no exaggeration to say, in most countries in the world. Yet differences of this kind have often been ignored or deprecated as "really" nothing but class differences in disguise, or somehow less "real" than class, or if not less real then surely less enduring, bound to disappear rapidly under the impact of industrialization, urbanization, and mass communications. Yet these differences and the conflicts they engender do not always disappear and may even sharpen with the passage of time, as in contemporary Belgium, Canada, and quite possibly in Britain.

This is not to argue that "class" differences are unimportant. It is to say that economic class is only one factor, often less important than others that can and quite evidently do yield distinct subcultures—ways of life, outlooks, norms, identifications, loyalties, organizations, social structures. What is more, these subcultures are often extraordinarily long-lived not only in the life of an individual (who may change his class identification more readily than his mother tongue or his religion) but also in the life of a society: for over a thousand years, classes and empires have risen and

---

be based, since it is hard to imagine an "ethnic" identification not based, at least remotely, on one of the other differences, i.e. religion, language, race, or physical stock. There are problems of precise definition here that I am deliberately trying to skirt. However, the terms ethnic subculture and subcultural pluralism are intended to be broad enough to extend to groups for whom objective differences in language, religion, race, or physical stock have been attenuated by time but whose identification with the "historical" group nonetheless remains rather strong. Examples might be nonreligious Jews in the United States or certain other groups with distinct regional roots whose attachments are at present not merely to a region but to a historically developed identity, such as English-speaking Scots, Welsh, or Protestant Irishmen in Great Britain or Scandinavians during periods when one of the Scandinavian peoples was subject to the rule of another without yielding its own separate identity as a people.

fallen while the linguistic boundaries within what are now Belgium and Switzerland have barely changed.

Presumably because an ethnic or religious identity is incorporated so early and so deeply into one's personality, conflicts among ethnic or religious subcultures are specially fraught with danger, particularly if they are also tied to region. Because conflicts among ethnic and religious subcultures are so easily seen as threats to one's most fundamental self, opponents are readily transformed into a malign and inhuman "they," whose menace stimulates and justifies the violence and savagery that have been the common response of in-group to out-group among all mankind. The junction of ethnic group or religion with regional subcultures creates an incipient nation whose spokesmen clamor for autonomy, and even for independence. Consequently many students of politics have agreed with John Stuart Mill that the boundaries of any country with a representative government must coincide with the boundaries of nationality; a considerable body of experience with multinational states lends impressive support to their argument.[2]

That subcultural pluralism often places a dangerous strain on the tolerance and mutual security required for a system of public contestation seems hardly open to doubt. Polyarchy in particular is more frequently found in relatively homogeneous countries than in countries with a great amount of subcultural pluralism. Perhaps the best evidence for this is to be found in a study by Marie R. Haug that classifies 114 countries according to an index of pluralism[3] and data

2. Cf. Walker Connor, "Self-Determination, The New Phase," *World Politics* 20 (October 1967): 30–53. Connor summarizes the dialectical development of the argument in Britain over the viability of representative institutions in multinational countries. Against Mill stands Acton, who held that the pluralism of multinational states provides an antidote to despotism and is a civilizing influence besides; Ernest Barker in turn supported Mill against Acton; finally, Alfred Cobban aligned himself with Acton against Mill and Barker. Connor himself strongly supports Mill and Barker against Acton and Cobban.
3. "Social and Cultural Pluralism as a Concept in Social System Analysis," *American Journal of Sociology* 73, no. 3 (November

derived from *A Cross-Polity Survey* by Banks and Textor.
Although there have been some changes of regime since the
early 1960s, when the data were collected, these can hardly
have been so great as to invalidate the general relationships.
Comparing the 26 countries where cultural pluralism (in
the numerical sense) is negligible with the 34 where it is
extreme reveals that:

> Among countries in which subcultural pluralism is
> negligible, more than half are also classified by Banks
> and Textor as integrated and homogeneous polities with
> little or no extreme opposition, communalism, frac-
> tionalism, or political nonassimilation (high in political
> enculturation).

> Among these countries, none is classified as a relatively
> nonintegrated or restrictive polity with a majority or
> near-majority in extreme opposition, communalized,
> fractionalized, disfranchised, or politically nonassimi-
> lated (low in political enculturation).

> Conversely, among countries in which subcultural
> pluralism is extreme, only 10 percent are high in politi-
> cal enculturation; almost two-thirds are low in political
> enculturation.

> Among countries in which subcultural pluralism is negli-
> gible, 60 per cent are also classified by Banks and Textor
> as having an effective allocation of power to functionally
> autonomous legislative, executive, and judicial organs
> (significant horizontal power distribution).

> Among these countries, only 18 per cent are classified

1967): 294–304. The construction of the index is shown in table
2, p. 297. The variables in the index are: language, race, religion,
sectionalism, and "interest articulation by non-associational groups,"
which include kinship, lineage, ethnic, regional, and religious groups.
This purely numerical index unfortunately cannot register the depth
of sharpness or subcultural cleavages, as in the Netherlands. See the
discussion below, p. 213.

as having complete dominance of government by one branch or by an extragovernmental agency (negligible horizontal power distribution).

Conversely, among countries in which subcultural pluralism is extreme, only one-third have a significant horizontal power distribution, while in 57 per cent one branch of government is without genuine functional autonomy or two branches have only limited functional autonomy.[4]

Our own classification of political systems (also based largely on Banks and Textor) yields about 34 polyarchies and near-polyarchies as of the early 1960s.[5] These make up a relatively large portion of countries with low subcultural pluralism (measured by Haug's index of subcultural pluralism) and a relatively small proportion of countries with marked or extreme subcultural pluralism. (Table 7.1)

4. The definitions are from Arthur S. Banks and Robert B. Textor, *A Cross-Polity Survey* (Cambridge: M.I.T. Press, 1963), pp. 88 and 106. The number of countries on which data were available varied. The percentages, number of countries, and level of significance for the chi square values are:

	PLURALISM:		CHI SQUARE
	NEGLIGIBLE	EXTREME	
Political enculturation:			
High: integrated polity	52.6% (19)	0.0% (31)	31.92 (d.f.6)
Low: nonintegrated polity	10.5% (19)	63.3% (31)	$p < .001$
Horizontal power distribution			
Significant	60.0% (25)	17.9% (28)	16.04 (d.f.6)
Limited	32.0% (25)	57.1% (28)	$p < .02$

Source: Haug, "Social and Cultural Pluralism," table 7, p. 303.
5. See the appendix for the way the classification of polyarchies and near-polyarchies was derived. The classification in table 7.1 is as of the early 1960s. Appendix table A-3 is a classification as of 1969.

It is revealing to consider the polyarchies and near-polyarchies (as of the early 1960s) that are classified in table 7.1 as having marked or extreme pluralism. Of the three countries with *marked* pluralism, in Belgium subcultural conflicts have intensified since the early 1960s and in the Philippines there has been a revival of guerrilla activities in the countryside (the third is Lebanon). Among the six polyarchies with *extreme* pluralism, Sierra Leone

Table 7.1. Polyarchy and Subcultural Pluralism

| | Amount of subcultural pluralism | | | |
	Low	Moderate	Marked	Extreme
Total N	26	28	27	33
Polyarchies and near-polyarchies	15	10	3	6
Percent	58%	36%	11%	18%

Note: Low defined as 0 or 1 on Haug's index of pluralism.
    Moderate defined as 2 or 3.
    Marked defined as 4 or 5.
    Extreme defined as 6, 7, or 8.

has ceased to be even a near-polyarchy; Malaya has divided into two countries; India has had profound conflicts over language; in Ceylon, communal conflicts and restraints on oppositions made it doubtful for a time whether Ceylon even met the standards of near-polyarchy; and Canada has witnessed the eruption of French-Canadian nationalism. Of the six, only Switzerland has been relatively serene; even there demands for a separate canton have recently risen among the French-speaking citizens of the Jura.

Nonetheless, if a competitive political system is less likely in countries with a considerable measure of subcultural pluralism, it would be going too far to say that it is impossible or that subcultural pluralism necessarily rules out an inclusive polyarchy.

One fact to keep in mind is that subcultural pluralism tends to be greatest, at present, among the less developed countries. Countries with extreme subcultural pluralism are predomi-

nantly new nations: 70 per cent have achieved independence
since 1945. Thus they often bear all the typical disadvantages
of the new nations: low per capita GNP, high employment
in agriculture, low urbanization, high illiteracy, low news-
paper circulation. They are, besides, relatively large in area.
(Tables 7.2 and 7.3)

Table 7.2. Subcultural Pluralism and Socioeconomic Development: I

	Pluralism		
	Negligible	Extreme	Chi square
Date of independence			
1913 or before	72.0%	24.2%	27.33
			(d.f.6)
After 1945	8.0%	69.7%	p < .001
N	(25)	(33)	
Per capita GNP			
$600 and above	50.0%	6.1%	42.08
			(d.f.9)
Under $150	3.8%	75.8%	p < .001
N	(26)	(33)	
Pop. in agriculture			
Over 66%	3.8%	72.7%	
33% or below	50.0%	9.1%	
N	(26)	(33)	

Source: Marie R. Haug, "Social and Cultural Pluralism as a Concept in
Social System Analysis," *American Journal of Sociology* 73, no. 3 (Novem-
ber 1967), tables 5, 6, 7, pp. 301–03.
Note: Percentages are calculated vertically.

As we have seen, low levels of socioeconomic development are themselves inimical to competitive politics. In fact,
in the early stages of nation-building, typically a variety of
factors interact to undermine the chances for a competitive
regime and to produce hegemony instead; subcultural pluralism is only one of these. Hence some of the association between subcultural pluralism and hegemony can reasonably
be attributed to other factors, such as the socioeconomic
level.

Yet competitive politics *can* exist even in countries with a very considerable degree of subcultural pluralism. Indeed, Belgium, Canada, and India, among others, have managed to develop and sustain polyarchies. There is, in addition, the compelling example of the Netherlands. There, differences in language, race, physical stock, ethnic identification, or

Table 7.3. Subcultural Pluralism and Socioeconomic Development: II

| | Pluralism | | | |
	Negligible	Extreme	Total N	Chi square
Urbanization				
20% or more in cities over 20,000	41.1%	12.5%	56	40.92
Less than 20% in cities over 20,000	0.0%	51.0%	49	d.f.3 p < .001
Literacy				
90% or above	52.0%	8.0%	25	37.68
Under 10%	0.0%	57.7%	26	d.f.9 p < .001
Newspaper circulation				
300 or more per 1,000 pop.	57.1%	7.1%	14	49.57 d.f.9
Under 10 per 1,000 pop.	0.0%	57.1%	35	p < .001
Area				
300,000 sq. mi. or more	9.7%	48.4%	31	15.73
Less than 75,000 sq. mi.	29.8%	12.8%	47	d.f.6 p < .02

Source: Haug, "Social and Cultural Pluralism," tables 4 and 5, pp. 300–01.
Note: Percentages are calculated horizontally.

region play no significant part; hence, numerically speaking, subcultural pluralism is not extreme. Yet religion is a plane of cleavage that has divided the country into three great spiritual families—(Catholic, Orthodox Protestant, and the remainder). These three subcultures have been voluntarily segregated to a degree unknown in any other inclusive polyarchy; yet the Netherlands has managed to sustain, and sturdily, a representative democracy.[6] Finally, among the countries with a high degree of subcultural pluralism in the numerical sense is the impressive case of Switzerland.

At least three conditions seem to be essential if a country with considerable subcultural pluralism is to maintain its conflicts at a low enough level to sustain a polyarchy.[7]

6. Hans Daalder, "The Netherlands: Opposition in a Segmented Society," in Robert A. Dahl, ed., *Political Oppositions in Western Democracies* (New Haven: Yale University Press, 1966), and Arend Lijphart, *The Politics of Accommodation* (Berkeley: University of California Press, 1968). There is, however, a good deal of evidence that subcultural segregation in the Netherlands is rapidly declining. Daalder mentions as examples: "Catholic University of Nijmegen will appoint a Calvinist as the new professor of political science; a merger of the separate unions is almost imminent; all groups are deemphasizing labels at breakneck speed." (Personal communication, 1969)

7. My analysis here has been strongly influenced by the experience of the Netherlands, described by Daalder and Lijphart in the works just cited, and Belgium, described by Val R. Lorwin, "Religion, Class and Language in National Politics," in *Political Oppositions in Western Democracies*. In particular, see the sections in Daalder, pp. 216–20, Lijphart, pp. 197 ff. and Lorwin, pp. 174–85. I have also profited from lengthy discussions with all three scholars and an opportunity to read works in process by Daalder and Lorwin, including Lorwin's "Segmented Pluralism: Ideological Cleavage and Political Cohesion," a paper presented to the Torino Round Table of the International Political Science Association, September 1969. An invaluable source is also Lijphart's "Typologies of Democratic Systems," *Comparative Political Studies* 1 (April 1968), pp. 3–44, where he sets out four "prerequisites for consociational democracy" having to do with elite attitudes and behavior (pp. 22–23):

1. Ability to recognize the dangers inherent in a fragmented system
2. Commitment to system maintenance
3. Ability to transcend subcultural cleavage at the elite level
4. Ability to forge appropriate solutions for the demands of the subcultures

In addition, he sets out six "conditions conducive to consociational democracy" (pp. 25–30):

1. Distinct lines of cleavage between subcultures
2. A multiple balance of power among the subcultures
3. Popular attitudes favorable to government by grand coalition

First, conflict is more likely to be maintained at moderate levels if no ethnic, religious, or regional subculture is "indefinitely" denied the opportunity to participate in the government, that is, in the majority coalition whose leaders form the "government" or the administration.

This requires in turn that among a sufficient number of members of each subculture, and particularly among the leaders, there exist desires for cooperation that cut across the subcultures at least some of the time. There are several common sources of incentives toward cooperation. One is a commitment to the preservation of the nation, its unity, its independence, and its political institutions. A second is the recognition on the part of each subculture that it cannot form a majority capable of governing except by entering into a coalition with representatives of other subcultures. This condition is satisfied if every subculture constitutes a minority.

The prospects appear to be worse for a country divided essentially into two subcultures than for a country divided into more than two. For if a country is split into two subcultures, then one will be a majority and the other a minority. Indeed, even if a country is divided into more than two subcultures, one might still comprise a majority. Strictly speaking, then, in order for each subculture to be a minority,

---

4. External threats
5. Moderate nationalism
6. A relatively low total load on the system

Jurg Steiner, who has used Swiss experience to test sixteen hypotheses about conditions favorable to peaceful resolution of conflicts in "subculturally segmented democratic systems" finds that the experience of Switzerland casts doubt on the first of Lijphart's six conditions just named, though not on the others. *Bedingungen für Gewaltlose Konflictregulierungsmuster in Subkulturell Segmentierten Demokratischen Systemen: Hypothesen Entwickelt am Beispiel der Schweiz* (Thun, Switzerland: mimeo, 1968), pp. 434–37. For his comments on Lijphart's other conditions, see pp. 432–34, 439–41, and 446–50.

it is a necessary but not a sufficient condition that there be more than two subcultures.

If a country is divided into majority and minority subcultures, then members of the majority have less need to be conciliatory toward the minority, since they can form a majority coalition among themselves. As a consequence, members of the minority may see no prospect of ever freeing themselves from the political domination of the majority; hence they, too, have little incentive to be conciliatory. Doubtless this is one of the factors that now contributes to the explosiveness of racial relations in the United States. If a minority subculture is also regionally concentrated, like French-speaking Canadians, then the dangers are even greater. For as militance grows among members of the minority, they will almost certainly begin to demand greater autonomy—and in the extreme case outright independence. In Belgium, where the two subcultures are regionally based, tendencies toward national separation have been contained not only by Belgian nationalism but by several other factors as well. For one, the Walloon minority has, with justification, never felt itself to be an oppressed minority, since it has been dominant socially, culturally, economically, and for many decades even politically. Recently, as the Flamands have begun to assert themselves and the Walloon minority has begun to feel more threatened, outright polarization is somewhat reduced by the existence of Brussels as a kind of third element. With 16 percent of the population of the country, the capital city contains both subcultures—a majority of Walloons and a Flemish-speaking minority. Although Brussels is itself a key issue in the relations of the two subcultures, it also serves as a force for conciliation.[8]

8. Lorwin stresses both aspects of Brussels, as issue and conciliator. As issue: "Brussels and its environs supply the leading issue of Flemish-Walloon contention. . . . A pole for Flemish immigration and the center of the nation's French-speaking dominance, Brussels became for *Flamingants* (militant pro-Flemish elements) both an obstacle to overcome and a *terra irredenta* to recover." As conciliator:

To produce more than two subcultures, and hence the possibility that each is a minority, does not require more than one major line of cleavage. To this extent, the number of different types of cleavage forms an inadequate measure of the extent of subcultural pluralism in a society. In the Netherlands, as we have just seen, religion forms a single plane of cleavage that has created and sustained the three *zuilen*—Catholics, Orthodox Protestants, and the remainder —none of which is a majority.[9] More than two subcultures can also be created if two (or of course more) planes of cleavage intersect to partition a population into, for example, four groups. Thus in Switzerland the German-speaking majority and the French-speaking minority are both divided into Catholics and Protestants, so that none of the resulting four groups is a majority; these four are subdivided further by region.[10]

In India, language, caste, and region generate a fantastic panoply of subcultures, each of which is a relatively small minority. (In a nation of 500 million a relatively small minority is often larger in absolute terms than most of the countries of the world.) As Kothari argues, India's extreme pluralism is not merely a source of difficulty but is also in some ways one of the strengths of the Indian polyarchy, for it now compels the leaders of every group to learn and

"Brussels has a 'national vocation.' Its very existence as a metropolis depends upon the performance of national political, administrative, commercial, financial, and cultural services. Out of interest and sentiment, Brussels wants (even if it fails to show the necessary linguistic tolerance) to maintain the unitary state. Conversely, advocates of regional separation *à deux* find Brussels a stumbling block." Lorwin, "Religion, Class, and Language in National Politics," pp. 172, 177.

9. In 1960, Roman Catholics constituted 40.4% of the population, the two major Protestant groups 37.6%, "No Church" 18.4%, and other Protestant sects, Jews, and "others," 3.6%. Daalder, "The Netherlands: Opposition in a Segmented Society," appendix table 6.5, p. 425.

10. Steiner. *Bedingungen für Gewaltlöse Konflictregulierungsmuster*, pp. 6–7, 432–33.

practice the arts of conciliation and coalition formation and prevents any single unified group from even approaching a monopoly of political resources.[11]

The condition that no subculture be indefinitely denied the opportunity to participate in the government can be met in two ways—by a system oriented toward unanimity, in which, as in Switzerland, every major party is represented in the government of the *Gemeinde,* the canton, and the federation, or as in Belgium and the Netherlands by a system of shifting coalitions that, over time, allows each group to shift out of opposition into the government—a system for which Lorwin has coined the "short and catchy name" *Allgemeinkoalitionsfähigkeit.*[12]

> The second requirement for reducing conflict in a country with considerable subcultural pluralism is a set of understandings or engagements, not always codified into formal constitutional provisions, that provide a relatively high degree of security to the various subcultures.

Among the most prevalent forms of mutual security arrangements are guarantees that the major subcultures will be represented in parliament in some rough approximation to their numerical weight, a guarantee that is frequently secured by using one of the various types of proportional representation for electing candidates. This kind of guarantee may extend even to the executive, as in the all-party Federal Council in Switzerland, or under the *Proporz* arrangement introduced in Austria under the Second Republic. Where participation in the executive is assured, the arrangement typically requires unanimity or (to put it differently) permits

11. Rajni Kothari, "India," in R. A. Dahl, ed., *Regimes and Opposition* (New Haven: Yale University Press, forthcoming 1971).
12. Lorwin, "Religion, Class, and Language in National Politics," p. 178.

each minority to exercise a veto over decisions affecting major subcultural concerns. Where the subcultures are more or less regional, mutual security may also be provided by federalism, as in Canada, India, and Switzerland; in Switzerland, considerable local autonomy provides still further protection to the subcultures.[13] Finally, mutual guarantees may be provided by specific constitutional provisions, pacts, or understandings that impose limits on the constitutional authority of any parliamentary coalition to regulate certain matters important to one or more subcultures, for example, language guarantees in Switzerland, India, and Canada or the guarantees and understandings in the Netherlands that concede a large measure of autonomy to the three *zuilen* with respect not merely to religion, newspapers, political parties, trade unions, and farm organizations, but also state-subsidized schools, social security programs, and the state-owned radio broadcasting stations and television network.[14]

> The third requirement is not only more conjectural but also more difficult to state precisely. The chances for a polyarchy are higher if the people of a country believe that a polyarchy is effective in responding to demands for coping with the major problems of the country, as these problems are defined by the population, or at least by the political stratum.[15]

13. Steiner points out that an important source of discontent in the Bernese Jura is that the Catholic, French-speaking inhabitants constitute a minority in these important respects not only within the country but also within the canton, where the majority are German-speaking Protestants. In the perceptions of the Jurassiens, therefore, the majority appears to be completely dominant. Steiner, *Bedingungen für Gewaltlöse Konflictregulierunsmuster,* pp. 433–34. Given this unusual situation, it is easy to see why the inhabitants of the Jura would want to form a separate canton, a solution that (to the outsider) appears to be quite in the Swiss scheme of mutual guarantees.
14. Even the revenue from the state tax on radio and television sets is distributed to the broadcasting companies of the *zuilen,* which have their own studies, staffs, and of course programs.
15. See the discussion in the following chapter, pp. 144–49.

For if demands on the government for "solutions" to major problems go unmet year after year, allegiance is likely to give way to disillusion and contempt, particularly when a "problem" involves extensive and acute deprivation among some considerable part of the population—galloping inflation, for example, extensive unemployment, acute poverty, severe discrimination, woeful inadequacies in education, and the like.

Now this requirement is not unique to polyarchy, nor is it even unique to countries with a considerable amount of subcultural pluralism; it is very likely a general requirement for all regimes—surely for all polyarchies. The reason for emphasizing it here, however, is that it may sometimes be inconsistent with the first two requirements. For to contrive a political system that works by unanimity and minority veto, or by shifting coalitions, and guarantees that no majority coalition will act adversely toward any of its subcultural minorities may be a perfect recipe for governmental immobility, for a system, that is to say, in which major problems, as these are defined by the political stratum, go unsolved because every possible solution is vetoed by some minority whose leaders feel that its interests are threatened. Although, as the experience of Switzerland and the Netherlands shows, immobility is not inherent, it is a serious complaint in some systems of this kind.[16]

Systems with marked subcultural pluralism may sometimes confront, then, a set of unhappy and even tragic choices: (a) a polyarchy that provides mutual guarantees to its minorities but cannot respond to demands for solutions to major problems sufficiently well to hold the allegiance of the people; (b) a hegemony that tries to meet these problems by

16. On Lebanon, for example, see the comments of Michael Hudson, *The Precarious Republic: Political Modernization in Lebanon* (New York: Random House, 1968), pp. 11–12, 87–88, 328–31, and Ralph E. Crow, "Religious Sectarianism in the Lebanese Political System," *Journal of Politics* 24 (August 1962): 489–520. On the general point, see Lorwin, "Segmented Pluralism," p. 16.

coercing, if need be, members of one or more subcultures; or if the subcultures are also regional, (c) separation into different countries. Only the last may enable polyarchy to survive among the dissenting minority. Thus the price of polyarchy may be a breakup of the country. And the price of territorial unity may be a hegemonic regime.

Political Institutions and Governmental Effectiveness

The extent to which political institutions are merely an outcome of all the other factors that have been discussed here, or are themselves in some degree an independent factor, is one of many questions that political scientists have not satisfactorily resolved. Although for about a generation political institutions have been more and more widely interpreted as mere epiphenomena, this period of reductionism in political science may now be coming to an end. However that may be, in order to assay the problem of governmental effectiveness in competitive regimes, some emphasis must, I think, be given to political institutions, even though I intend to skirt completely around the formidable problem of "explaining" how countries with competitive systems come to their specific governmental arrangements.

In polyarchies, two kinds of institutional arrangements seem to have important consequences for the "effectiveness" of the government. One of these has to do with the relationship between the executive and the other major political forces in the country, including a relationship that has often been the source of major problems in competitive regimes —between the executive and the legislature. It seems to be true that all the nineteenth-century competitive regimes that have managed to survive as polyarchies in the twentieth century have developed strong executives armed with extensive capacities for action. All, including France, have rejected the classic model of assembly government. Whether de facto or de jure, everywhere responsibility for coordinating policies and establishing priorities, and much of the responsibility for innovation, has shifted toward the executive. The other significant institution is the party system. It is a defensible, if, alas, vague hypothesis that the costs of toleration are reduced where party systems appear to contribute more to integration and action than to fragmentation and paralysis. Although it is exceptionally difficult to cast this proposition in operational terms, it seems clear that highly fragmented multiparty systems (Sartori's "extreme" or "polarized" pluralism)[17] can lead to unstable or weak coalitions that are unable to cope with major problems and thereby exaggerate in the eyes of the public and even the political elites the partisan or game aspects of political life. These results in turn may stimulate a loss of confidence in representative democracy and the willingness to tolerate political conflicts.[18]

About a third of the contemporary polyarchies meet the problem of party fragmentation with two-party systems of one sort or another. Among the remaining two-thirds a substantial number have successfully avoided extreme fragmentation by:

A party system with two large, dominant parties and one or several small parties as in the German Federal Republic.

17. In various works, Giovanni Sartori has carried out an extensive comparative analysis of the causes and consequences of highly fragmented multiparty systems. See his "European Political Parties: The Case of Polarized Pluralism," in Joseph LaPalombara and Myron Weiner, *Political Parties and Political Development* (Princeton: Princeton University Press, 1966) pp. 137–76; his *Partiti e sistemi di partito* (Florence: Editrice Universitaria, 1965); and his "The Typology of Party Systems," in Stein Rokkan and Erik Allardt, eds., *Cleavages, Parties and Mass Politics* (New York: The Free Press of Glencoe, 1970).

18. Some data and argument supporting this interpretation will be found in Jack Dennis, Leon Lindberg, Donald McCrone, and Rodney Stiefbold, "Political Socialization to Democratic Orientations in Four Western Systems," *Comparative Political Studies* 1 (April 1968): 71–101, esp. 91–92.

A party system with one normally dominant government party that gains close to 50 percent of the popular votes and seats in the parliament, with the opposition fragmented into three or more parties, as in India, Japan, and the Scandinavian countries.

A special coalition of the two major parties, as in Austria until recently and in West Germany from 1966 to 1969.

A high-consensus, unanimity-oriented system as in Switzerland, where all major parties are included in the executive.

But countries that experiment with competitive politics do not always succeed in preventing fragmentation of the party system. In any country where competitive politics is accompanied by a highly fractionalized party system (which in a parliamentary system is likely also to produce a weak executive) the chances for a shift toward a hegemonic regime are rather high. In the past decade, near-polyarchies in both Greece and Argentina foundered in part, it seems, because party fragmentation made for a regime that because of its inability to deal effectively with the country's problems was unable to win or to hold the allegiance of enough of the population to prevent a coup d'etat from establishing a dictatorship. And in France, the classic home of assembly government, the Fourth Republic foundered because of its failure to solve the excruciating problem of Algeria.

8. THE BELIEFS
OF POLITICAL ACTIVISTS

To the extent that the factors described in the preceding chapters propel a country toward a hegemonic regime or toward public contestation and polyarchy, they must operate, somehow, through the beliefs of the people, particularly those who are most involved in political life. At the very least, then, the beliefs of the political activists are a key stage in the complex processes by which historical sequences or subcultural cleavages, for example, are converted into support for one kind of regime or another.

Assumptions

The relationships examined in this chapter might be represented as follows, where the simple arrow means "explains" or "accounts for," and the arrow — P → means "affects the probability of":

I	II	III	IV
Factors determining beliefs $\rightarrow$	Political Beliefs $\rightarrow$	Political Actions — P →	Regimes

The question is, then, the extent to which beliefs (II) determine the political actions (III) of people in a country and thus affect the chances for a particular kind of regime (IV), defined here according to the extent of hegemony, public contestation, and polyarchy. To the extent that beliefs do affect regimes, we shall want to know what factors determine beliefs (I). There are many problems with this paradigm, but the paradigm itself helps us to get at these problems.

Let me begin by making clear that I use the term "beliefs" in a broad sense. I am not going to distinguish between beliefs and knowledge. By knowledge we usually mean beliefs that seem to us well grounded in truth, perhaps incontrovertible. Most of us are willing to call a physicist's beliefs about physics his "knowledge" of physics; yet many of us would be less charitable toward his beliefs about politics. In politics one man's "knowledge" is often another man's disbelief.

So far as I am aware, no thoughtful person denies the relevance of beliefs to action. Beliefs guide action not only because they influence or embody one's more distant goals and values—one's religious salvation, for example, one's security in old age, or the independence of one's country— but because beliefs make up our assumptions about reality, about the character of the past and the present, our expectations about the future, our understanding of the hows and whys of action: in short, our "knowledge."

The importance of the purely cognitive element in our beliefs, whether beliefs about politics or about other things, can hardly be overestimated. Knowledge of the rules of a game, for example, has not only normative but also cognitive significance, as many a foreigner has discovered in the United States upon attending his first game of baseball. The foreigner may not give a hoot whether the rules of baseball are "good" or ought to be observed, but because he does not know what the rules are he is totally unable to make sense of what is happening before his eyes. An American watching a game of cricket is equally lost. As in baseball or cricket, so too in politics: what we believe influences not only what we want to happen but what we think actually happens. In its emphasis on "is" rather than "ought," Marxism may be an extreme case, but it serves nicely to make the point. While Marx's writings unquestionably have moral import and appeal, their manifest content is almost exclusively cognitive, not moral. To the Marxist, Marx's work explains what has happened, is happening, and will happen; only by implication does it specify what ought to happen.

It seems evident, too, that individuals' beliefs influence collective actions and hence the structure and functioning of institutions and systems. It is difficult to see how a polyarchy could exist if a majority of the politically active strata of a country believed strongly that a hegemonic regime was more desirable and could be achieved by supporting antidemocratic leaders and organizations. In a hegemonic regime, presumably the leaders, at least, must prefer hegemony to any single alternative.

As these examples suggest, the way in which different beliefs are distributed among the people of a country is also important. Probably a polyarchy requires a much more widespread belief in the general desirability of the system than is required to sustain a hegemonic regime. But if it is true that in all systems different people have unequal impact on political outcomes, then it is important to know who holds what beliefs. Surely Lenin's beliefs, and later Stalin's, had very much more influence on developments in Russia in this century than the beliefs of, say, two randomly selected Russian peasants. The way the institutions of government have operated in the United States since 1787 has been determined much more by the beliefs of the fifty-five men at the Constitutional Convention of 1787 than by the beliefs of fifty-five average citizens of Philadelphia that year. I realize that my assumption runs the risk of opening up the old controversy over the role of the Great Man in history, a question I do not wish to pursue here. But I hope that most readers will share my assumption. In any case, in this chapter I am going to be mainly concerned with the beliefs of the people most involved in political action, such as activists, militants, and in particular those with the greatest manifest or implicit power, actual or potential, the leaders or potential leaders. This concern does not mean that the beliefs held among the less influential strata are irrelevant, but only that a stronger case can be made for treating the beliefs of the politically most active and involved strata as an important explanatory factor.

The case is strengthend by evidence on several other aspects of political beliefs. Within a particular country, the more rudimentary and unorganized an individual's political beliefs are, the more uncertain the relation, if any, between belief and action. To take some hypothetical examples, a person whose belief system in effect contains the essentials of Mill's argument on liberty is very likely to oppose a regime that threatens censorship of the press or the suppression of political parties. One whose beliefs contain in effect the central arguments of the Communist Manifesto is likely to favor attempts by working-class organizations to contest a bourgeois party or regime. But it is very difficult to predict the kind of regime, movement, or party that would be opposed or supported by one whose whole political credo can be summed up as "the times are bad and people like me are badly off in this country." [1]

Most people, it appears, have quite rudimentary political beliefs. Rich and complex systems of political belief are held only by small minorities. On the present evidence, it is reasonable to think that while this is true in all countries, the lower the average level of formal education in a country, the smaller the minority is that has complex beliefs about politics. In general, the likelihood that one holds a complex set of interrelated beliefs about politics increases with one's level of education and with one's interest and involvement in

1. Philip E. Converse, "The Nature of Belief Systems in Mass Publics," in David E. Apter, ed., *Ideology and Discontent* (New York: The Free Press of Glencoe, 1964), pp. 213 ff.

politics. It seems obvious, in fact, that the purely cognitive
component—knowledge of a variety of aspects of political
life, including the rules of the game—must be greater among
leaders and activists than among, say, politically apathetic
inhabitants of a country.[2]

To sum up, it is reasonable to think that activists and
leaders are more likely than most other people

1. to have moderately elaborate systems of political
   beliefs
2. to be guided in their actions by their political beliefs
3. and to have more influence on political events, including events that affect the stability or transformation of regimes

Several questions arise:

First, what kinds of beliefs among activists crucially affect
the chances for public contestation and polyarchy?

Second, how do these beliefs come about?

Third, can an explanation of how political beliefs come
about account for them so fully that beliefs can be treated
simply as intervening variables? To put the question the other
way round, is it useful to treat the political beliefs of activists
as an *independent* explanatory factor, comparable in significance to those described in earlier chapters?

Some Crucial Beliefs

It is an unhappy fact that no one can answer these questions satisfactorily at present. To be sure, it is possible to
say something about how people in different countries vary
in their attachment to certain beliefs, that is, about variations
at II in the paradigm presented a few pages back. But satisfactory evidence on variations in beliefs among (and within[3])

2. Ibid., pp. 218 ff.
3. Since beliefs are rarely if ever uniformly held in a given country,
we are concerned with "significant" variations or differences in
"modal types." The conceptual and methodological problems in-

countries is still limited to a few countries, most of which, as might be expected, are polyarchies. Evidence about beliefs in hegemonic regimes is slight; often we use indirect evidence from Italy or Germany as a substitute, on the assumption that beliefs of Italians or Germans may help to account for their experiences with fascism and nazism.

Because of the small numbers of countries studied and the concentration on polyarchies, it is impossible at present to demonstrate conclusively that variations in beliefs (at II) significantly affect the chances for polyarchy or hegemony (at IV). The problem is compounded by uncertainties about the intervening relationships with behavior (at III).

Strictly speaking, then, assertions about the impact of beliefs on the character of a regime must be treated as hypotheses that cannot yet be tested satisfactorily against reliable and relevant data. Nonetheless, the possible role of beliefs is too great to be ignored. For there are plausible reasons for thinking that certain beliefs do affect the chances for hegemony or polyarchy. Since the evidence is so fragmentary, I intend to do no more than to offer a few illustrations.

Legitimacy of polyarchy

Let me begin by offering three propositions.

First, the greater the belief within a given country in the legitimacy of the institutions of polyarchy, the greater the chances for polyarchy.

Although such a statement may seem so nearly self-evident as to require no discussion, a few comments will serve to

volved are analogous to those in the study of "the modal personality" of a country or a culture. Cf. Alex Inkeles and Daniel J. Levinson, "National Character: The Study of Modal Personality and Sociocultural System," *The Handbook of Social Psychology,* ed. Gardner Lindzey and Elliot Aronson, 2d ed. (Reading, Mass.: Addison-Wesley, 1969), 4: 418–506.

round it out. To believe in the institutions of polyarchy means to believe, at the very least, in the legitimacy of both public contestation and participation. In practice, these two dimensions of polyarchy are somewhat independent not only historically, as I pointed out in chapter 1, but also as beliefs. Around the time of the reform of the British Parliament in 1832, many Whigs and Liberals affirmed by word and deed their belief in the legitimacy of the institutions of public contestation that had been evolving in Britain for more than a century. If the legal basis for some of these forms of contestation was less clear than it is today—the freedom of the press to criticize the government, for example—in practice the boundaries were fairly broad, and these defacto freedoms were supported by most Whigs and Liberals. What most sharply distinguished Whigs and Liberals from Radicals, however, was the Radical commitment to a very broad, even universal, suffrage. Probably most Whigs and Liberals in the 1830s believed that the Reform Act went quite far enough; yet that reform left about six adult males out of seven without the franchise—a degree of exclusion the Radicals found unacceptable. It is not too much to say, then, that in the 1830s most Whigs and many Liberals did not believe in the legitimacy of polyarchy. They believed firmly instead in the legitimacy of what I have called a competitive oligarchy.

It is also possible to believe in the legitimacy of inclusion but not of public contestation. Peron's dictatorship in Argentina sought to do what no previous regime had done, to incorporate the working strata into Argentine life—economic, social, and political. Paradoxical as it may seem, since 1930 the only elections in Argentina that have been reasonably honest, fair, and widely participated in by the electorate, the outcome of which has not been set aside by the military, occurred during Peron's dictatorship. Not that Peron believed in or supported polyarchy; under his rule, oppositions were increasingly suppressed. Yet Peronism stood and even today stands for the full inclusion of the working strata in the politi-

cal system, and although it may grant legitimacy to dictatorship it denies legitimacy to any system that excludes or dis-
criminates against the working strata or their spokesmen.

As with other beliefs, the views of activists and leaders are
likely to be more crucial than those of other people. Yet
since even inactive or excluded strata may sometimes be
mobilized, their beliefs are very far from irrelevant. As with
other beliefs too, the complexity and richness of beliefs about
the legitimacy of polyarchy no doubt increase with education,
political interest, and involvement. Even in well-established
polyarchies, very young children can hardly be expected to
believe in "democracy"; the word and the concept have no
meaning, after all, to most four-year-olds. But evidence indicates that in the United States, Italy, and Germany, by the
time they finish school a substantial majority of young people
agree that "democracy is the best form of government." Nor
is this belief devoid of concrete detail; they have also begun
to learn something about the content of that commitment.
Thus a substantial proportion of American children in the
early grades appear to believe that political conflict does more
harm than good, but only a small minority of older students
express this belief. To many American children, competing
political parties at first seem unnecessary and undesirable or
downright confusing, but as they develop they tend to acquire
a belief in the desirability of competing parties. The idea
that people should be allowed to make speeches "against our
kind of government" is unfamiliar and uncongenial to young
children, but a great many older children have learned to
accept it.[4]

With all that is now known about political beliefs, it would
be wildly unrealistic to expect, even in a country like the
United States where a democratic ideology has been the domi-

4. Jack Dennis, Leon Lindberg, Donald McCrone, and Rodney
Stiefbold, "Political Socialization to Democratic Orientations in Four
Western Systems," *Comparative Political Studies* 1 (April 1968):
78, 86, 89.

nant belief system for generations, that many people would possess an elaborately worked-out democratic theory. Scratch the average democrat, and you will not find a Locke, a Rousseau, a Jefferson, or even a Lincoln. Nonetheless, the legitimacy of polyarchy or the belief that "democracy is the best form of government" probably does not exist in a total vacuum. As a belief, it is not ordinarily insulated completely from other beliefs. Thus it is a reasonable conjecture, supported by a certain amount of evidence, as we shall see in a moment, that an individual is more likely to believe in the legitimacy of polyarchal institutions if he also holds certain other beliefs. But before we examine these, let me first add two more propositions:

> Countries vary a great deal in the extent to which activists (and others) believe in the legitimacy of polyarchy.

> These variations are to some extent independent of the social and economic characteristics of a country: two countries with a great many similarities in their social and economic orders may vary significantly in the extent to which activists (and others) believe in the legitimacy of polyarchy.

Argentina: the not-so-deviant case.[5] To illustrate and to lend

5. The argument and data in this section are derived from the following sources: "Political Oppositions in Argentina" an unpublished seminar paper by Guillermo O'Donnell, who first suggested to me some of the main lines of interpretation that follow; Carlos Alberto Floria, "El Comportamiento de la Oposicion en la Argentina"; Natalio R. Botana, "Las Crisis de Legitimidad en Argentina y el Desarollo de los Partidos Politicos"; Mariano Grondona, "Algunas observaciones sobre la evolución reciente del sistema político argentino"; and Rafael Braun, "La representatividad de los partidos políticos y la interpretación del interés publico por parte de las fuerzas armadas: un dilema argentino" (all papers presented at the Primer Encuentro Internacional de Ciencia Política, Buenos Aires, August, 1969); Cias Alberto Floria, "Una Explicación Política de la Argentina," *CIAS, Revista Mensual del Centro de Investigación y Acción*

some support to these propositions, particularly the last, it is instructive to compare Argentina with, let us say, Sweden. Outwardly, Argentina's political development in the late nineteenth century followed a path to polyarchy very similar to that of Sweden, Britain, and a number of other stable polyarchies. To be sure, Argentina's early history is hardly analogous to Sweden's; at the very least, Argentina squeezed into a few decades what occurred over centuries in Sweden: a decade of revolution and struggle for independence from 1810 to 1820, a decade of what Germani has called *anarquía, caudillismo, guerras civiles,* followed by two decades of a unifying autocracy.[6] For the next eighty years, however, Argentina had all the external appearance of a developing polyarchy. It operated under the constitution of 1853 (as it has continued to do, formally, down to the present day). It is true that participation was restricted to a small minority, but participation in elections does not appear to have been more restricted in Argentina than in Britain until the Reform Act of 1867 or in Sweden or the Netherlands until late in the century. Toward the end of the century, the rapidly expanding middle class began to make itself felt in political life. Organized parties came into existence as powerful electoral forces —particularly the Radicals who, as spokesmen for the middle classes, insistently demanded entry into the system. In

Social 16 (November 1967); Mariano Grondona, *La Argentina en el Tiempo y en El Mundo* (Buenos Aires: Editorial Primera Plana, 1967); Gino Germani, *Politica y Sociedad en una Epoca de Transicion* (Buenos Aires: Paidos, n.d.).; Dario Canton, "Military Interventions in Argentina, 1900–1966" (Paper presented to the Conference on Armed Forces and Society Working Group, International Sociological Association, London, September 1967), and his "Universal Suffrage as an Agent of Mobilization" (Paper presented to the VIth World Congress of Sociology, Evian, France, September 1966); and James W. Rowe, "The Argentine Elections of 1963" (Washington, D.C.: Institute for the Comparative Study of Political Systems, n.d.).
6. *Politica y Sociedad,* p. 196, and in his "Hacia una Democracia de Masas," in Torcuato S. Di Tella et al., *Argentina, Sociedad de Masas* (Bueno Aires: Editorial Universitaria de Buenos Aires, 1965), p. 211.

1911, about the same time as Sweden and a few years before the Netherlands, Argentina effectively guaranteed universal male suffrage. As a result, election turnout took a large jump—from 21 percent of all male citizens over eighteen in 1910 to 69 percent in 1912. Although turnout fell off during the next dozen years, it was roughly comparable to that in the United States and not much lower than it was in Sweden during the 1920s. Moreover, it rose again to 81 percent in 1928 and 75 percent in 1930. Thus in electoral participation Argentina was also comparable with a number of other polyarchies. What is more, with the victory of the Radical party's presidential candidate in 1916, Argentina appeared to manage without violence the dangerous transition from competitive oligarchy to a polyarchy based on universal suffrage.

There were still other factors favorable to polyarchy. According to the criteria so frequently used today to predict the chances for "stable democracy," Argentina provided solid grounds for optimism. Its population was highly urbanized, literacy was low, education was widespread, the country was moderately prosperous (its GNP per capita was probably the highest in Latin America), and it had a large middle class. On all these counts, Argentina was at least as well off as the three countries where polyarchy has proved to be more durable than in Argentina—Costa Rica, Chile, and Uruguay. Nor does that deus ex machina of much theorizing about democracy help us greatly: landholdings were concentrated, to be sure, but apparently less than in Chile, possibly less even than in Costa Rica, and very likely less than in Australia.

As it did for most other countries, the onset of the Great Depression in 1929 created serious problems for Argentina. But other polyarchies were also hit by economic crisis. Some that were also highly dependent on international trade, like Sweden, and even some that were heavy exporters of agricultural products, like Australia and New Zealand, nonetheless met the crisis with actions that retained, restored, perhaps even enhanced the confidence of their citizens in the effectiveness of their governments. In Argentina, things went differently. Although the notables lost few of their privileges under Radical governments, their parties steadily lost votes and representatives. In the late 1920s, conservatives had increasingly attacked the institutions of polyarchy in Argentina —universal suffrage, political parties, the Chamber of Deputies, the ineffectiveness and *personalismo* of the President. Then came economic crisis. A military coup brought the Argentine experiment with polyarchy to an end. Since 1930, polyarchy has never been effectively restored.

It is puzzling that polyarchy collapsed in Argentina but not in Sweden, Australia, and New Zealand, or for that matter in Costa Rica or, if we take the whole period into account, in Chile and Uruguay. I am not aware of any wholly satisfactory explanation for the failure of polyarchy in Argentina. Yet one thing seems clear: the differences in regimes cannot be explained by appealing to the usual explanatory factors—the level of socioeconomic development, urbanization, education, size of the middle class, per capita income, and so on. Although a full explanation would surely be very complex, one crucial factor does emerge with striking clarity: Argentinians appear never to have developed a strong belief in the legitimacy of the institutions of polyarchy. Consequently, when the regime confronted serious difficulties it was easily swept aside by dictatorships that were supported first by conservative elites, the so-called oligarchy, and later under Peron by the working classes—neither of which had ever acquired a very deep conviction about the legitimacy of polyarchy.

As every student of Argentine history is aware, despite outward appearances Argentina's polyarchy did not develop from 1853 to 1930 according to the standard Western European model. The description presented a moment ago is correct—yet it is also highly misleading, for it ignores two interrelated factors deeply implicated in the failure of polyarchy to acquire legitimacy in Argentina: (1) throughout their period of dominance, the notables openly rejected elections as the legitimate foundation of their power to govern; and (2) a large part of the population remained isolated and alienated from the political system. Thus, as it traversed the path from competitive oligarchy to polyarchy, Argentina failed to accomplish what some of the European countries achieved during their transition: neither the Argentine elites, the middle strata, nor the working classes were ever converted to a belief in the legitimacy of polyarchy.

1. The notables failed utterly to develop and transmit a belief in the legitimacy of certain central institutions of polyarchy. Although the more remote factors are elusive,[7] one thing stands out clearly: By their own conduct, the notables taught the Argentinians that elections need not be binding on the losers or the potential losers. Thus they denied legitimacy to a central institution of polyarchy. For throughout the long period of seemingly "constitutional" government from the 1860s to the electoral reform of 1911, the notables regularly and publicly flaunted both constitutional and legal requirements for universal suffrage. According to law and constitution, "voting was universal, for men only, with no qualifications regarding literacy, wealth, property, etc." [8] The notables evidently assumed, no doubt correctly, that if these requirements were ever enforced, their own governing position would be weakened or destroyed. As in Spain during the same period (and with similar consequences) elections were uniformly conducted with massive fraud and violence. The

7. Floria mentions as derivatives of the Spanish tradition "the common disrespect for the law," the practice of "caciquismo," which "organized illegality under the slogan: 'for one's friends even when they are in the wrong, and against one's enemies even when they are in the right,' " and the practice of resorting to force when no legal means are available. He also refers to a nineteenth-century liberal tradition that reconciled "contempt for the common man with faith in democracy." "El Comportamiento," p. 6.
8. Canton, "Universal Suffrage," p. 4.

notables not only excluded the mass of the population from participating in political life; they were unwilling even to permit conflicts among themselves to be settled through elections. They interpreted differences among themselves (such as the exent to which Buenos Aires should dominate the provinces) as "zero-sum" conflicts with consequences far too grave to be determined by mere elections.

Thus from the beginnings of the "constitutional" regime, the leaders of the country denied that elections were a legitimate way of displacing a government: as a practical matter, they provided no alternative to revolution.

It is true, of course, that in other countries where polyarchy later acquired considerable legitimacy, notables had resorted to illegality, corruption, even violence, to win elections. Elections in Britain in the eighteenth century were hardly a model of fairness. But Argentina was different in three respects. First, in sheer mass and extent, fraud and violence were by all accounts extraordinary—not far from those famous elections in Spain in the nineteenth century when the outcome of the vote was announced in advance.[9] Second, as in Spain, by openly flouting the very constitution and laws that ostensibly gave their regime its legitimacy, the notables helped to undermine the legitimacy of any regime based on elections. Finally, unlike Britain, in Argentina there was no transition period between rule by notables and full suffrage during which the political strata came to accept the legitimacy of honest elections. The lesson the notables transmitted, then, was this: when elections turn out badly, the losers are not obliged to accept the results.

This was the legacy the middle and working classes inherited when they were finally allowed into electoral politics by the reform of 1911. That reform, which came about under pressure from the Radicals (pressure that included abortive revolts in 1893 and 1905) effectively enforced an already

9. Gerald Brenan, *The Spanish Labyrinth* (Cambridge: Cambridge University Press, 1962), p. 5.

existing constitutional provision for universal male suffrage, provided for a secret ballot, and created electoral courts of federal judges to oversee the elections. But where it is the norm that those who lose the election may reverse the results by force, polyarchy rests on fragile foundations. And such was the case in Argentina. That little has changed since 1930 is vividly demonstrated by the brief interlude of non-dictatorship from 1955 to 1966. In 1962, when the Peronistas were allowed to present candidates for Congress and some provincial governorships, they gained the largest share of the votes. Thereupon President Frondizi annulled the election; even so, he was arrested and thrown out of office by anti-Peronist military forces discontented with the election results and fearful of a repetition of Peronism. When elections were scheduled in 1963 for a president to replace Frondizi, Peronist candidates were prohibited. However, when it began to appear in 1966 that the Peronistas might win many provincial governorships in the forthcoming elections, instead of waiting to annul the elections the military took over, evidently with very wide support among notables and middle classes fearful of a return to Peronism and tired of a system of fragmented parties. The new dictatorship under General Onganía sought to put an end to these evils by suppressing all political parties and elections and ruling by decree.

2. Excluded from politics by notables who showed open contempt for electoral processes, the great bulk of the population remained isolated and alienated from the political system—hardly likely to rush to its defense to prevent a military takeover. But isolation and alienation were vastly amplified by another factor: the enormous number of noncitizens, who remained psychologically and legally outside the electoral process. The rate of immigration to Argentina far exceeded that to the United States.[10] Yet where quasi-universal suffrage and competitive parties in the United States en-

10. Germani, *Politica y Sociedad,* pp. 247, 265.

sured that immigrants would soon be made citizens in order that they might vote, in Argentina the incentive of the immigrant to acquire citizenship was reduced by the fact that until 1911 even if he were to become a citizen he would still be excluded from politics, and by a variety of other factors. In any case, because most immigrants did not become citizens, a large part of the population remained legally and psychologically outside the Argentine polyarchy. In 1914 nearly a third of the population of Argentina were foreigners; in Buenos Aires, which dominates the political life of the country, half the people were foreigners. Among adults, the proportions were even higher—72 percent in Buenos Aires, 51 percent in five of the most thickly settled provinces, 20 percent elsewhere. Among male adults (who as citizens would have been entitled to vote) the percentages were higher yet: perhaps four out of five adult males in Buenos Aires were noncitizens and thus automatically excluded from participating in the political life of the country. The immigrants were, of course, disproportionately concentrated among the working classes. Thus Argentina had a large proletariat and even a sizable middle class with not great attachment to the Argentine political system.

The upshot of Argentina's political development, then, is that belief in the legitimacy of the institutions of polyarchy— and particularly in the binding character of elections—is shallow, especially among the elites, but perhaps also among the people as a whole. For example, the belief in free elections among key segments of the population is too weak for the country to engage regularly in elections and abide by the results. A survey taken in greater Buenos Aires in March 1966, shortly before the military took over, reveals a good deal. (Table 8.1) It is important to keep in mind that the Peronistas could be expected to win a third or more of the votes: thus to ban their participation was to prohibit the largest group of voters in Argentina from having its own candidates. Nearly a fifth of greater Buenos Aires thought it was right to do so; almost as many more expressed no opposition to the idea. But what is interesting, though hardly surprising, is the extent to which the question of banning Peronists was a class issue. The table shows that the idea of banning Peronist candidates was strongest among the upper strata, where opposition to Peronism was strongest, and weakest among lower strata, where support for Peronism was

Table 8.1. "Would you consider it good or bad if the government were to ban Peronist participation in future elections?"

	Wrong	Right	Don't know, no answer
	64%	19%	17%
By education			
Illiterate or primary education	65%	16%	19%
Secondary education	63%	24%	13%
Academic education	50%	35%	15%
N = 1004			

Source: Encuestas Gallup de la Argentina, March 1966, reported in *Polls* 2 (Spring 1967), p. 22.

greatest. Only half the more educated group opposed the ban; this was also the segment that would support the military take-over. The fact that the least educated opposed the ban can hardly be read as a commitment to free elections on their part; it would be interesting to know how many might have supported a total ban on elections of any kind under a Peronist regime.

Thus a somewhat cynical but not overly exaggerated formulation of a basic norm in Argentine politics would be this: I believe in elections as long as I can be sure that my opponents will not win.

Authority

A number of writers have stressed the importance of beliefs about or attitudes toward authority.[11] Thus in the theory

11. Inkeles and Levinson, "National Character," p. 448 ff.

that he has been developing for some years, Eckstein assigns central importance to the patterns of authority that prevail within a country. Eckstein has hypothesized that democracy would be more stable if the authority patterns in the government were "congruent" with the patterns in other institutions and associations in the country.[12] Presumably "congruent" authority patterns would also make it easier for hegemonic regimes to carry on.

The idea is highly plausible, certainly, that beliefs about the nature of authority relationships between government and the governed are crucial to the chances for the emergence of different kinds of regimes. To make the point in extreme form: if most of the inhabitants of a country believe that the only proper relation of people to their government is one of complete hierarchy, of rulers to subjects, of command and obedience, the chances that the regime will be hegemonic are, surely, high. Given such views, there can hardly be a place for public contestation. And it may also be true, as Eckstein can be read as saying, that people find it hard to reconcile markedly different beliefs about authority; it is stressful to be required to believe in the validity of hegemonic authority in one relationship and democratic authority in another. Eckstein, who chose Norway for a limited test of his theory, has argued that Norwegians have been singularly successful in handling their conflicts and cleavages because they almost uniformly believe in (and adhere to) democratic authority relationships.

> Since democratic norms pervade Norwegian life in the family, in schools, in economic and friendly societies, pressure groups and parties, local and national government, one need not wonder that Norwegians regard it as both natural and moral, a general "way of living,"

12. Harry Eckstein, *Division and Cohesion in Democracy: A Study of Norway* (Princeton: Princeton University Press, 1966), app. B (1961), and passim.

not merely a form that has merit in national governance.[13]

Norway may represent one end of a scale. Yet polyarchy seems to be consistent with considerable variation in beliefs about authority.[14] In fact since polyarchy requires both open conflict among organizations and a capacity for inventing and accepting compromise solutions, it is arguable that this combination of conflict and conciliation may be facilitated if a considerable measure of hierarchic authority is acceptable within organizations. Lijphart has emphasized the strong tendency of the Dutch "to be obedient and allegiant—regardless of particular circumstances," a quality without which the strongly organized cleavages in the Netherlands might long since have destroyed polyarchy in the Netherlands.[15] Even the democratic Norwegians are described by Eckstein as deferential toward "specialized functional competence," which "leads to a particularly high valuation of the expert and the specialist." [16] At least since Bagehot, Englishmen have been characterized as deferential toward their "social betters" and toward governmental authority.[17] Americans are thought to be a good deal less deferential toward government and social elites than Englishmen[18] and may be less deferential toward expertise than Norwegians.

13. Ibid., p. 173.
14. Ibid., p. 189.
15. Arend Lijphart, *The Politics of Accommodation: Pluralism and Democracy in the Netherlands* (Berkeley and Los Angeles: University of California Press, 1968), pp. 144 et seq. See also the comments of Hans Daalder, "The Netherlands: Opposition in a Segmented Society," in Robert A. Dahl, ed., *Political Oppositions in Western Democracies* (New Haven: Yale University Press, 1966), p. 197.
16. Ibid., p. 166.
17. Ibid., pp. 156, 183. See also Richard Rose, *Politics in England* (Boston: Little, Brown, 1964), pp. 38–41.
18. Some interesting fragmentary evidence on the tendency of English children to see the world as more hierarchial than American children is in Fred I. Greenstein and Sidney Tarrow, "An Approach to the Study of Comparative Political Socialization: the Use of a Semi-

Nonetheless, it is most unlikely that polyarchy is equally consistent with all beliefs about authority. Certainly some extreme patterns are much more favorable to hegemony. The beliefs of the ruling tribal group in Ethiopia, the Amhara, provide an example. According to Levine:

> The complex of beliefs, symbols, and values regarding authority constitutes a key component of Amhara political culture. Throughout Amhara culture appears the motif that authority as such is good: indispensable for the well-being of society and worthy of unremitting deference, obeisance, and praise. . . . Obedience is the prime objective in the socialization of Amhara children . . . This experience in the family is continuous and consistent with the rest of Amhara culture . . . Family patriarch, parish chieftain, wealthy landlord, ecclesiastical dignitary, political dignitary, military officer—all are perceived in the imagery of fatherhood; all are the objects of comparable attitudes regarding the obeisance which is due them and the benefits which may be expected from them . . . All of these themes are realized in the most complete form and on a grand scale in connection with the highest authority figure of all, the emperor. The incumbent of this role has been the recipient of the most extreme forms of obeisance. It has been customary, for example, for Ethiopian subjects to prostrate themselves and refrain from lifting their eyes in his presence.

Views like these are hardly conducive to public contestation.

> Amhara culture proscribes direct and honest public criticism of any authority. In authoritarian relationships —and again, all political interaction among the Amhara

---

Projective Technique" (Paper presented to the meetings of the American Political Science Association, September 1969).

is contained within authoritarian relationships—there are only three alternatives: complete deference, acquiescence, and flattery; criticism by devious and covert means; or outright rebellion.

In these circumstances, it is hardly surprising that ideas favoring the institutions of polyarchy fall on totally barren soil:

> Despite the existence of Western-educated individuals who have promoted the idea of parliamentary representation in Ethiopia for more than sixty years, the idea runs so counter to the authoritarian cast of Amhara political culture that electoral procedures are simply not taken seriously.[19]

Effectiveness

Another set of relevant beliefs, as I suggested in the last chapter, are those having to do with expectations about the effectiveness of different regimes in dealing with critical problems.[20] Since we are dealing here primarily with the beliefs of activists and leaders, a "problem" exists and is "critical" if it is perceived as such by a significant proportion of activists or leaders. (Naturally this way of defining a "critical problem" might be unsatisfactory in a different context.)

Expectations about governmental effectiveness can be a more or less fixed element in the political culture of a country: the young may be regularly socialized into believing that their government is, on the whole, highly effective or chronically ineffective. Thus by the time they reach the eighth grade in school a high proportion of white Americans

19. Donald N. Levine, "Ethiopia: Identity, Authority, and Realism," in Lucian W. Pye and Sidney Verba, eds., *Political Culture and Political Development* (Princeton: Princeton University Press, 1965), pp. 250–51, 253.
20. Cf. Seymour Martin Lipset, *Political Man* (Garden City: Doubleday, 1960), p. 78.

acquire the belief (or at least they did until recently) that their government is effective. In one major study, only 2 percent of the eighth-grade students believed that the American government very often makes mistakes; almost 60 percent believed that the government makes mistakes rarely or almost never. Almost three-fourths believed that the government "knows more than anyone" or "knows more than most people." [21] Given the enormous impact of this socialization process, it is not surprising that in response to the question in Almond and Verba's five-nation survey, "Speaking generally, what are the things about this country that you are most proud of," 85 percent of the Americans mentioned their governmental and political institutions. Americans not only mentioned pride in political institutions far more often than anything else, but the American proportion far exceeded that of other countries.[22] And political activists in the United States were even more likely than other people to express pride in American political institutions.[23]

Although I have not been able to find strictly comparable cross-national data on expectations about governmental effectiveness, there can hardly be any doubt that in some countries a significant proportion of the population, including the activists, do not have much confidence in the capacity of the government to deal effectively with the country's prob-

21. David Easton and Jack Dennis, *Children in the Political System: Origins of Political Legitimacy* (New York: McGraw-Hill, 1969), p. 133. See also their article, "The Child's Image of Government," in *The Annals of the American Academy of Political and Social Science* 361 (September 1965): table 6, p. 54.
22. The figures were: U.S., 85%; Britain, 46%; Germany, 7%; Italy, 3%; Mexico, 30%. Gabriel A. Almond and Sidney Verba, *The Civic Culture* (Boston: Little, Brown, 1965), table III.1, p. 64.
23. Even with education controlled, American respondents classified as high or medium in "subjective competence" expressed pride in political institutions much more frequently than those low in "subjective competence." Ibid., table VIII.4, p. 199. "Subjective competence," in turn, is highly related to political activity and involvement. Cf. tables VI.2, p. 144; VIII.1, p. 189, and VIII.2, p. 193; and chap. X, passim.

lems.[24] And just as American children are taught to believe in the effectiveness of their government, so in some countries children learn quite the opposite.[25]

Nonetheless, even if beliefs about governmental effectiveness are often acquired through early socialization, it does not follow that they must remain unchanged. The performance of a government may itself change—or may be perceived to change. The skepticism of villagers in Italy, France,

24. For example, interviews in 1964–65 of "167 members of the Iranian political elite identified through a two stage reputational analysis," to the question, "On the whole, do you think that the Iranian political system is working very well, not too well, or badly?" the responses were:

Very well	15.6%
Fairly well	31.7
Not too well	26.3
Badly	15.0
Don't know, etc.	11.4

Marvin Zonis, "Political Elites and Political Cynicism in Iran," *Comparative Political Studies* 1 (October 1968): 363.

In a survey by DOXA in Italy in 1967, in response to the question, "Do you feel that things in Italy go well or badly with regard to the performance of the government Administration (Ministries, public officials, etc.)?" the answers were:

Very well	2%
Well enough	19
Neither well nor badly	22
Rather badly	26
Very badly	8
Don't know	22

In comparison with other countries, the performance of the Administration was judged as "Better than in other countries" by 16%, worse by 34%, and don't know by 49%. A similar response was given to a question about the honesty and devotion of Italy's statesmen. *Polls* 3, no. 4 (1968): 62, #13, #15, #18.

25. In the village in Provence studied by Wylie, the children "constantly hear adults referring to the Government as a source of evil and to the men who run it as instruments of evil. There is nothing personal in this belief. It does not concern one particular government composed of one particular group of men. It concerns government everywhere and at all times." Laurence Wylie, *Village in the Vaucluse,* rev. ed. (New York: Harper and Row, 1964), p. 208.

or India is rooted in centuries of experience with their own governments. Yet as the performance of the government changes, villagers in southern France or in India also change; they come to believe that the government need not be merely an inept or evil force, but that it can help in dealing with problems.[26] Or confident expectations like those held by Americans can be reversed by failure. Given the unbelievable faith of young Americans in their government described a moment ago, it is scarcely to be wondered at that when young people were confronted by failures of the government in dealing with the crucial problems of race, poverty, and war, a number lost confidence in "the system" and became alienated, cynical, or radical.

Where beliefs about the effectiveness of government are uncertain or shallow, as is often true with new regimes, inept performance is even more dangerous. Thus the inability of newly established polyarchies in Italy, Germany, and Spain to cope effectively with palpable problems—even to maintain public order—generated doubts about the effectiveness of polyarchy and spurred the shift toward dictatorship. In the personal life histories that Abel collected in Germany in 1934, he found ample evidence that opposition to the republic was, after 1929, "reinforced by the belief that the growing number and severity of the problems confronting the German nation were largely due to the inefficiency of the government." [27]

Beliefs about governmental effectiveness may be influenced not only by the performance of one's own government but also by the perceived successes or failures of other gov-

26. To some extent, this may have occurred in Wylie's village. See his comments on "Peyrane Ten Years Later," in ibid., pp. 364–65. See also the changes reported by Mrs. Wiser in the village of Karimpur in India in William and Charlotte Wiser, *Behind Mud Walls, 1930–1960* (Berkeley: University of California Press, 1963), p. 224.
27. Theodore Abel, *The Nazi Movement* (New York: Atherton Press, 1966 [1938]), p. 121.

ernments, ancient or contemporary. Philosophers, publicists, propagandists, ideologues, and many other people all exploit the experiences of other governments to convince their fellow citizens of the relative effectiveness of various kinds of regimes. Like many later writers, Machiavelli and Rousseau used republican Rome as a standard. Montesquieu made Britain his model—and influenced Americans. Like Britain in the eighteenth century and the United States in the nineteenth century, in the twentieth century a variety of performances has influenced perceptions—particularly among intellectuals—of the relative effectiveness of different kinds of regimes. In the 1930s the successes of dictatorships in Italy, Germany, and the USSR were in competition with the achievements of a "middle way" in Sweden and the New Deal in the United States. In Latin America the influence of authoritarian models has often been great: PRI in Mexico, Peron in Argentina, Castro in Cuba, and most recently the reformist military junta in Peru.

The evidence indicates, then, that beliefs about governmental effectiveness are strongly influenced both by political socialization and by the way the performance of different regimes is perceived.

Beliefs about governmental effectiveness may reinforce, weaken, or alter prevailing beliefs about authority.[28] If a government is perceived as effective, its successes are likely

28. Eckstein's formulation is different from but not inconsistent with this one. He hypothesizes that "congruence between [the government's] authority pattern and the authority patterns of other social units in the society" is a necessary but not sufficient condition for "high performance by a government." In Eckstein's formulation, governmental performance is broader than the concept of effectiveness used here; it includes not only output efficiency and strife avoidance, which would be roughly equivalent to my concept of effectiveness, but also durability, legitimacy, and permeation, which is defined as "the ability of a polity to derive resources from, and to carry out its directives in the various segments of its social space." Harry Eckstein, "Authority Relations and Governmental Performance: A Theoretical Framework," *Comparative Political Studies* 2 (October 1969): 283–87

to enhance the prestige of the authority patterns it embodies; the converse is true if it fails. (Figure 8.1)

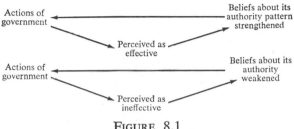

FIGURE 8.1

Since all governments fail some of the time, socialization builds up a reservoir of confident expectations that function as a reserve during periods of adversity. In new regimes, these reservoirs are low or even empty; in old regimes with a record of considerable achievement, the reservoirs are likely to be high. In Italy from 1919 to 1923, in Weimar Germany and in Republican Spain, new polyarchies had few reserves to draw on, whereas a reservoir of confidence in the capacity of the government to deal with problems helped polyarchy in Britain and the United States to survive the challenge of mass unemployment in the 1930s.[29]

29. Although this is conjectural, the evidence is extremely persuasive. I am unable to find relevant survey evidence earlier than a Fortune Poll taken in the U.S. in March 1940. At that time, about 15% of the labor force, or over eight million persons, were still unemployed. The poll asked:

Which one of the following most nearly represents your opinion of the American form of government: (1) Our form of government, based on the Constitution, is as near perfect as it can be, and no important changes should be made in it. (2) The Constitution has served its purpose well, but it has not kept up with the times and should be thoroughly revised to make it fit present-day needs. (3) The systems of private capitalism and democracy are breaking down, and we might as well accept the fact that sooner or later we shall have to have a new form of government.

Trust

Another element of belief that is often emphasized is "the extent to which members of a political system have trust and confidence in their fellow political actors." [30] Thus LaPalombara has stressed the importance of distrust in the Italian political culture: "the general atmosphere is one of fear, suspicion, distrust, and hostility." "I am compelled to assert," he writes,

> that on the basis of the evidence at my disposal the attitudes Italians maintain are essentially Hobbesian and that the history of the country suggests that, when the state of nature becomes too intolerable, it is also a Hobbesian solution concerning government to which Italians turn. The fact that republican government remains relatively intact . . . [does not mean] that the Republic can survive many more years on its culturally uncertain and problematical foundations.[31]

Levine has also called attention to the high levels of distrust among the Amhara in Ethiopia:

Unbelievable as it may seem in retrospect, even the poor preferred the first and overwhelmingly rejected the third:

	STATE-MENT #1	STATE-MENT #2	STATE-MENT #3	DON'T KNOW
National total	64.2%	19.2%	5.2%	11.4%
Prosperous	79.9	14.2	2.4	3.5
Upper middle class	71.4	19.8	3.7	5.1
Lower middle class	64.1	20.5	5.2	10.2
Poor	58.4	18.6	7.6	15.4

Hadley Cantril, and Mildred Strunk, *Public Opinion, 1935–1946* (Princeton: Princeton University Press, 1951), p. 980.
30. Sidney Verba, "Conclusion: Comparative Political Culture," in Pye and Verba, *Political Culture,* p. 535.
31. Joseph LaPalombara, "Italy: Fragmentation, Isolation, and Alienation," ibid., pp. 290, 297.

The particular features which dominate the Amhara's image of generic human nature are man's inherent aggressiveness and his untrustworthiness . . . Related to this view of man's powerful latent hostility is the notion that man is untrustworthy.[32]

In at least three ways, mutual trust favors polyarchy and public contestation while extreme distrust favors hegemony. In the first place, polyarchy requires two-way or mutual communication, and two-way communication is impeded among people who do not trust one another. Thus Almond and Verba found much higher levels of trust among their American and British respondents than in Germany and Italy. Probably authoritarian regimes in Germany and Italy sharply eroded mutual trust; as LaPalombara's comments quoted above suggest, the transformation of polyarchy into hegemony may also have been facilitated by a relatively low level of mutual trust. At any rate, Almond and Verba also found that the percentage reporting that they did not feel free to discuss politics with anyone was markedly higher in Germany (32 percent) and Italy (34 percent) than in Britain (12 percent) and the United States (18 percent).[33]

Second, a certain level of mutual trust is required in order for people to join together freely in order to promote their goals. Organizations based on command, with authority downward, may be possible (though not necessarily efficient) with mutual distrust; organizations based on reciprocal influence are difficult to form and maintain in an atmosphere of distrust. Thus Levine argues that the extreme distrust prevailing among the Ethiopians helps explain "the lack of organizations for the articulation and aggregation of interests in Ethiopia." This lack, he points out,

32. "Ethiopia," pp. 257, 258.
33. *The Civic Culture,* table III.8, p. 83. For responses on trust and distrust, see table IX.2, p. 213. As in many other tables, the data on Mexico are less easily explained. Thus the percentage of Mexican respondents who did not feel free to discuss politics was 21%—only slightly above the United States.

is the result not only of the authoritarian character of
the regime, supported as this is by traditional Amhara
attitudes toward authority. It also reflects the difficulty
Ethiopians have in undertaking any sort of concerted
action, particularly in the political sphere. Here again
the Amhara conception of human nature is a factor of
more than academic significance. The mutual distrust
and lack of cooperation which inform the political climate of the country are directly related to a very low
regard for man's capacity for solidarity and consensus
. . . The idea that it is possible to transcend the prevailing atmosphere of anxiety and suspicion by trusting
one another . . . has been slow to appear and extremely rare.[34]

Finally, conflicts are more threatening among people who
distrust one another. Public contestation requires a good deal
of trust in one's opponents: they may be opponents, but they
are not implacable enemies. "A sense of trust," Richard
Rose writes of Britain, "is pervasive in the political culture.
. . . At the level of government, trust is important between
colleagues and partisan opponents because it reassures all
that the particular group in office will not take advantage
of the absence of constitutional restraints upon the powers
of government. To do so would not be a violation of law,
but of trust, and political leaders value their reputation for
trustworthiness." [35]

Cooperation

Trust is obviously related, as these remarks make clear,
to the capacities of a people for engaging freely and easily

34. "Ethiopia," pp. 277–88.
35. *Politics in England,* p. 43. Rose has also written, "This depth of
trust is evidenced by the maintenance for centuries of a stable system
of government without a written constitution." "England, The Traditionally Modern Political Culture," in Pye and Verba, *Political
Culture,* p. 96.

in cooperative actions.[36] As with trust, beliefs about the possibility and desirability of cooperation vary a great deal, and, as Levine's comment suggests, there are good reasons for thinking that an inability to cooperate reduces the chances for polyarchy.

The relevant units for cooperation or conflict need not be individuals but aggregates—factions, parties, social classes, regions, and the like. What we are concerned with, then, are the beliefs that people have about the prospects of cooperation and conflict among relevant actors in political life, whether these are individuals, organizations, or other actors. Keeping this in mind, it will be useful to distinguish three different ways in which someone might view cooperation and conflict among the relevant political actors. At one extreme, relations among actors may be viewed as a strictly competitive (zero-sum) game, where the central rule is: what you gain, I lose, and what I lose, you gain. Since we have everything to lose and nothing to gain by cooperating, we believe that the best strategy for an actor to follow is strict competition: never compromise or cooperate but try to win completely on every issue. According to LaPalombara, this is how Italians tend to view politics:

The fact is that the typical Italian feels that elections are contests among mutually and fundamentally antagonistic groups—between the "we" and "the enemy." It is assumed that the winners will take advantage of and exploit the losers. For many the election is described

36. As some social psychologists have shown. Thus an attitude survey among college students found that a person who scored high on trust in people is likely to believe that international conflict can be reduced or settled by cooperation and mutual understanding; low scores are likely to feel that the only way to handle international affairs is through coercion, force, and power. Morris Rosenberg, "Misanthropy and Attitudes Toward International Affairs," *Journal of Conflict Resolution* 1, no. 4 (December 1957): 340.

as essentially a life-and-death struggle between opposed
and irreconcilable ways of life.[37]

Political activists in the two dominant parties probably
hold this view even more strongly than people less involved
in politics. A recent study of Communist and Christian Democratic party activists shows that a preponderant majority of
both view the world essentially in Manichean terms as a
conflict between dichotomous forces of good and evil—the
good represented by their own party, of course, and evil by
the other.[38]

At the other extreme, relations among actors may be seen
as strictly cooperative. Here the central rule is: not only is
there no conflict between us but our interests are identical
or so intertwined that we stand to gain or lose together.
Hence the best strategy is to cooperate completely and avoid
all conflict. Weiner suggests that some such view as this is
an important element in the beliefs of Indian elites:

> For reasons which must lie deep in the psychology of
> Indians, India's national party leaders, intellectuals,
> and bureaucrats look upon conflict within their society
> as intrinsically undesirable. While the notion of com-
> petition and conflict is central to American political life
> and thought, notions of cooperation, harmony and, to

37. "Italy," pp. 290–91.
38. Francesco Alberoni, Vittorio Capecchi, Agopik Manoukian,
Franca Olivetti, and Antonio Tosi, *L'attivista di partito* (Bologna:
Il Mulino, 1967), pp. 381–87. The 108 activists in the Christian
Democratic (DC) and Communist (PCI) parties were classified as
follows according to their "vision of the world":

	DC	PCI	Total
Absolutely dichotomous	3	17	20
Predominantly dichotomous	14	21	35
Conceives of reality as a struggle or fight among positions but has a more articulated sensitivity to the alternatives	28	14	42
In no way dichotomous	9	2	11
	54	54	108

use a favorite Indian word, "synthesis" are central to Indian thought. This is not to say that there is more cooperation and less conflict in India than in the United States, but simply that while in general Americans easily adapt to situations of conflict, the Indian elite generally finds such situations intolerable.

. . . Indian historical writings tend to stress the unities of the past and minimize the conflicts and the struggles over power. Indian intellectuals generally envision the pre-British village as a harmonious social and political unit. And contemporary historical writings on the struggle for independence tend to underplay the great internal dissensions which existed.

Most of the national leadership believes that every effort should be made to eliminate conflict within rural India. No progress, so the argument goes, can be achieved in the villages without a spirit of harmony and cooperation. Similarly, conflict should be minimized or eliminated at all levels of society, for it is only as the country is united that it can move forward.[39]

A third view sees relationships as cooperative-competitive. Conflict, competition, and cooperation are all viewed as normal aspects of social relationships which contribute to a healthy, vigorous, progressive society. In this view there are great gains to be secured from cooperation, but because one cannot agree with everyone on everything some conflict is inevitable. Nor is conflict necessarily bad; it is often a part of a larger process in which the actors in conflict all end up better off. The important strategy in a conflict is to search for mutually beneficial solutions. Far from being a betrayal of principle, a compromise is essentially a good thing, and a spirit of compromise vital.

Belief in the virtues and possibilities of cooperative-competitive relationships is central to English liberal thought. It

39. Myron Weiner, "India: Two Political Cultures," in Pye and Verba, *Political Culture*, pp. 235–36.

was at the heart of both Adam Smith's revolutionary notion of the beneficent results of competition and J. S. Mill's classic defense of the benefits to be derived from the liberty to express clashing opinions.

What can we conclude about the consequences of these beliefs for hegemony and polyarchy? It would be astounding if the first view did not seriously impede cooperation among the various actors. Experiments by social psychologists have in fact found this to be the case.[40] And this is of course pre-

40. One well-known game used in experiments is the Prisoner's Dilemma. This is a two-person game with four possible outcomes: (1) A's best alternative, which is the worst for B. (2) B's best alternative, which is the worst for A. (3) The worst alternative for both. (4) A satisfactory alternative, better for each than the worst but somewhat less satisfactory for each than his best. An example would be:

	B chooses alternative	
	x	y
	(4)	(1)
p	A wins \$9 B wins \$9	A loses \$10 B wins \$10
A chooses alternative		
	(2)	(3)
q	A loses \$10 B wins \$10	A loses \$9 B loses \$9

Communication between the players is forbidden. Clearly if A trusts B and tries to be cooperative by choosing p, B might betray him and chose y, as in (1). So too if B trusts A and chooses x but is betrayed by A, as in (1). If each distrusts the other and they refuse to cooperate, both end up losing, as in (3). Thus they can both avoid losing and win, as in (4), only if both trust one another and try to cooperate. In one experiment with a game of this kind, Morton Deutsch found that players who were each told to act as if their opponent's welfare as well as their own was important, and were also informed that their opponent had received the same instruction, were more likely to take the risk involved in trusting their oponents and cooperating in order to achieve outcome (4), even in the absence of communication and personal knowledge of their opponent. When each was told to do as well for himself as possible, and to do better than the other, they were more likely to end up with the worst outcome (3). Morton Deutsch, "Trust and Suspicion," *Journal of Conflict Resolution* 2, no. 4 (December 1958): 265. In a later experiment by Scodel et al., when 22 pairs of players were told to win as much as possible over 50 trials, only 2 of the 22 pairs collaborated, and collaboration did

cisely what many observers of Italian politics conclude.
LaPalombara, for example, concludes that

> one consequence . . . at an organizational participatory
> level is extreme polarization of feeling which is in part
> reflected in the proliferation of political parties . . .
> The fragmentation that grows out of this mutual sus-
> picion and antagonism is dramatically portrayed when
> we look at Italy's secondary associations. In the field
> of labor, for example, [the labor organizations] . . .
> reproduce and intensify in the arena of organized labor
> the intense feelings that characterize interpolitical party
> relationships . . . [whether] one is speaking of agri-
> cultural organizations, professional associations, athletic
> clubs, youth groups, women's federations, university
> student movements—really the entire gamut of volun-
> tary associations—one is likely to find them fragmented
> into at least Communist, Socialist, Catholic, and Fascist
> factions.[41]

If the strictly competitive view impedes the degree of cooperation and trust required for polyarchy, the opposite view,
that all relationships are or ought to be strictly cooperative
is by no means free of difficulties for the operation of a polyarchy. For it tends to undermine certain key institutions in a
polyarchy of their legitimacy, particularly the political parties.
Political parties necessarily engage in conflict; they may even
exacerbate conflict. But if political conflict is an unredeemed
evil, then surely competing political parties are an evil. This
is, in fact, the public ideology in many countries ruled by
hegemonic regimes; in communist countries, certain aspects

not increase as the game went on. According to the experiments, the
fact that many players saw the game as competitive prevented them
from giving their opponent any chance to beat them by trying to
establish cooperative relations. Alvin Scodel et al., "Some Descriptive Aspects of Two-Person, Non-Zero-Sum games," *Journal of Conflict Resolution* 3, no. 2 (June 1959): 114.
41. "Italy," pp. 291–93.

of Marx's thought provided a logical and persuasive foundation on which Lenin and his successors were able to erect
a theoretical and practical justification for repressing all
parties other than the single ruling party.[42]

Even among those who believe strongly in democracy, a
belief in strict cooperation and the evils of conflict is likely
to undermine the legitimacy of political parties. Given the
beliefs about cooperation and conflict in Indian culture, it
is not surprising that a number of Indian intellectuals, particularly those of Gandhian inspiration, are advocates of
partyless democracy. The most distinguished advocate of
this view is Jayaprakash Narayan, "a strong exponent of
what he calls a 'communitarian' society, in which party politics would be eliminated, and where popular elections would
be replaced by a system of indirect elections from village
councils up to the national parliament."

> During the past few years [Myron Weiner wrote in
> 1965], Jayaprakash and many of his followers have
> carried his critique of parliamentary democracy to many
> parts of India. Parliamentary democracy, he has argued,
> with its system of political parties, has intensified con-
> flict at all levels of Indian society, divided India's vil-
> lages, aggravated caste and communal tensions, and en-
> couraged men to seek power for its own sake. He fer-
> vently believes that it is possible to increase the powers
> of local government (a position he strongly advocates)
> without at the same time increasing local conflict if only
> political parties would voluntarily abstain from par-
> ticipating in village life. . . .
>
> Even those who reject Jayaprakash's solution as Uto-
> pian are prepared to accept his criticisms of the par-
> liamentary system and his basic assumption that har-
> mony is a prerequisite for national development . . .
> Several . . . versions of this view . . . find support

42. Cf. Robert A. Dahl, "Marxism and Free Parties," *Journal of
Politics* 10, no. 4 (November 1948): 787–813.

> among some intellectuals and national leaders. One . . .
> is that the present system of party government should
> be replaced by a "national" government which would
> consist of all of India's political parties. The argument
> that . . . political conflict would be transferred from
> outside of government to within government is countered
> with the reply that in a "national" government all the
> political parties would have to give up their own po-
> litical ambitions in order to serve the common goal of
> national unity and national development.[43]

Obviously it would be wrong to label such views antidemocratic, but it is equally obvious that beliefs of this kind
are hostile to polyarchy. Conceivably, beliefs of this kind,
if acted on, might produce a system more democratic than
polyarchy (though I think this is highly unlikely); meanwhile they weaken the legitimacy of polyarchy.

Some Indians may, of course, hold both views: they may
see politics as strictly competitive, given the current state
of things, and yet they may ardently desire that politics
should actually be strictly cooperative. That many Italians
may feel much the same way is suggested by the fact that
30 out of 54 Christian Democratic activists viewed society
as a meeting of forces that ideally could work together har-
moniously.[44] An interesting feature of Leninism is the way
that it combines both views: in bourgeois societies, politics
in its most elementary aspect is a strictly competitive, zero-
sum game played between bourgeoisie and proletariat, but
as soon as the proletarian revolution eliminates classes, politics must necessarily become strictly cooperative. It is not
surprising, then, that in Italy activists in the PCI overwhelmingly perceive social reality as a collision between "antagonistic groups and interests, a class struggle between bourgeoisie and proletariat, an opposition between capital and

43. "India," pp. 236–37.
44. Alberoni et al., *L'attivista di partito*, p. 356.

labor." [45] It would be more surprising if many of them, particularly older and more orthodox militants, did not also believe, with Lenin, that a successful proletarian revolution would bring about a society ruled by harmonious cooperation, in which, therefore, competing parties would be unnecessary.

While extreme beliefs in either strict competition or strict cooperation probably generate an unfavorable environment for polyarchy, the range of beliefs about cooperation and conflict that are compatible with polyarchy may be quite broad. The operation of polyarchy and public contestation require both cooperation and conflict in highly visible institutions such as elections, parties, and parliaments. Hence one would expect polyarchy to be favored by beliefs that emphasize the possibility and the desirability of both conflict and cooperation, particularly, perhaps, where political conflict can be seen as an element in, and restrained by, a higher order of cooperation.

I am not aware of any cross-national data that bear directly on this question, but scattered evidence on attitudes toward compromise may be relevant, for in the general sense of the term, compromise is a normal and desirable consequence of conflicts bounded by cooperation. Although the evidence is weak, there do seem to be significant differences among countries in beliefs about compromise. Certainly in some countries with long and sturdy traditions of polyarchy and public contestation, compromise is honorable in both word and deed. For example, "Compromise is traditionally considered the Swedish technique in politics, and the word 'compromise' evidently sounds pleasing to Swedish voters." [46] Or consider the Netherlands:

45. Ibid., p. 347.
46. Nils Stjernquist, "Sweden: Stability or Deadlock?" in Robert A. Dahl, ed., *Political Oppositions in Western Democracies*, p. 139. It is worth nothing that the well-known book on Sweden by Dankwart A. Rustow is titled *Sweden: The Politics of Compromise* (Princeton: Princeton University Press, 1955). Rustow comments: "In Sweden

> Dutch politics is a politics of accommodation. That is
> the secret of its success. The term accommodation is
> here used in the sense of settlement of divisive issues
> and conflicts where only a minimal consensus exists.[47]

The Dutch, and particularly the leaders, take the existence
of "ideological differences as basic realities which cannot
and should not be changed." This imposes an obligation on
leaders to search for (and nonleaders to accept) compromises that can be agreed to by all the blocs.[48]

That a belief in the virtues and possibilities of compromise
prevails in many polyarchies seems obvious. Such a belief
has been central to American politics. The Swiss system
could not operate without it. In Britain, where the parties
follow strictly competitive strategies in elections and cabinet
formation, cooperation is facilitated by a spirit of compromise.[49]

It would be interesting to have more evidence about countries in which "compromise" is condemned or disdained. As
one possible instance, the Spanish cognate *compromiso* covers a variety of meanings rather different from those of the
English word, and the meaning closest to English usage is
generally said to carry with it a somewhat unfavorable
connotation (as is the term "to *be* compromised" in English). To the extent that these differences in language reflect
differences in outlook, as seems to be the case, then parties
and politicians may gain respect for their compromises in
Sweden but contempt in Spain and Latin America. Where

---

perhaps more than anywhere else the technique of compromise has
been an essential ingredient in the art of proposing the terms on
which men can live together. Many of her outstanding politicians . . .
have been accomplished masters of that technique" (pp. 230–31).
47. Lijphart, *The Politics of Accommodation,* pp. 103, 124, 125.
48. Ibid., p. 124.
49. "The practise of settling political differences peacefully has
existed for so long that it has come to be expressed in basic cultural
norms concerning compromise, self-restraint, and national duty
before party duty." Rose, *Politics in England,* p. 157.

compromises are disdained, cooperation is difficult and conflicts are more likely to go unresolved. If conflict is unbearable, then hegemony may be seen as the best way to compel
cooperation.

Explaining Beliefs: A Misleading Paradigm

As I warned, the beliefs I have described are no more than
illustrations. I have not touched at all upon the possible consequences of more coherent bodies of belief that may unite
the specific fragments just described into a more comprehensive and unified outlook, theory, or ideology. If the evidence at hand is inadequate to support hypotheses about
variations in discrete beliefs of the kind just mentioned and
their consequences for regimes, to link belief systems or
ideologies with regimes would be even more speculative.

It might be argued that the attempt to isolate beliefs as
a factor in accounting for differences in regimes is a vain
enterprise, since beliefs themselves are best interpreted as
merely intervening variables. After all, it might be said, if
we can explain how beliefs come about, and if beliefs help
to explain how regimes come about, we can account for
variations in regimes by explanatory factors more "basic"
than beliefs. The point can be clarified by the paradigm suggested earlier.

If it is true that:

A. Factors determining $\to$ Political beliefs
      beliefs

$$\to \frac{\text{Political}}{\text{Actions}} - P \to \text{Regimes}$$

then it seems reasonable to argue that:

B. Factors determining
      beliefs   ——————— P ———————$\to$ Regimes

The simplified paradigm B is, however, thoroughly misleading. In the first place, it assumes that we know a great
deal more than we do. In actual fact, existing theory and
data are quite unable to demonstrate the validity or even the
plausibility of B. It therefore represents a kind of reduction
that is unwarranted on scientific grounds.

No doubt the most popular explanation for beliefs is to
attribute them to self-interest. The difficulty with this particular form of reductionist explanation is not so much that
it is wrong as that it is nearly meaningless. It may very well
be true that wholly altruistic beliefs are rare; indeed, it is
difficult to imagine how anyone could adhere to a belief that
ran counter to the "interests" of the self at all levels, conscious and unconscious. But that is exactly the problem:
to say "self-interest" is, despite the illusion of precision, to
say very little.[50] What one identifies as the "self" varies from
one individual to another, from one situation and role to
another, and from one culture or subculture to another.
In the culture of "amoral familism" of South Italy described
by Banfield, for relationships outside the family the "self"
is the family, and the villagers act as if they were following
this rule:

> Maximize the material, short-run advantage of the nu-
> clear family; assume that all others will do likewise.

The villagers also act according to certain implications of
this rule:

> 1. *In a society of amoral familists, no one will further
> the interest of the group or community except as it is
> to his private advantage to do so . . .*

50. "The self comprises all the precious things and persons who are
relevant to an individual's life, so that the term selfish loses its original connotation, and the proposition that man is selfish resolves itself into the circular statement that people are concerned with the
things they are concerned with." Gardner Murphy, "Social Motiva-
tion," in G. Lindzey, ed., *Handbook of Social Psychology* (Reading,
Mass.: Addison-Wesley, 1954), 2: 625.

> 2. . . . *Only officials will concern themselves with pub-*
> *lic affairs, for only they are paid to do so. For a private*
> *citizen to take a serious interest in a public problem*
> *will be regarded as abnormal and even improper.*[51]

Yet there is nothing universal about "amoral familism." For example, in the kibbutz in Israel studied by Spiro, the identification of a member with his family is weakened both by his identification with the kibbutz as a whole and, for the *sabra* who has been reared in the kibbutz, with the group of sixteen children with whom one is reared from kindergarten through high school, the *kevutza*. The strength of these emotional ties is indicated by the fact that for the sabras the incest taboo extends to the kevutza and even to the whole kibbutz and by a wealth of evidence that the sabras have a strong sense of responsibility for the kibbutz and its members.[52]

If the "self" is somewhat elastic, one's "interest, what one should do to serve the self," is even more so. For one thing, conceptions of interest depend on cognitive beliefs, and these are shaped by many different factors: because of cultural influences, for example, a person with a burst appendix might rub sheep fat on his belly or call a doctor. Consequently, conceptions of self-interest or group interest vary a good deal. Thus it is not particularly helpful to explain

51. Edward C. Banfield, *The Moral Basis of a Backward Society* (Glencoe: The Free Press, 1958), pp. 85–87. Italics in the original.
52. "In not one instance has a sabra from [the kibbutz studied by Spiro] married a fellow sabra nor, to the best of our knowledge, has a sabra had sexual intercourse with a fellow sabra . . . In no instance have sabras from the same kevutza had sexual intercourse with each other. The reason given by the sabras for their exogamy is interesting: they view each other, they say, as siblings." Melford E. Spiro, *Children of the Kibbutz* (New York: Schocken Books, 1965), p. 347. See also his *Kibbutz, Venture in Utopia* (New York: Schocken Books, 1963), p. 219. Although Spiro is critical of many aspects of the kibbutz and the discrepancy between ideal and reality, he leaves no doubt about the strength of the sabra's attachment to his kevutza and to the kibbutz. See, e.g., *Children of the Kibbutz*, p. 365.

beliefs as expressions of self-interest, for what is seen as self-interest depends on one's beliefs.[53]

Probably the commonest form of the explanation by self-interest interprets beliefs as a reflection of an individual's position in the society and economy. Innumerable studies, both systematic and casual, reveal tendencies of this kind, but they also show that the correlation between an individual's beliefs and his socioeconomic characteristics is almost always quite weak. The significant finding is not that there exists some relationship, but how weak and uncertain the relationship proves to be.[54]

It is tempting to think that if "self-interest" and socioeconomic position are psychologically too naïve to serve as explanatory factors, a more sophisticated psychological explanation will suffice. Can the beliefs of a political activist be adequately explained as a reflection of his personality structure? One of the leading investigators of the relations between politics and personality cautions against reductions of this kind, arguing that:

> Personality structures ≠ political belief ≠ individual political action ≠ aggregate political structures and processes

where ≠ means "does not necessarily predict." He goes on to say:

> I do not mean to imply an absence of empirical connection across these various links . . . Rather, what needs to be emphasized is that the connections *are* empirical . . . and that the relationships are neither

53. Cf. Clifford Geertz's comment on the "interest theory" as a determinant of ideology: "The main defects of the interest theory are that its psychology is too anemic and its sociology too muscular." "Ideology as a Cultural System," in Apter, ed., *Ideology and Discontent*, p. 53.
54. For example, see Donald D. Searing, "The Comparative Study of Elite Socialization," *Comparative Political Studies* 1 (January 1969): 471–500, particularly 488–89.

necessarily strong nor positive, especially those that cross more than one of the links.

The weakness of the first of these links is that

> As is often pointed out, persons with similar underlying personality characteristics are capable of holding different political beliefs, and those with similar beliefs may differ in underlying personality characteristics. The psychic elements of underlying personality and belief are capable of independent variation.[55]

Political Culture as an Explanation

If a spirit of reductionism led social scientists for a time to play down the effects of beliefs on the character and behavior of different kinds of regimes, more recently a focus on the importance of political culture has indirectly given renewed emphasis to the importance of political beliefs.

Political culture has been defined as "the system of empirical beliefs, expressive symbols, and values which defines the situation in which political action takes place. It provides the subjective orientation to politics." [56] It is now rather widely recognized that differences in the political cultures of various countries help to account for the differences in the nature of their political systems.

The relationship between political culture and beliefs, as I use the term here, is fuzzy. Certainly many of the beliefs held by political activists can be regarded as a part, or a product, of a country's political culture. But the focus in this chapter on the beliefs of political activists may be distinguished in two respects from the recent concern for political culture. First, studies of political culture tend to concentrate exclusively on stable and persistent outlooks produced by socialization into an on-going system of beliefs; hence the

55. Fred I. Greenstein, *Personality and Politics* (Chicago: Markham, 1969), pp. 124–26.
56. Sidney Verba, in Pye and Verba, *Political Culture,* p. 513.

investigation of political cultures may easily neglect sources of change in beliefs. Because alien, esoteric, or unorthodox beliefs in one period may become part of the political culture at a later time, the processes that make for changes in beliefs are as important as those processes, like socialization, that make for stability. Second, although students of political culture call attention to differences between elite and mass political cultures, they have mainly paid attention to the more widespread and diffuse aspects of the widely shared political culture of a country; up to now, they have paid a good deal less attention to the beliefs of political elites and activists. As a result, we know little about differences in the cognitive beliefs of activists in various countries.

Nonetheless, by taking advantage of the insights and evidence provided by the recently reviving interest in political culture, it may be possible to develop a better understanding of some of the possible causes of both stability and change in the beliefs of political activists.

Acquiring Political Beliefs

Virtually all moral and religious training is founded—correctly, I think—on certain simple assumptions, to wit:

Most people acquire their beliefs during a period when they are particularly receptive. Typically, a person is highly receptive during, and only during, the first two decades of his life. At the end of this period, one's outlook becomes fixed or crystallized. Thereafter, one's beliefs are likely to remain rather stable.

When social scientists concerned with political culture place such a heavy emphasis on the importance of early socialization, they tread the ancient path of Aristotle on ethics and the churches on religion.[57]

57. "The Virtues then come to be in us neither by nature, nor in despite of nature, but we are furnished by nature with a capacity for receiving them, and are perfected in them through custom . . . So

It would be wrong, of course, to assume that political beliefs are fully formed and crystallized beyond change after the early period of youthful socialization is finished. Changes may occur later, either gradually or, in the more infrequent case, abruptly. Ordinarily, it appears, when beliefs change in later life the change is gradual, as with the classic transformation of the youthful radical to the middle-aged conservative. A gradual change of this kind need not involve the kind of crisis one associates with "a loss of belief." Instead, one might say that new beliefs fill up the space that has been left by the erosion of the old. With a rapid change of beliefs in a mature person, however, there is more likely to be an interlude between the old and the new when one suffers from a sense of having lost his beliefs. Loss of beliefs is, it seems, accompanied by a painful state too unpleasant to sustain. Hence, loss of belief is likely to coincide with a period of high receptivity—even an active search for new beliefs to replace the old. The urgency of the search insures that the period of receptivity is short. Ordinarily it is soon followed by the acquisition of new beliefs, which, because the threat of loss is unbearable, may be even more rigidly held than the old.

Although a young person may also suffer a sudden loss of belief, typically the youthful period of receptivity seems to be a process of gradual or intermittent acquisition, reality testing, relearning, and crystallization as the youth is initiated into the beliefs that prevail in the major institutions of socialization in his society or subculture—the family, school, church, work-place, peer group. "Very young children in Britain first learn to think of the Queen as the effective ruler of Britain . . . To the young child the Prime Minister is merely a helper of the Queen . . . This view of the rela-

---

then, whether we are accustomed this way or that straight from childhood, makes not a small but an important difference, or rather I would say it makes all the difference." *The Ethics of Aristotle* (London: Dent, 1911), pp. 26–27 tionship between the Queen and the Prime Minister erodes with increasing age, but it diminishes much more rapidly among middle class children than among working class children." The average adult Englishman, then, has acquired the cognitive belief that the Queen reigns but does not rule; the normative belief that, as one twelve-year-old put it, "the Prime Minister is a person who rightfully sort of governs the country and he's got men under him"; and quite possibly an affective or emotional warmth toward the monarchy and neutrality vis-à-vis the Prime Minister.[58]

It may be useful therefore to distinguish two different kinds of periods of relatively high receptivity to the acquisition of beliefs: the normal period of youthful socialization and the more abnormal situation that occurs when, having already acquired a belief, one loses it and feels a sense of loss. What factors influence the content of the political beliefs an individual acquires during his periods of receptivity?

Exposure

One obvious determinant is the extent to which one is exposed to a particular political outlook, which depends in turn on a number of things. The chance of being exposed to a particular idea depends, of course, on whether the idea is present in one's own environment. Two necessary conditions are, clearly, that the idea has been formulated and that it has been diffused to the individual's environment. So much seems obvious enough.

Invention and diffusion provide a person with available models. Schemes of representation, for example, existed well before the eighteenth century, but the model of representative government for the state did not. That model had still to be articulated—invented, if you like. After it was formulated during the eighteenth century, it struck many sensitive

58. Fred I. Greenstein, V. M. Herman, Robert Stradling, and Elia Zurick, "Queen and Prime Minister—the Child's Eye View," *New Society* 14 (October 23, 1969): 365–68.

political observers—Jefferson and Madison in America, James Mill in England—as a brilliant new discovery that solved a hitherto unsolvable problem: how to combine democracy with the large state. To take another example, the idea of a constitutional convention was wholly novel, as Palmer has pointed out, until the American Revolution stimulated the calling of conventions to write or rewrite the various state constitutions and, of course, the Constitutional Convention of 1787 in Philadelphia.

What most impressed the French was the very act of constitution-making itself, the constituting or reconstituting of government through the principle of the people as a constituent power. What they learned from America was the possibility of having a constituent assembly or convention. The very word "convention" in this sense . . . came into the French language through translation of the American state constitutions. For the subjects of government to repudiate and dismantle their governments, revert to a state of "nature," and then by deliberate planning to constitute governments anew, to invent and delimit new offices and authorities and endow them with written grants of power, was at least in a juridical sense the very essence of revolution, the practical acting out of the social contract, and the assertion of the sovereignty of the people.[59]

The extent to which one is likely to be exposed to a particular belief during youth, the normal period of high receptivity, depends on the amount of influence that the bearers of the belief have on the process of socialization, particularly in the family, church, school, and university.[60] A notable

59. R. R. Palmer, *The Age of the Democratic Revolution: A Political History of Europe and America, 1760–1800, The Challenge* (Princeton: Princeton University Press, 1959), p. 267.
60. "Just as *what* is taught is vital in the socialization effect of education, so is *who* teaches. In Chile, the Bonilla-Silvert survey of primary and secondary school teachers indicated that their numbers

instance was the extraordinary influence of English or English-established schools, colleges, and universities on the political perspectives of many Indian intellectuals, scholars, journalists, teachers, administrators, and political leaders who helped to gain acceptance for liberal democratic ideas and institutions before and after independence.[61] The effect of the English universities was amplified by their indirect influence on Indian universities. The perspectives of the Westernized, or Anglicized, Indian were often profoundly at odds with the character and actual development of India. If, as a result, the net impact of English education on India's political development can never be precisely determined, surely it is no exaggeration to say that if Indian intellectuals and other leaders had been as deeply exposed during their higher education to antidemocratic or illiberal ideas, the chances for polyarchy in India would have been significantly reduced.

Prestige

As this example suggests, the particular beliefs that an individual acquires during his periods of receptivity, whether in youth or later on, depend not only on the amount of exposure but also on the relative prestige of the ideas and beliefs to which he is exposed. The prestige of a particular political belief seems to depend among other things on the prestige of its advocates and antagonists and on the successes and failures of the people, organizations, and institutions that symbolize the belief. Like Benjamin Franklin in Paris, the bearer of a belief (in this case a belief in the virtues and potentialities of representative government and political equality) may himself acquire esteem as the representative

included more downward-mobile than upward-mobile people, and that these downward-mobile teachers' attitudes rated very high on *traditional* values." Alfred Stepan, "Political Development Theory: The Latin American Experience," *Journal of International Affairs* 20, no. 2 (1966): 232.
61. Weiner, "India," pp. 239–40.

of a new idea and at the same time enhance the esteem in which the idea itself is held because of his own special prestige—in Franklin's case, as savant, natural genius, wit, and friend of the great, the famous, and the fashionable. Gandhi's prestige in recent decades has many sources other than his advocacy of nonviolent resistance, but the prestige of that idea has doubtless been enhanced by its association with the saint-like Gandhi. So too with his martyred follower, Martin Luther King.

In lending prestige to a belief or detracting from it, intellectuals and scholars once again occupy a strategic position; to those who do not independently investigate the validity of a belief, the intellectual, scholar, scientist, or other accredited expert often provides the needed validation. And it is, of course, the relative prestige of writers and scholars within the educational system of a country that gives them a relatively high degree of influence over political socialization. In the United States, for example, critics of the "Liberal Establishment" from both Right and Left contend that the content of the curriculum from kindergarten through the universities is far more "liberal" than is the country as a whole. The charge is very likely true, for American intellectuals and scholars are not only more "liberal" than the general population, but they have more influence on the content and practices of the educational institutions, though much less than many of them would like.

The relative prestige of an idea also depends on what are thought to be its achievements. These are embodied in people, institutions, or organizations. Although systematic data on the relative prsetige of belief systems are lacking, some well-grounded impressions may suffice to make the point. Palmer writes of the impact of the American Revolution on Europeans:

> There were many in Europe, as there were in America, who saw in the American Revolution a lesson and an

encouragement for mankind. It proved that the liberal ideas of the Enlightenment be put into practice. It showed, or was assumed to show, that ideas of the rights of man and the social contract, of liberty and equality, of responsible citizenship and popular sovereignty, of religious freedom, freedom of thought and speech, separation of powers and deliberately contrived written constitutions, need not remain in the realm of speculation, among the writers of books, but could be made the actual fabric of public life among real people, in this world, now.

Thus was created an American myth, or mirage, or dream, "the first of these great movements of secular mysticism," to quote a recent author, "which modern man has been experimenting with for the last two hundred years." [62]

Later, as Tocqueville testified, the simple fact that democracy appeared to be working successfully in the United States weakened the arguments of antidemocrats. Throughout the nineteenth century, the relative prestige of democratic beliefs seems to have been high throughout Europe and the Americas.

Because polyarchal institutions were historically associated with capitalism, the onset of the Great Depression doubtless reduced the prestige not only of capitalism but of polyarchy as well. Although the apparent achievement of reformist governments in a number of countries with polyarchal regimes—the New Deal in the United States, the reforms of Labor governments in Sweden and elsewhere—probably restored some of the prestige to polyarchy, the seeming triumphs of one-party hegemonic regimes in the USSR, Italy, and Germany in the 1930s undoubtedly enhanced the prestige of these regimes and the ideologies they purported to re-

62. *Age of the Democratic Revolution,* pp. 239–40.

flect.[63] However incredible it may seem in retrospect, the
USSR under Stalin was regarded by some distinguished
Western intellectuals and writers of liberal, left, or socialist
persuasions as the embodiment of what Sidney and Beatrice
Webb unhappily chose to call a New Civilization.[64] If the
defeat of the Axis powers in World War II was a severe blow
to the prestige of fascism and nazism, through its sacrifices
and military victories the Soviet Union emerged in a heroic
and creditable light, while in Italy and France the dedicated
and effective participation of communists in the resistance
helped the party, particularly in Italy, to acquire very considerable prestige. In Latin America, the failure of competitive political systems either to bring about structural reforms or to endure, the solid achievements of PRI in Mexico,
Castro's revolution in Cuba, reformist juntas like that of
Peru—all have had an impact on the relative prestige of
polyarchy and hegemony. To offer a final example, the involvement of the United States in the Vietnam war seems to
have drastically lowered the prestige of polyarchy (though
not necessarily of democratic beliefs) among young people
in the United States and probably elsewhere.[65] In fact, this
final example may serve to illustrate the general argument:
a young person growing up in the United States in the late
1960s in all likelihood would not only be exposed to beliefs
different from those of a young person in, say, 1950 or 1900,
but the relative prestige of polyarchy, particularly as embodied in American institutions, would be lower. Hence the
proportion of young people who believed in something other

63. For Argentina, see Mariano Grondona, *La Argentina en el
Tiempo y en el Mundo* (Bueons Aires: Primera Plana, 1967), pp.
146–47.
64. Sidney and Beatrice Webb, *Soviet Communism: A New Civilization?* (London: Longmans, Green, 1935).
65. Kenneth Keniston, *Young Radicals* (New York: Harcourt, Brace
and World, 1968), p. 123. Jean-Marie Domenach, "L'idéologie du
Mouvement," *Esprit,* 36° Annee (August–September 1968), pp. 39 ff.

than polyarchy, at least as practiced in the United States, was probably greater than in certain earlier periods.

Consistency with previous beliefs

A third factor determining the chances that an individual will acquire a particular political belief is the extent to which he feels it to be consistent with his present beliefs.[66] To be sure, even if a new idea is inconsistent with an already accepted belief, if one finds the new belief attractive he may reject the old or conclude that the new and the old are not really inconsistent. Nonetheless, if the new view is thought to conflict with one's existing beliefs, obviously the chance that one will adopt it is reduced. This is what happens, in fact, when a period of high receptivity comes to an end and one emerges with a more or less crystallized set of beliefs. Thereafter, one consciously or unconsciously tests new beliefs for consistency with the old and, ordinarily, rejects the new ones when they are felt to be inconsistent. When new ideas conflict with old, firmly held beliefs, an enormous weight of contradictory perceptions is required in order to bring about a loss of belief; and it sometimes appears as if the level of contradiction behind the dam of old beliefs had been secretly rising, until finally the dam itself is swept away and nothing remains except disbelief. It is easy to see, too, why the general culture and the specific political culture into which an individual is socialized are so important in explaining political life, as social scientists have recently re-emphasized. For the culture consists of those very beliefs, perspectives, and habits of mind that are successfully transmitted to the young and therefore provide the conscious and unconscious assumptions against which new beliefs are tested—and usually found wanting.

It is this need for subjective consistency in beliefs that

66. Robert E. Lane and David O. Sears, *Public Opinion* (Englewood Cliffs: Prentice-Hall, 1964), pp. 44 ff.

helps to give ideas a certain life of their own, an autonomous development not wholly under the control or manipulation of social interests. Although there is unquestionably more determinism in social and political beliefs than in highly abstract belief systems like those of mathematics and physics, once a social or political principle becomes firmly embedded in the political culture, it can serve quite literally as an axiom from which new unanticipated, and seemingly inescapable conclusions can be drawn. The "functions" originally fulfilled by a principle, the "interests" initially served by it, can no longer control or dominate the conclusions to be drawn from it.

Beliefs about political equality and inequality often take on this axiomatic quality. Wherever principles of political equality were used by spokesmen for the middle classes to justify their entry into the political system, it was not long before spokesmen for excluded groups drew the logical consequences, showed the inconsistency of the exclusion, and insisted that middle-class governments had to honor their own sacred principles or lose their legitimacy. In fact, certain clusters of political belief so regularly show up in different circumstances that they appear almost to reflect the necessity with which certain conclusions follow from certain premises. To believe in political equality among a large association of people seems to carry with it, as if by implication, a number of principles; to make the same point more cautiously, the attempt to devise principles consistent with political equality narrows the choice down to a very much smaller subset.[67]

67. It is difficult to believe, for example, that democratic ideas were simply invented once at a given time and place and that subsequent repetition is nothing more than a result of diffusion. Consider the following case: In 1781 "a reforming committee at Westminster . . . drew up a report that went beyond any of the new American state constitutions in its democratic theory of representation. The report, drafted by John Jebb, demanded universal manhood suffrage, the use of the ballot rather than oral voting, the annual election of Parliament, representation of voters in proportion to numbers in equal electoral districts, payment of wages to elected representatives, and

Consistency with experience

"Internal" consistency, whether according to familiar principles of logic or by more subjective and personal criteria, is not, of course, the only kind of consistency one requires. A fourth factor bearing on the likelihood that one will adopt a particular political belief is the extent to which one feels that the belief is consistent with one's own experiences. Experience is particularly important for the credibility of the cognitive aspects of belief, for if one's own perceptions of reality conflict with those maintained in the new belief to which one is exposed, then in order to reduce the strain one must reject either one's own perceptions, the existence of a discrepancy, or the validity of the new idea. While each of these evidently occurs, the last is without doubt the most common. Here again, it is obvious how important is the culture in which the individual is reared, for he is conditioned to interpret the events of his life in a particular way. What one experiences is partly shaped by one's own culture; thus people from different cultures may experience the "same" event in quite different ways. So too, people with different political perspectives—whether weakly organized, fragmented belief systems or coherent ideologies—may perceive the same happening in very different ways, and thus each person may accumulate experiences that confirm his existing beliefs.[68]

---

removal of all property qualifications for election to the Commons. Here were all six points of the People's Charter to be famous in England over fifty years later." Palmer, *Age of the Democratic Revolution,* pp. 208–09.

68. The phenomenon is, of course, familiar to psychoanalysts, psychiatrists, and psychologists. "All day long we unconsciously *selectively* perceive the world about us. Man can prevent unpleasant perceptions by varying his attention and by wishful perceiving or thinking. . . . The simplest form of denial is blotting out the perception by withdrawing our attention from it . . . People frequently *'fill in the blanks'* with wish-fulfilling perceptions." Irving L. Janis, George F. Mahl, Jerome Kagan, and Robert R. Holt, *Personality Dynamics, Development, and Assessment* (New York: Harcourt, Brace and World, 1969), p. 354. Italics in the original.

Nonetheless, except for psychotics and to a lesser extent young children, selective perception is limited by reality.[69] Among the views to which he is exposed, the youth selects those that seem to conform most closely with his own experiences. In spite of selective perception, this process continues throughout life, and dramatic discrepancies between personal experiences and beliefs can lead to a change in beliefs. Personal experiences have led to the collapse of armies: the Russian in 1917, French in 1940, German in 1945. German soldiers on the Western front surrendered individually, then in small groups, and finally in vast straggling droves throughout April 1945 rejected the desperate propaganda from Berlin urging them to fight on, for they were convinced by battlefield experience that further resistance was futile. Yet only a few months earlier, many of the same soldiers had been fighting doggedly. During the 1960s in the United States, a significant number of young people, after experiencing what Keniston has called a "confrontation with inequity," lost their confidence in liberal reformist politics and adopted more radical views:

> Whether it was working with the unemployed in the inner city, in voter-registration drives in the South, with Negro families in the slums, or in a detailed study in American policies in Vietnam, these young radicals were forced into an immediate personal confrontation with the injustices of American life and policies.[70]

Some experiences are widely shared, others are idiosyncratic. Differences in historical experience are one source of

69. "The price of this defensive gain [denial] can be high: an inability to live in the real world. But denial usually stops short of the hallucinatory extreme of psychosis: in the adult, wishful thinking and even the tendency to it are usually restricted by being tested against reality. Not so with the child, however, whose behavior conforms more to the pleasure principle than to the reality principle." Ibid., p. 354.
70. Keniston, *Young Radicals,* p. 127.

the famous generation gap, since those whose outlook is shaped by a special historical experience find it increasingly difficult with the passage of time to convey to oncoming generations the meaning and "reality" of that experience. Even if "old soldiers never die," they often lose their audiences. It has often been observed that by the late 1960s the "meaning" and the risk of totalitarian rule began to seem very different to people under thirty in Western Europe and North America and to older persons, particularly Europeans, who had lived through the high period of totalitarian triumph of the 1930s and to whom the risks of a country regressing to barbaric despotism would always remain great. To many of these older people, polyarchy seemed both more fragile and more precious than it did to younger people who had never experienced extreme despotism but only polyarchy, with all its shortcomings when measured against democratic ideals.

Accidental or idosyncratic experiences may also play a decisive role. When Lenin was seventeen, his older brother, Alexander, was hanged for taking part in a plot by university students to kill the tsar. According to his sister, Lenin was "hardened" by Alexander's execution and began thinking seriously about revolution.[71] In trying to account for the development of Gandhi and his doctrine of Satyagraha (literally "truth force," variously translated as nonviolent resistance or militant nonviolence), Erikson places special emphasis on Gandhi's experiences in South Africa and a strike in Ahmedabad in 1918.[72] The way an American president handles his job—his "style"—is, according to Barber, "a reflection of the ways of performing which brought him success at the time, usually in late adolescence or early adulthood, when he emerged as a personality distinctive from his

71. Edmund Wilson, *To the Finland Station* (New York: Harcourt, Brace, 1940), p. 361.
72. Erik H. Erikson, *Gandhi's Truth* (New York: W. W. Norton, 1969).

family heritage, in a role involving relatively intensive participation in a socially organized setting." The early "success" that triggers the development of the later style (and the career that leads to the presidency) is often rather accidental.[73] In his interviews with young people who participated in the "Vietnam Summer" in 1967, Keniston found it necessary to emphasize not only the "psychological meaningfulness of the development of radicals" but also "the importance of what, from a psychological point of view, appear to be 'accidents.'"

> The development of these young radicals was often profoundly affected by things that "happened" to them through no plan, motive, or design of their own: a major family illness; the psychological problems of brothers or sisters; a chance to move to another school in another city. No one can weigh exactly the impact of such events upon a developing individual: much depends on his stage of development and his sensitivities at the time. In several instances, for example, major family upheavals in early adolescence deprived young radicals of parental attention, forcing them to become independent long before most adolescents do. In another case, the "accident" of going to a private school reinforced psychological tendencies that might not otherwise have been strengthened.[74]

Another Paradigm

I have been emphasizing some factors—exposure, prestige, consistency with previous beliefs and experience—that help determine whether a particular individual will acquire a particular belief during his particular period (or periods) of

73. James David Barber, "Classifying and Predicting Presidential Styles: Two Weak Presidents," *Journal of Social Issues* 24 (July 1968): 52 and passim.
74. *Young Radicals,* p. 226.

receptivity. But these same factors may also be conceived of as influencing a number of people during the same period of time; thus they help to produce those broad and decisive changes in outlook that historians describe when they write about the Renaissance, the Enlightenment, or the growth of democratic ideas.

One can hardly exaggerate how badly off we are as we move into this terrain. If it is difficult to account satisfactorily for the acquisition of individual beliefs, it is even more difficult to account for historical shifts in beliefs. Theories about individual beliefs explain, at best, why some people hold certain beliefs some of the time; they do not account for anything like *all* individuals or *all* beliefs. Yet historical explanations leave even more of the phenomena unexplained. If the data are inadequate for testing theories about how individuals acquire their beliefs, the data and even the concepts needed for explaining historical changes are far worse. One can identify an individual, and it makes some sense to say, for example, that "Robinson acquired democratic beliefs as an adolescent." But what is the equivalent of Robinson when we speak of historical changes? Concepts like "European society" or "the American people" are much too broad or ill defined. Clearly one is referring to some subset of persons, but the subset is extremely difficult to specify with much precision. Frequently what one seems to have in mind are those people in a country, or in some set of countries, who make up what might be called the ideational elites, the creators and special bearers of ideas—intellectuals of various sorts, philosophers, poets, ideologues, pamphleteers, publicists, journalists, scientists, and so on. One may also have in mind the political elites, whose beliefs are of exceptional importance in political life because of the exceptional influence of their bearers. But the boundaries of these elites are imprecise, and we lack information about their members. It is not surprising, then, that because of their concern with rigor and their dissatisfaction with the "softness" of historical description, generalization, and explanation, most social scientists have turned away from the historical movement of ideas. As a result, their own theories, however "rigorous" they may be, leave out an important explanatory variable and often lead to naïve reductionism, as if one tried to explain the collective behavior of the players in a game of football by attributing it mainly to each player's toilet training in infancy.

In a rough way, the elements discussed in the preceding section can be used in trying to account for changes in the frequency or intensity of a particular belief among a group of political activists. In a country, even in a world region such as Europe, periods of relative stability in certain political beliefs give way to periods of instability, breakdown, receptivity, which are then followed by crystallization of new beliefs and, for a time, relatively stable beliefs once again. Thus Paulson writes of the Italian village near Rome that he calls Castelfuoco:

> At the end of World War II the people of Castelfuoco entered a period of popular ferment never before equalled. Many hoped that the war had finally crushed the old order. The aristocrats faced political death and final economic collapse. The old rural civilization . . . approached extinction. The crudities and coercion of fascism had been unmasked before the world.
>
> Into this moment of intense search for a society more just, more clean, looking more to the future than to the past, the communists stepped vigorously . . .
>
> Along with a new *classe dirigente,* the communists offered a meaningful commitment for those who, in the post-World War II period, faced the shock of deep spiritual crisis. The crisis had been maturing for a generation but suddenly, with the collapse of fascism and the quest for a new order, people had no place to turn . . .
>
> The communists . . . have found a commitment in

the ideal of a better society. This commitment is contagious and inevitably makes its holders "missionaries" . . . In the postwar spiritual and political vacuum, facing an opposition more or less tied to the status quo, they have an immense power to penetrate the minds of the masses.[75]

However, it would be misleading to insist too narrowly on the analogy with individuals. Although an aggregate of individuals may be thought of for some purposes as if it were a single actor, some imporant differences must be kept in mind. Even during periods of relative stability in ideas, some activists and members of the ideational elites are receptive to new ideas. Conversely, during periods of receptivity, not all activists are open to the new belief—and certainly not the whole population. Even in Castelfuoco, which has one of the highest percentages of Communist votes in Italy, only about half the votes go to the Communist party; from a third to a quarter go to the Christian Democrats, a tenth to Socialists, and the rest are scattered among other parties.[76] Hence crystallization does not necessarily lead to a single dominant view, as one would expect with the individual actor. On the contrary, conflicting beliefs may crystallize as with religion during the Reformation or the political cleavages between communists and noncommunists that hardened in Italy and France after 1945. A period of "stability" in beliefs may not entail political stability or tranquillity; it may mean religious wars, ideological conflict, violence.

Moreover, individual beliefs may change without affecting the aggregate distribution, which seems to be approximately the case in some countries, at least in the short run, with party loyalties. Individuals, in fact, may die and be replaced;

75. Belden Paulson with Athos Ricci, *The Searchers: Conflict and Communism in an Italian Town* (Chicago: Quadrangle Books, 1966), pp. 321–26.
76. Ibid., p. 112.

because of the processes of socialization, when beliefs are embodied in an institution, like a church or political party, the distribution and even the relative intensity of beliefs may remain substantially unchanged in spite of individual turnover. As Rokkan and Lipset point out:

> *The party systems of the 1960s reflect, with few but significant exceptions, the cleavage structures of the 1920's. This is a crucial characteristic of Western competitive politics in the age of "high mass consumption": the party alternatives and in remarkably many cases the party organizations, are older than the majorities of the national electorates. To most of the citizens of the West the currently active parties have been part of the political landscape since their childhood.*[77]

This crystallization into beliefs that with the passage of time are increasingly out of joint with perceptions of reality prepares the way for a loss of faith among the mature and receptivity to new alternatives among the young.

Finally, because people die and are replaced by young persons who may have different beliefs, the distribution of beliefs among the politically active or the ideational elites may change even if every individual keeps the beliefs he acquires early in life. In fact, it may be this process of replacing the old cohorts by new ones that accounts for most large-scale historical change in beliefs. The shift in the United States during the 1930s from a normally Republican to a normally Democratic majority seems to have been of this kind.[78] If, as in Castelfuoco, the youthful cohorts enter with new views at the same time as the aging cohorts suffer a loss of belief,

77. Seymour M. Lipset and Stein Rokkan, "Cleavage Structures, Party Systems, and Voter Alignments: An Introduction," in Lipset and Rokkan, eds., *Party Systems and Voter Alignments* (New York: The Free Press of Glencoe, 1967), p. 50. Italics in original.
78. Angus Campbell, Philip E. Converse, Warren E. Miller, and Donald E. Stokes, *The American Voter* (New York: Wiley, 1960), pp. 153–54.

then the total amount of change is, of course, greatly magnified. Indeed, each may reinforce the other: weakening belief among the old encourages new beliefs among the young, which in turn leads to loss of belief among the old. Despite a common romantic view that the process always represents a healthy rejuvenation, it is in fact morally and politically neutral. If it strengthened democratic as against aristocratic views in the United States during the Jeffersonian period (as seems likely), the process may also have weakened beliefs in democracy in Athens between Demosthenes and Pericles. And some such process very likely took place in Germany between the First World War and Hitler's seizure of power.[79]

Thus, while the notion of receptivity, crystallization, and stability in beliefs can be applied to aggregates, the analogy with individuals must be treated with caution. Nonetheless, whether we deal with an individual or an aggregate of individuals, the chance that the actor will acquire a particular belief during a period of receptivity seems to depend on:

1. The amount to which the actor is exposed to the belief, which in turn
   a. requires that the belief has been formulated and diffused to the actor's environment; and
   b. depends on the amount of influence that the bearers of the belief exert on processes of socialization.
2. The relative prestige of the belief, which depends on
   a. the personal prestige of its advocates and antagonists; and
   b. the successes and failures of the people, organizations, and institutions that symbolize the belief.
3. The extent to which the new belief is consistent with the actor's perceptions of reality as these are shaped by

79. Abel, *The Nazi Movement,* pp. 172–74.

    a. the actor's present beliefs; and
    b. the actor's experiences.

This paradigm suggests several observations.

First, all of the conditions described in previous chapters that affect the chances for hegemony, public contestation, and polyarchy must do so by influencing beliefs via the connections listed above. Thus the historical path to the present taken by a country helps to determine the successes and failures that symbolize a belief, the relative prestige of that belief, and so the chance that it will be acquired by an individual who is exposed to it during a period of receptivity. Again, in a country with several distinct subcultures, members of a particular subculture acquire beliefs and experiences that help to shape their perceptions of reality and thus the acceptability of additional beliefs to which they may be exposed.

Second, while the conditions discussed in earlier chapters partly determine the extent to which activists are receptive to beliefs affirming the relative desirability of public contestation and participation, they do not fully determine the content of such beliefs. For example, no satisfactory explanation for polyarchy in India is possible, I think, that fails to take into account the peculiar impact of Anglo-American political ideas on Indian political elites during the critical period of national development preceding and following independence, an impact that came in part from the salient role of English norms in the political socialization of key leaders. Or again, the triumph of nazism in Germany is hard to explain without taking into account the independent effect of nazi ideology. Obviously there were other factors, but there is force in the argument of Theodore Abel that the importance of ideology "as a determinant is at least equal to that of the general discontent which existed at the time." [80]

Third, there are accidents and uncertainties both in the acquisition of beliefs and in the acquisition of power. To-

80. Ibid., p. 174.

gether, they enormously compound the difficulties of explanation. The preceding analysis reveals some of the sources of uncertainties in the process of acquiring *beliefs*. As to the acquisition of *power,* that process is, except to an insistent determinist, obviously full of accidental and uncertain elements.

When we say that an event is an "accident" we do not necessarily imply that it is without a cause. It does mean, however, that the theory with which we operate does not enable us to predict or explain such events. Our theory can only take them into account after they occur: it cannot subsume them under some more general law, hypothesis, or conjecture. To be sure, some kinds of accidents are subject to fairly accurate statistical prediction; they are, in this sense, "lawful." But many accidents are not: assassinations, for example. But even where statistical predictions are reasonably accurate, they may furnish little or no help to a theory that seeks to account for certain kinds of historical happenings in which "accident" plays a salient role.

Consider again the case of Lenin. Unless one assumes that his arrival in Russia in April 1917 had no effect on history, then history was subject to chance. What if the German government had not wanted him to return? Or if his train had been blown up? These accidental events—accidental because no theory makes them lawful, predictable events—would then have changed the course of history by whatever amount Lenin's presence in Russia after April 1917 changed the course of history. One must be a fanatical determinist, I think, to insist that there were no accidental elements in Lenin's acquisition of power.

Aside from the accidents (or nonaccidents) that affect the chances that a particular individual will gain power, highly uncertain trains of events may affect the chances for a whole regime. For example, unless one assumes that the course and outcome of the Second World War were completely determined, one must reckon with the possibility that polyarchal regimes would not have been imposed in Italy, Austria, Germany, and Japan, nor hegemonic regimes in Poland, Czechoslovakia, Hungary, and elsewhere. Suppose that the Axis powers had won the war? Or secured a negotiated peace? Or that the Soviet armies had not occupied Czechoslovakia?

When I try to take into account the complexities, uncertainties, and gaps in our understanding of the processes by which the politically influential acquire their beliefs and gain power, I am driven to two conclusions. Neither will seem the least bit surprising to anyone who already takes for granted the importance of "ideas" in history. Yet both conclusions run directly counter to the reductionism that prevails in much of contemporary social science:

> At present and for an indefinite future no explanatory theory can account satisfactorily for the beliefs of political activists and leaders.

> Consequently, just as any theory that attempts to account for variations in regimes in different countries must take as major independent variables such factors as the socioeconomic level of a country, the nature and extent of inequalities, the extent of subcultural cleavages, and other factors discussed in previous chapters, so too must such a theory, as a practical matter, treat the beliefs and "ideas" of political activists as a major independent variable.

9. FOREIGN CONTROL

The destiny of a country is never wholly in the hands of its own people. In some cases, domination imposed by people from outside the country can be so decisive as to override the effects of all the other conditions that have been discussed so far.

Every country exists in an environment that contains other countries. Under every regime, policy makers must take some account of the possible actions and reactions of policy makers in other states. In this sense even the most powerful states are in some degree limited by the influence, control, or power of other states. Moreover, most countries participate to some extent in a multinational economy; consequently policy makers usually take into account the actions and reactions of people outside their own country who may affect the local economy. Countries heavily dependent on international trade or foreign investments—often small countries —are particularly subject to the actions of foreigners.

Because the influence of the international environment on the development of hegemony or polyarchy is extremely complex, I wish to deal here with only one form of external influence, foreign domination. To distinguish that form more sharply, let me specify three ways in which the actions, reactions, or expected actions of foreigners may affect the chances of polyarchy or hegemony in a particular country.

First, the actions of foreigners may and almost certainly will have some impact on one or more of the conditions discussed in previous chapters. The beliefs of political activists, paths to the present, the level of socioeconomic development, the degree of economic concentration or dispersion, inequalities, even the extent of subcultural cleavages—all are open to influences by foreign actors.

Second, the actions of foreigners may drastically alter the options available to a regime without necessarily altering the form of the regime. As I have already said, existence in an international environment alters and reduces the options available to any regime in every country. However enormous is the might of world powers like the United States and the Soviet Union, neither can escape the consequences of actions by the other. For that matter, the power of these superpowers is limited not only by one another but by a great many other actors on the international scene. The day's news will invariably furnish any number of examples: the inability of the United States to defeat the forces of the National Liberation Front in Vietnam or of the Soviet Union to drive the Western powers out of Berlin, the difficulty of the major powers in agreeing on a plan for controlling nuclear weapons, etc., etc.

Nor are the effects of foreigners confined only to foreign affairs. In making decisions about domestic economic policies, American policy makers, for example, have had to consider the deficit in the balance of payments, the role of the dollar as an international currency, the impact on the American economy of currency devaluations, actual or threatened, by other countries, and so forth.

If the options of great powers are sometimes reduced by the actions of foreigners over whom they have little or no direct control, the situation is even more acute for countries with more limited power resources, such as small or less developed countries, particularly small *and* less developed countries. Thus where the postwar Labor government in

Britain did not shrink from nationalizing several major industries out of fears about the impact of nationalization on foreign investment, President Frei's Christian Democratic government in Chile had to consider the very real possibility that nationalization of the copper industry might drastically reduce foreign investments and access to world markets.

To the extent that the actions of foreigners reduce the options available to a country, the people lose the capacity to govern themselves. Nonetheless, a polyarchal regime might exist in a country whose options were narrowly constricted by the actions of foreigners. Indeed, internally the political system might be highly egalitarian, consensual, highly participatory, strongly protective of personal and political liberties, and thus highly "democratic" by the usual criteria. Yet the scope of "democracy" might be very narrow simply because so few alternatives were available. One thinks of the difference between a local government in a polyarchy and the Greek conception of the autonomous city-state: the political system of a small town in a modern country governed by a polyarchal regime may itself be a polyarchy, may even be highly "democratic," but the town has very little autonomy. The form of polyarchy is unchanged, but its content is drastically altered.

Third, people in one country may deliberately seek to use their resources to impose a particular kind of political regime on another country: outright foreign domination. They will probably affect the content of politics, too, but the point I wish to emphasize here is that by their actions foreigners may massively affect the chances for hegemony or polyarchy, pretty much independent from any of the conditions discussed in the previous chapters.

Each of these kinds of external influence would be an appropriate subject for an entire volume. Consider the first. To unravel all the ways in which the international environment significantly influences the conditions described in previous chapters would obviously be a major task, and I do not intend to undertake it here. The second kind of international influence is of great importance in the contemporary world, particularly for small countries. With increasing international integration, the Scandinavian countries, for example, will lose more and more of their autonomy. One can even foresee the time when they may be local or regional governments in a larger political system. But this topic is also too complex for adequate treatment in this book.

The third is probably the most directly relevant to the purposes of this book. For in estimating the chances for hegemony or polyarchy, it would obviously be important to know whether foreign powers were attempting to impose or intended to impose a particular regime. In the period immediately following the Second World War, a large number of European regimes were to some extent imposed: hegemonies in Eastern Europe, polyarchies in Germany, Austria, and Italy. A purely autonomous political development over a long period has never been possible in Czechoslovakia; local circumstances favorable to a competitive political regime have too often been overridden by outside domination. Much the same has been true in Poland.

The interaction between local conditions and foreign domination is complex. How is it that Finland is a polyarchy? A part of the Swedish realm for six centuries, a part of the Russian Empire (the Grand Duchy of Finland) from the Napoleonic Wars to the Russian Revolution, twice at war with the Soviet Union, first in 1939–40 and then from 1941 to 1944, twice defeated, a cobelligerent with Germany in the Second World War, how is it that this small nation of five million people exists as a polyarchy alongside a country with fifty times its population, a superpower ruled by a hegemonic regime? If the Russians had been prepared to pay the costs it hardly seems open to doubt that they could have imposed a hegemonic regime on Finland in 1944–45. If in the Soviet view the expected costs exceeded the expected gains, this was not only because the gains were lower than in Poland and

Czechoslovakia but perhaps partly because the Finns, long accustomed to living under a liberalized regime, could be counted on to make the costs high over the long run.

These examples suggest that concrete historical statements, or predictions based upon a particular configuration of international forces at a specific time, may be more fruitful than theoretical generalities about the interplay between foreign domination and polyarchy. Nonetheless, if we focus on overt rather than covert domination, and if we confine our attention exclusively to relatively direct consequences for polyarchy (and thus ruthlessly exclude from consideration a number of consequences that would be important from other points of view), it is possible to advance a few general statements that seem to be supported by the available evidence.

In the first place, a high proportion of the countries in which polyarchy existed in 1970 had been occupied or otherwise subject to foreign military intervention at least once since achieving independence. As table 9.1 indicates, among the older countries more polyarchies than nonpolyarchies have been subject to overt foreign military domination. As an inspection of table 9.2 will quickly reveal, the reason, of course, is that most European countries that were polyarchies in 1970 had been overrun and occupied as a result of the Second World War (one of these, Belgium, had also suffered the same fate during the First). However, it should also be kept in mind that four of these countries, though governed by polyarchies as of 1970, had been ruled by hegemonic regimes at the time of capitulation.

Second, it does not appear to be true, as is sometimes thought, that a period of overt foreign domination by a hegemonic power inevitably wreaks irreparable damage on a polyarchy. As tables 9.1 and 9.2 indicate, the damage certainly need not be fatal. In fact, a period of foreign domination may strengthen national unity, foster a climate of reconciliation among hostile groups, and speed the incorporation of strata struggling for more recognition and power.

Table 9.1. Occupation and Military Intervention,
Polyarchies and Nonpolyarchies

Political regime in 1970

Independence gained:	Polyarchy	Near-polyarchy	Non-polyarchy	Total
Before 1900				
Occupied or subject to military intervention at least once since independence	8	1	6	15
Never occupied or subject to military intervention since independence	7	3	22	32
1900–1945				
Occupied, etc.	3	—	5	8
Never occupied, etc.	5	—	7	12
Other				
After 1945				
Occupied, etc..	1	1⎫	51	⎫
Never occupied, etc.	5	1⎭		⎬59
Total N				126

Note: The basic data on independence and occupations are from Bruce M. Russett, J. David Singer, and Melvin Small, "National Political Units in the Twentieth Century: A Standardized List," *American Political Science Review* 62 (September 1968): 932–51. Under their classification "Dependent," they omit some overt military interventions of short duration (e.g., the USSR in Romania in 1944, the U.S. in Lebanon in 1958 and the Dominican Republic in 1965) and certain special cases (e.g., Italy, 1943–46) that I classify as occupation or military intervention. The classification of polyarchies, near-polyarchies, and nonpolyarchies is from appendix table A-3. A few micro-states are omitted.

In Belgium, the German invasion and occupation during the First World War brought Socialists into the government for the first time; they remained even after the war was over. The war also led directly to universal suffrage in Belgium. Under the old system of plural voting, as Lorwin writes,

Workers and peasants who had suffered in the trenches or in deportation could have cast one ballot each, while

Table 9.2. Independence among Present Polyarchies
and Near-Polyarchies

	Full polyarchies	Near-polyarchies
I. *Independent before 1900*		
A. Independence never interrupted by occupation or military intervention	Chile Costa Rica Sweden Switzerland United Kingdom United States Uruguay	Colombia Turkey Venezuela
B. Occupied or military intervention	Belgium Denmark France West Germany Italy Japan Luxembourg Netherlands	Dominican Republic
II. *Independence gained 1900–1945*		
A. Independence never interrupted	Australia Canada Iceland Ireland New Zealand	
B. Occupied or military intervention	Austria Finland Norway	
III. *Independent 1945 or later*		
A. Independence never interrupted	Jamaica Trinidad Israel India Philippines	Malaysia
B. Military intervention	Lebanon*	Cyprus

* At request of own government.

war profiteers could have cast two or three. Instead, the King and the government called the voters to the polls on a one man, one vote basis. The parliament they elected legitimized the change by constitutional amendment.

Lorwin goes on to describe the impact of the Second World War:

> If the First War marked the full acceptance of the Socialist Party, the Second marked that of the labor unions. Under the Nazi occupation, clandestine personal contacts among leaders of industry and Catholic, Socialist, and Liberal trade unions produced a "pact of social solidarity" of symbolic and practical importance. The pact was implemented after the Liberation by wide advances in social legislation and collective bargaining . . . Union and industry representatives came to exercise powers of administration in a number of quasi-public social welfare agencies.[1]

In the Netherlands, the first Socialist ministers came into the government in 1939 under the threat of nazism, and in that country, Belgium, and Norway, invasion and occupation also produced all-party governments-in-exile.

Needless to say, it would be utterly fatuous to draw the conclusion that overt foreign intervention is a good thing for a polyarchy. Even if one were to put to one side all the other costs, which have sometimes been enormous, not only is polyarchy superseded temporarily by hegemonic rule, but the longer-run consequences are by no means all beneficial. Some cleavages may be intensified. Lorwin writes that in Belgium during the Second World War "the Germans encouraged Flemish separatism, leaving a train of political booby traps for the Belgian nation after the war." [2] If reconciliation and national unity may sometimes facilitate the acceptance of hitherto excluded strata and greater generosity toward their demands, opposition leaders may be so fully drawn into coalition building that they unduly soften their

1. Val R. Lorwin, "Belgium: Religion, Class, and Language in National Politics," in Robert A. Dahl, ed., *Political Oppositions in Western Democracies* (New Haven: Yale University Press, 1966), pp. 158, 165.
2. Ibid., p. 161.

demands, leaving a legacy of relative inequalities and resentments as a cause of later crises.

Despite these qualifications one must not lose sight of the
simple proposition that overt foreign intervention is not necessarily fatal to an already existing polyarchy and may actually strengthen it in some respects.

In the third place, it is patently untrue that polyarchy has

Table 9.3. Polyarchy, Dependence, and Independence:
29 Present Polyarchies

Polyarchy or near-polyarchy inaugurated before independence	Polyarchy inaugurated after independence but during overt foreign domination	Polyarchy inaugurated "autonomously": after independence and not during overt foreign domination
Australia	Austria	Belgium
Canada	West Germany	Costa Rica
Iceland	Italy	Chile
India	Japan	Denmark
Jamaica		France
Lebanon		Israel
New Zealand		Luxembourg
Norway		Netherlands
Trinidad and Tobago		Sweden
Philippines		Switzerland
		United Kingdom
		Uruguay

Special cases:

Finland
Ireland
United States

come about only through strictly autonomous developments
within an already independent country. As table 9.3 indicates, of the 29 countries with polyarchal regimes in 1970,
in only 12 was polyarchy inaugurated after independence
and not during a period of overt foreign domination. In 4
countries, as we have seen, polyarchy was inaugurated during military occupation or intervention after the Second

World War. In addition, in 10 countries, including some
where polyarchy is now very deeply rooted, substantial
strides toward polyarchy were taken while the country was
at least nominally subject to a foreign power.

Fourth, foreign domination frequently produces a boomerang effect. There can hardly be any doubt that an important consequence of nazism among countries where polyarchy was temporarily set aside by the occupiers was temporarily to strengthen attachments to democratic ideas and
to increase hostility to the antidemocratic ideology of nazism.
There is good reason to think that the Soviet occupation of
Czechoslovakia has made many Czechs hostile to orthodox
Soviet Marxism and enhanced the attractiveness of at least
some aspects—especially the libertarian features—of polyarchy. The boomerang effect may radiate far beyond the
victims of intervention. The actions of the United States
in Guatemala, Cuba, Vietnam, and the Dominican Republic,
together with a widespread perception of the U.S. as economically aggressive and domineering, has probably helped
in many parts of the world to discredit the institutions of
polyarchy and belief in its capacity for social justice.

Fifth, the circumstances in which it was possible for polyarchy to be inaugurated during a period of overt dependence
(or to be preserved for subsequent revival) were historically
unusual and seem much less likely to reoccur in the fore-
seeable future. To see why this is so, consider the rather
schematic set of possibilities in table 9.4.

The first situation is roughly comparable to that of Belgium, Denmark, the Netherlands, Norway, and France un-

Table 9.4. Some Circumstances of Foreign Domination

In the country subject to domination:

The previous regime was:	The conditions favor:	The dominant country seeks to inaugurate:
1. Polyarchy	Polyarchy	Hegemony
2. Polyarchy	Hegemony	Hegemony
3. Hegemony	Polyarchy	Polyarchy
4. Hegemony	Hegemony	Polyarchy

der nazi domination. An important aspect of that domination was its comparatively short duration and limited scope. Most of the political leadership survived. Among the general population, the boomerang effect was powerful: nazism came to be widely loathed; hegemony was the rule of the enemy and occupier, the cause of defeat, privation, humiliation, suffering.

If there is good reason for thinking that in a country where it has existed for some time and the underlying conditions are favorable to it, polyarchy is likely to be rapidly restored after a relatively brief period of overt domination, the outcome is bound to be more uncertain if the period is long and the foreign power systematically wipes out everyone who holds democratic beliefs.

In the second situation envisaged in table 9.4, the restoration of polyarchy would be very much less likely. The foreign power would find it easier not only to impose a hegemonic regime but also to withdraw in due time from overt domination, leaving behind a hegemonic ally. By going native, the hegemony would accommodate itself to the spirit of nationalism. Although there are no clear-cut cases, Poland provides at least a partial example. A country with only the briefest interludes of near-polyarchy during the French Revolution and its aftermath, dominated and divided for a century thereafter by Russia and Prussia, Poland's latest experience with polyarchy had already terminated in presidential absolutism[3] before the country was overrun by the German and then Russian armies. Unlike the situation in the occupied countries of Western Europe, in Poland polyarchy is simply not there waiting to be revived, and the conditions for creating it anew are certainly far from favorable.

Turning now to situations in which the dominant power seeks to inaugurate polyarchy in a country where the previous regime has been hegemonic, the third case in table 9.4 pretty

3. The term is Gordon Skilling's: *The Governments of Communist East Europe* (New York: Crowell, 1966), p. 28.

clearly poses much less of a challenge than the fourth. Even if conditions were by no means wholly favorable for polyarchy in Austria, Germany, Italy, and Japan in the wake of the Second World War, on a comparative basis each was a prime candidate for polyarchy. Comparatively speaking, re-establishing polyarchy in these countries was an easy job. In fact, the very smoothness with which polyarchy was rein-augurated probably encouraged American policy makers to adopt simplistic and overoptimistic assumptions about the prospects of inaugurating polyarchy elsewhere, a delusion that was reinforced by the seeming success of American aid to Greece and Turkey beginning in 1947.

On a comparative basis practically all of the countries that have achieved independence since 1945 have highly unfavor-able conditions for polyarchy. Nonetheless, in 1970 Jamaica, Trinidad, India, the Philippines, and Lebanon were all gov-erned by polyarchal regimes, and Malaysia and Cyprus by near-polyarchies. Although it would be folly to predict much stability for these regimes, their existence does raise a ques-tion as to the circumstances under which foreign intervention may facilitate the development of polyarchy in a country where many of the conditions are highly unfavorable to it.

Several factors seem to have helped the development of polyarchy in these countries. For one thing, in all these coun-tries a substantial proportion of the political activists were predisposed to favor the institutions of polyarchy. In India, for example, in the years preceding independence there was an astonishing degree of agreement among leaders and ac-tivists on the proposition that India must be a democracy in the Western sense. As the last chapter has shown, to explain why the political activists of a country hold the beliefs they do during a particular historical period is highly complex. So complex is the process by which political activists acquire their beliefs that an outside power, particularly when it is itself a polyarchy, can have only limited success in generating support for a particular ideology; the foreign power is caught in a tough network of historical and cultural forces that frequently it can do very little to manipulate.

Moreover, in these countries prolonged and massive coercion was not employed by the foreign power against the subject population. Thus the boomerang effect was to some extent avoided. At any rate polyarchy was not discredited by association with the brutalities of a hated outside force. Thus it was possible in these countries for the rudimentary institutions of polyarchy or near-polyarchy to be introduced and to function over a period long enough for the political activists to acquire skill in operating them and a vested interest in maintaining them.

These were historically uncommon circumstances, and today they seem to be absent in most countries where the underlying conditions are unfavorable to polyarchy. The end of formal colonialism means that the outside power today must move into a nominally independent country where nationalism is probably strong and the boomerang effect is likely to be powerful. A substantial proportion of political activists are likely to favor a hegemonic regime of some sort. Public contestation, which may allow deadly enemies to enhance their following, will seem to be a luxury at best, at worst downright pernicious. Even if the outside power intervenes at the behest of the local government, it will be invited in precisely because that government cannot, unaided, put down its opponents. Thus the outside power is drawn into massive coercion . . .

10. THE THEORY: SUMMARY AND QUALIFICATIONS

If the argument of the previous chapters is correct, then the chance that a country will be governed at the national level for any considerable period of time by a regime in which opportunities for public contestation are available to the great bulk of the population (that is, a polyarchy) depends on at least seven sets of complex conditions. These are summarized in table 10.1, which necessarily ignores the subtleties and qualifications in the argument.

In principle it would be possible—and as better data become available no doubt it will be possible—to rank the various countries of the world according to these variables. For the sake of exposition let us suppose that countries were ranked in deciles. If about one country in five is governed by a polyarchy, we should expect that in the 1960s and 1970s a very high proportion of the countries in the upper deciles would be polyarchies and negligible proportions in the last two or three deciles. Thus a country with a profile like that of A in figure 10.1 would almost certainly be a polyarchy, and probably a typical polyarchy would have a profile rather like that of A. Conversely, one would predict with complete confidence that a country with a profile like B would not be a polyarchy; very likely it would be a hegemony. Doubtless too, most countries with profiles like that

Table 10.1. Conditions Favoring Polyarchy

	Most favorable to polyarchy	Least favorable to polyarchy
I. Historical sequences	Competition precedes inclusiveness	Inclusiveness precedes competition Shortcut: from closed hegemony to inclusive polyarchy
II. The socioeconomic order:		
A. Access to		
1. Violence	Dispersed or neutralized	Monopolized
2. Socioeconomic sanctions	Dispersed or neutralized	Monopolized
B. Type of economy		
1. Agrarian	Free farmers	Traditional peasant
2. Commercial-industrial	Decentralized direction	Centralized direction
III. The level of socioeconomic development	High: GNP per capita over about $700–800	Low: GNP per capita under about $100–200
IV. Equalities and inequalities		
1. Objective	Low, or Parity and dispersed inequalities	High: Cumulative and extreme
2. Subjective: relative deprivation	Low or decreasing	High or increasing
V. Subcultural pluralism		
1. Amount	Low	High
2. If marked or high	None a majority None regional None indefinitely out of government Mutual guarantees	One a majority Some regional Some permanently in opposition No mutual guarantees
VI. Domination by a foreign power	Weak or temporary	Strong and persistent
VII. Beliefs of political activists		
1. Institutions of polyarchy are legitimate	yes	no
2. Only unilateral authority is legitimate	no	yes
3. Polyarchy is effective in solving major problems	yes	no
4. Trust in others	high	low
5. Political relationships are:		
strictly competitive	no	yes
strictly cooperative	no	yes
cooperative-competitive	yes	no
6. Compromise necessary and desirable	yes	no

of C in figure 10.2 would be polyarchies, and most polyarchies would have a profile like A or C or some combination of the two. Again, a country with a profile like D would
almost certainly not be a polyarchy, and probably a high
proportion of countries like B and D, or some combination
of B and D, would be hegemonies.

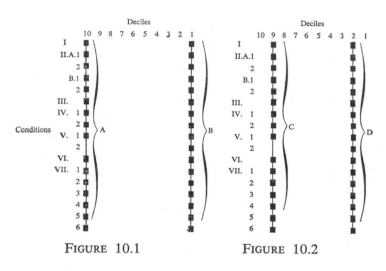

FIGURE 10.1   FIGURE 10.2

The analysis in previous chapters suggests, however, that
we would have a number of important deviant cases with
profiles very different from these. Thus some polyarchies
would not be in the upper deciles on all variables; the outstanding exception would surely be India, which would probably fall in the lower deciles on conditions IV and V, and
(because of the traditional peasant society in which about
80 percent of the Indians live) fairly low on condition III.
India's profile might look something like that in figure 10.3.
Moreover, some hegemonies would be very high on one or
more characteristics; East Germany, for example, would
rank high on both IV and VI, and perhaps fairly high on
V; it might be approximately like that shown in figure 10.4.

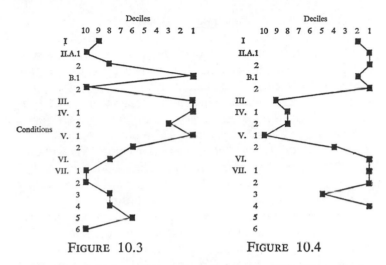

FIGURE 10.3   FIGURE 10.4

Denmark might be characterized by figure 10.5; although the shortcut from a traditional hegemony to a polyarchy should have caused difficulties, all the other factors are highly favorable. As a final illustration, Argentina would perhaps look like figure 10.6.

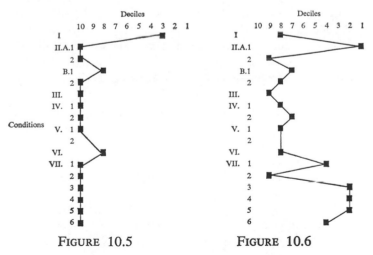

FIGURE 10.5   FIGURE 10.6

Some Qualifications

Why are these profiles, the reader may enquire, allowed to stand as hypothetical or, better, impressionistic representations of the data? In fact, why have I not tested the theory by actually undertaking the rankings that would provide an actual profile for every counry or at least for a sufficiently large number of countries to provide a moderately good test of the theory? The answer points directly to one of the severe limitations of the theory: I have not done so because, given the kinds of data now available, the results would, I believe, be misleading and illusory. To be sure, it is possible to find satisfactory data on some of the variables —notably on the level of socioeconomic development. No doubt one reason why so much attention has been given to the relationship between regime and socioeconomic level is simply that reasonably acceptable (if by no means wholly satisfactory) "hard" data are available from which to construct indicators. This is a perfect example of how the availability of data may bias the emphasis of theory. As I indicated in chapter 5, to focus on socioeconomic levels exaggerates the importance of this factor and obscures the importance of others. For example, data on objective and subjective inequalities are very poor, and as I indicated in chapter 8, only the most fragmentary comparative information is available on the beliefs of political activists in various countries, particularly in countries with hegemonic regimes. The poverty of data may well be overcome in the next several years as a result of various studies now under way. Meanwhile, to construct profiles for a large number of countries would, I think, lend a spurious validity to a theoretical exploration that necessarily rests at present on a rather modest foundation of data.

The weaknesses in the data impose another serious limitation having to do with the formulation of the theory itself: I have made no attempt to assign weights to the various explanatory variables. Clearly this is a matter of great theoretical (and practical) significance, and it cannot be gainsaid that the defect is a grave one. Once again, it would be possible and indeed easy to create a mask in order to put a strong face on a slack-jawed theory. It is tempting, for example, to interpret the theory as a multiple regression equation. But in the absence of satisfactory data from which to construct the predictor variables, the values of the constants would be fictitious. The sophisticated reader would know that we had remained where we had started out, while the innocent reader might be deceived into believing that the theory is more precise than in fact it can be.

11. POSTSCRIPT: SOME IMPLICATIONS FOR STRATEGIES OF CHANGE

To the extent that I have been able to answer it, the last chapter completes the answer to the question posed at the end of the first chapter. The book really ends there.

Yet the argument of the book seems to me to have some implications for strategies of change. Although the problem of how to transform hegemonies into polyarchies would be a whole subject by itself, it may be useful to tease out of the general argument a few conclusions, general as they may be, that are more directly relevant to action.

One can hardly reflect on the various conditions that seem to account for differences in regimes without concluding that a country that has had little or no experience with the institutions of public contestation and political competition and lacks a tradition of toleration toward political oppositions is most unlikely to turn into a stable polyarchy in the space of a few years. It is also true that countries with a long history of toleration, competitive politics, and broad participation rarely turn into hegemonies.

It is unrealistic to suppose, then, that there will be any dramatic change in the number of polyarchies within a generation or two. Some hegemonic regimes may be transformed into mixed regimes, some nearly-hegemonic mixed regimes may become near-polyarchies, and some near-polyarchies may become polyarchies. Doubtless, too, there will be some movement in the opposite direction, but short of extensive conquest by imperialistic hegemonies the number of polyarchies is unlikely to diminish much. As with a great many things, the safest bet about a country's regime a generation from now is that it will be somewhat different, but not radically different, from what it is today.

This view of regimes is sobering, perhaps, and some readers may feel that it is unduly pessimistic. It is far removed, certainly, from the boundless optimism of much democratic thought, particularly among Americans. Yet it is worth recalling that the Age of the Democratic Revolution, as Palmer has called the last third of the eighteenth century, ended without any enduring "democracies"—or, in the language of this book, polyarchies—except in the United States. Even in the United States, it is no great exaggeration to say that what is called the American Revolution only legitimized or, in some cases, speeded up a bit the processes of democratization that had already been taking place in the colonies, processes that were by no means completed by the end of the struggle for independence. I am not arguing that the revolutionary movements had no long-run effects, nor that these effects were unimportant or undesirable; in the long run the revolutionary movements of the eighteenth century helped to create some of the conditions for polyarchy, particularly in the matter of beliefs and the dispersion of inequalities. But they failed pretty completely in their major objective, which was to achieve lasting representative republics based upon popular suffrage—that is, polyarchies. The revolutions that swept over Europe in May 1848 also had long-run consequences, but they too failed to build durable polyarchies.

Implications for Foreign Assistance

It follows that policy makers in a country like the United States who may wish to transform the government of another country from a hegemony or mixed regime into a polyarchy face formidable and complex problems, not the least of which is our lack of knowledge about the long causal chain running from outside help to internal conditions to changes of regime.

The most promising situation would exist in a country where the seven sets of conditions described earlier produce a highly favorable profile (for example, a country like C in figure 10.2), but where for some reason an unpopular dictatorship has imposed itself on the country. In spite of the illusions of some American policy makers and publicists, countries like this are a statistical rarity. The least promising situation would exist in a country where the seven sets of conditions produced a decidedly unfavorable profile. This, of course, is precisely the case in a preponderant share of the countries that most desperately need economic aid.

If the most promising situation is rare and the least promising commonplace, it is nonetheless true that some countries have a mixed profile—more favorable for polyarchy in some respects, less favorable in others. Radically different as they are in many ways, Argentina, Cuba, Czechoslovakia, Greece, Yugoslavia, Spain, and Taiwan illustrate the point.

It is worth asking, therefore, how policy makers in, say, the United States might facilitate the transformation of countries like these into polyarchies. There appear to be three main strategies: (1) to invade and occupy the country, forcibly displace the government and replace it with a polyarchy, and then protect the new government as long as may be required; (2) to support democratic—that is, revolutionary —movements within the country, with funds, weapons, or other resources; (3) to support the existing government with funds, weapons, or other resources and bring pressure on it to change.

The first strategy has had a few striking successes and many failures. In the form of colonial domination and tutelage over a lengthy period, it has helped to create polyarchy in India, the Philippines, Jamaica, and Puerto Rico. Military defeat followed by occupation and the restoration of polyarchy helped to create polyarchies in Italy, Germany, Austria, and Japan. Over against these successes there is a long string of failures. The revolutionary governments established with the aid of the French in the later stages of the French Revolution all collapsed. Though many of the new ex-colonial countries began their independence in recent decades with an experiment in polyarchy, the number now governed by dictatorships far exceeds the number governed by polyarchies. Moreover, the first strategy has probably been rendered obsolete by developments since World War II. Colonialism in its classic form of direct domination has all but disappeared, while "neo-colonialism" in the form of economic and political penetration of nominally independent and sovereign countries has not so far been conducive to the establishment of polyarchy. Attempts to establish polyarchy by direct military intervention of the kind following the defeat of the Axis dictatorships in World War II may prove to be, and one devoutly hopes will be, historically unique. The tragedy of Vietnam has demonstrated how illusory is the belief that the United States can on its own volition establish polyarchy in another country by force.

For a great many reasons the second strategy also runs a high risk of failure. The government of one country attempting to involve itself in the revolutionary political movements of another is likely to be clumsy, inept, ignorant, politically insensitive, and trapped against its will in the factional disputes of the revolutionaries. In particular, to suppose that the American government could skillfully manage such complex relationships is, since the disaster of the Bay of Pigs, highly implausible. Then, too, in dealing with revolutionaries, dictatorships have most of the advantages in resources. It is not too much to say that if revolutionary forces within the country have the popular base necessary for a polyarchy, they do not need much outside support, and if they do not have a popular base then no amount of outside support short of outright invasion and occupation (and not necessarily even that) will enable them to build a polyarchy. Then, too, throughout most of the world democratic movements are no longer revolutionary, and nowadays revolutionary movements are rarely democratic. On the contrary, in much of the world, where the profile of conditions is highly unfavorable to polyarchy, revolutionaries who overthrow a hegemonic regime are very likely to replace it with another. That the new hegemony may be better or worse than the old is highly relevant in judging the desirability of revolutionary action, but it is irrelevant to the success of the second strategy. Finally, only a new government willing to pay the price of hostile relationships with regimes different from its own is likely to find the strategy acceptable. Even governments that emerge out of a revolution tend to abandon the strategy because of the advantages of stabilizing their relationships with other countries, irrespective of regime. Needless to say, governments of well-established polyarchies are unlikely to risk much in behalf of revolutionaries; no country came to the aid of the Hungarian revolution in 1954 or the Czechs in 1968.

The third strategy has no more prospect of success than the others. It is one thing to aid a beleagured polyarchy to survive, as in India, Israel, or Chile. But it is quite another to aid a hegemonic or mixed regime on the assumption that aid can be used as a lever for transforming the regime. Dictators and oligarchs are not easily beguiled by foreign assistance into destroying their own regimes. In this respect, whatever the long-run effects may be on the conditions for polyarchy in various countries, as a strategy for transforming

nonpolyarchies into polyarchies the American foreign aid
program must be adjudged a total failure. So far as I am
aware, it has not a single such success to its credit.

Suppose then that in a country governed by a polyarchy
the political leaders, activists, or citizens in general wish to
advance the prospects for polyarchy in other countries. What
can they do? In particular, what about economic and technical aid provided with the cooperation of the country in need
of assistance?

It is important to distinguish among the grounds on which
economic and technical aid might be given. In the first place,
a powerful case can be made entirely on moral and humanitarian grounds. In addition to altruistic considerations, a
powerful case can also be made that over the long run it is
in the rational self-interest of the wealthy to eradicate misery,
frustration, and suffering among the poor, that any well-off
country should provide assistance to any less well-off country where the aid would be used for the reduction of misery.
If assistance were rendered on these grounds, the nature,
ideology, and foreign policies of the regime would be irrelevant. And unless international organizations proved to be
less efficient in allocating and administering funds, there
would be no reason why aid should not be administered by
international or multilateral organizations rather than purely
national ones.

Second, no doubt something of a case can also be made
(in the end it is perhaps a special instance of the arguments
on moral and humanitarian grounds or from self-interest)
that in the very long run socioeconomic development facili-
tates polyarchy. But for the reasons discussed in earlier
chapters, the socioeconomic level of a country is only one
of a number of variables bearing on the chances of polyarchy, and the relationship between the one and the other
is very far from simple, direct, or well understood. Because
of the tenuous, uncertain, and long-run nature of this relationship, assistance on these grounds to any particular coun-

try that is not already close to a full polyarchy is a gamble with a highly uncertain payoff. It may be reasonable to demand that citizens of the most affluent polyarchies should undertake the gamble. But given the enormous uncertainties in the lengthy causal running chain from assistance to polyarchy, with rare exceptions it would be virtually impossible to show that assistance to underdeveloped country X is more likely to lead eventually to polyarchy than assistance to underdeveloped country Y. Once again, the conclusion seems to follow that aid should be granted on the basis of a country's need and capacity to use it, without regard to the nature or ideology of the regime. And here, too, there is no self-evident reason for channeling aid through a national agency rather than through international organizations.

Third, a strong case can be made on moral grounds that citizens of affluent polyarchies should provide assistance if it is requested by the government of a needy country that has already established a polyarchy or even a near-polyarchy that is close to arriving at a comparatively high degree of liberalization and participation.

Finally, then, there is the question of providing economic, technical, or military assistance to specific hegemonic or mixed regimes on the assumption that these kinds of aid will bring about a transformation of the regime into a polyarchy, or something very close to it. The whole burden of this book, I believe, argues against the rationality of such a policy. For the process of transformation is too complex and too poorly understood to justify it. The failure of the American foreign aid program to produce any transformations of this kind over two decades gives additional weight to this negative conclusion.

It would be a serious misinterpretation, however, to read this argument as an objection to economic and technical aid. On the contrary, there is every reason, I believe, why the wealthy countries should allocate a substantial part of their increasingly fabulous riches to reduce misery and suffering in poorer countries. But the justification for such action is morality and compassion, or rational self-interest, and not the prospect that outside assistance can be used as a lever to pry democratization and liberalization out of a hegemonic regime.

Implications for Political Action

Suppose, now, that we look at the problem from the perspective of someone within the country. Assume that a hypothetical Innovator in a country governed by a hegemonic or mixed regime wishes among other things to lower the barriers to effective participation and political oppositions—wishes, that is, to move the country closer if not necessarily all the way to full polyarchy. What if anything does the analysis contained in the previous chapters offer our Innovator?

Virtually nothing, certainly, in the way of advice about how to acquire the power needed for political innovation in the context of a specific personal, national, and historical situation: whether to seek reform or revolution, to work within, alongside, outside, or against the existing regime, to acquire and use power as a member of the governing class or as clandestine member of a conspiratorial opposition, etc. But beyond these crucial tactical problems of acquiring the necessary power for change, there are questions of strategic objectives, of the specific ways in which power, once acquired, can be used in order to move closer to polyarchy in a particular country. As always, tactics and strategy cannot be sharply separated; in principle, strategic objectives should govern the choice of tactics, and yet the choice of tactics may prove decisive in the achievement of objectives.

Even if the argument of this book is unhelpful for matters of tactics, it does, I think, have some implications for strategy that may be useful for our Innovator. Let me now suggest several of these.

Taking Stock

Suppose the Innovator begins simply by taking stock. Perhaps the most obvious conclusion he might draw from the preceding chapters is that in any given country at any given time, the possibilities are limited. In some countries, a wise and even courageous citizen might simply throw up his hands in despair and await the further unfolding of history until the moment became more propitious for his endeavors.

Enthusiastic democrats will doubtless say that such a statement is excessively pessimistic. But I believe that more lasting harm has been done to the prospects of democracy by ignoring the odds than by facing them squarely. Surely the political events of this century have fully vindicated the older view that democracy is not bound to triumph irresistibly over all the obstacles placed in its path by the history and current condition of a people.

Yet nothing in the preceding pages endorses a mindless pessimism nor, certainly, the bias, so common among Americans, which holds that representative democracy requires a unique conjunction of exceptionally rare conditions such as only a few peoples, like the Americans themselves, are fortunate enough to be endowed with. For what stands out sharply in a world perspective is the variety of circumstances in which polyarchies, if I may revert to that term once again, are operating today.

In sum: according to the view presented here and supported at least in a modest way by the evidence available to me, the extent to which the opponents of a government have an opportunity to contest the conduct of that government is chancy but not accidental. And if the prospects for oppositions are mainly determined by factors beyond their immediate control, the degree of freedom oppositions enjoy can sometimes be altered by deliberate human choice.

The preceding chapters have emphasized seven kinds of

factors which by their variation may favor either polyarchy or hegemony. To repeat, if the Innovator lives in a country where all seven elements favor political competition, the chances for a polyarchy are of course very high, even if not a sure thing. If he lives in a country where all the elements favor hegemony, then the chances for a competitive regime, and particularly for an inclusive polyarchy, are naturally very low, while chances for a hegemonic regime are very high.

In his choice of tactics and strategic objectives, the Innovator must of course consider the profile of his country and the limitations and possibilities it suggests. In a country with a highly favorable profile and considerable experience with competitive politics under a mixed regime it would be reasonable to work for changes that would allow the operation of a full polyarchy. In a country with a highly unfavorable profile, the immediate introduction of a full polyarchy would be a utopian objective; for even if the existing hegemony were overturned or fell into dissolution and thus enabled a group of innovators to adopt a constitution prescribing the institutions of polyarchy, that constitution could hardly be expected to be effective, and the institutions it prescribed would be empty or ephemeral. Yet even in a situation so depressing for the democrat, an Innovator might bring about certain changes that would permit greater participation and contestation and thus over a much longer period increase the prospects for polyarchy.

Mutual guarantees

Opponents in a conflict cannot be expected to tolerate one another if one of them believes that toleration of another will lead to his own destruction or severe suffering. Toleration is more likely to be extended and to endure only among groups which are not expected to damage one another severely. Thus the costs of toleration can be lowered by effective mutual guarantees against destruction, extreme coercion, or severe damage. Hence a strategy of liberalization requires a search for such guarantees.

The prescription stresses the search rather than the specifics, since in each country the problem is so different that it would be foolish to offer a general solution. The first steps toward liberalization in a hitherto highly hegemonic regime are bound to be different from the next steps in a quasi-hegemony. In a full hegemony the first step may be nothing more or less than some kind of understanding that in conflicts within the ruling groups the losers will not be punished by death or imprisonment, exile, or total destitution. In this respect the change in the USSR from Stalin's hegemony to the post-Stalinist system was a profound step toward liberalization.

As we have already seen, among polyarchies the nature and explicitness of the guarantee to potential antagonists vary widely; in highly homogeneous countries explicit arrangements are less important than in countries with deep subcultural cleavages, where constitutional and institutional structures may be required to give adequate security to the subcultures. What is more, the cleavages and the institutions for managing them are rarely static: in India the state boundaries were redrawn from 1956 onward to conform more closely to major linguistic boundaries; in the Netherlands, *verzuiling* is very far from an unchanging phenomenon, and since it was identified it has been declining. What is persistent in the Netherlands or in the very different system of Switzerland, what is a cornerstone of the developing system of regional (state) governments in India, what has been evolving with the Walloons and Flemish in Belgium, and what is increasingly demanded by French Canada is a system of mutual guarantees that provide security to major subcultures.

In a country with subcultural cleavages and a hegemonic

regime, the Innovator who seeks to liberalize the system also confronts the problem of mutual guarantees. In their moves toward liberalization in 1968, before the Soviet invasion and occupation, the leaders of the one-party hegemonic regime in Czechoslovakia had endorsed the idea of a federal system that would allow the two territorial and linguistic groups—the Czechs and Slovaks—each to have its own province within the nation. Moreover, a proposed new constitution for the ruling Communist party would have met the problem of subcultural pluralism not only by reorganizing the party along federal lines but also by a provision for a mutual veto over certain decisions taken by the Central Committee. While decisions of the Central Committee would ordinarily be taken by majority vote, decisions concerning "the existence, sovereignty, or superior national or territorial interests" would have to be approved by at least half of the representatives of each subculture in the Central Committee, each group voting separately. Since the Slovaks composed only about 18 percent of the party members, in effect the opposition of slightly more than 9 percent of the party could, in principle, block a decision of this kind.[1] Thus the Czechs and Slovaks appeared to be moving toward a "consociational" solution to the problem of protecting a subcultural minority in a system intended to be much less hegemonic and more responsive to popular pressures.

As in polyarchies, the closer a country approaches a system of mutual veto the more it runs the risk of *immobilisme*. The risk of *immobilisme* is the price a country with potentially hostile subcultures pays for tolerating the political expression of its cleavages. In many countries, obviously, those who opt for or against liberalization are not prepared to pay the price. Yet in the long run the price may be lower than it first appears. For the experience of some "consociational" countries shows that a system of mutual guarantees can

1. See the report by Michel Tatu in *Le Monde* (Sélection Hebdomadaire, August, 8–14, 1968), pp. 1, 4.

gradually reduce the fears and hostilities of the subgroups, help to generate a broader and deeper support for the institutions of participation and public contestation, strengthen a sense of common nationhood, and in time allow the political energies absorbed in subcultural conflicts to be channeled to the other important problems of the society.

Executive authority

When barriers to public contestation and participation are lowered, interests and demands will appear which the government has hitherto ignored. If public contestation and participation are to be effective, the authority of political institutions responsive to these new interests and demands must be increased. But to reduce the likelihood of immobilism and deadlock, the executive must retain a considerable measure of power for rapid and decisive action, especially in emergencies. Thus the executive must have authority that in a realistic sense is beyond the capacities of transitory majorities in parliament to curtail and yet not beyond the reach of influence of substantial and persistent coalitions, whether minorities or majorities.

This prescription, which is necessarily vague, directs the Innovator's attention to what has invariably been one of the most formidable problems of constitution makers who are trying to develop a competitive political system. The formulation above is an extremely general statement of the problem and the solution—or rather the direction in which a solution must be sought. The most familiar special case of this problem in representative governments is of course the classic question of the relations between executive and legislature. Operating with a theory of representative democracy that emphasized the exclusive legitimacy of the elected assembly as the supreme representative of the people's will, nineteenth-century constitution makers found it difficult to provide for an executive with independent sources of authority. In this century, however, most polyarchies have rejected as unworkable the model of assembly government with a weak, subordinate executive; in practice governments in polyarchies and especially their executives have been armed with very great powers for vigorous and decisive action. It is now all too clear that any attempt to emulate assembly government is likely to lead to disaster and, in time, a clamor for the rapid creation of hegemonic controls.

In a general way, then, the movement in polyarchies has been from a dependent executive to what is de facto if not de jure an independent executive. The problem for our Innovator is exactly the opposite. Political leaders who are too independent must be made more dependent for their authority on political institutions responsive to a variety of interests and demands. The ancient and recurring lesson from hegemonies is that too much independence is oppressive. The lesson of polyarchies is that too little independence can lead to governments so ineffectual as to stimulate support for hegemonic rule.

It is doubtful whether the strategic objective can be formulated much more precisely than these very general remarks. Given the enormous variations from country to country, a more detailed strategy would obviously have to be formulated to fit the situation of a particular country.[2]

Preventing fragmentation

> *Since the costs of toleration are raised by excessive fragmentation into competing political parties, a strategy of liberalization requires a search for a party system that avoids a great multiplication of parties.*

2. An attempt to do exactly this for Argentina is contained in an article, "Del gobierno revolucionario al orden constitucional," *Criterio* 61 (Buenos Aires, June 13, 1958): 371–75. Although I had not seen the article when I first wrote this chapter with its recommended strategies, there is sufficient similarity to reassure me that the strategies recommended here are in fact relevant for at least some countries.

The Innovator must consider with very great care the probable pattern of cleavages that might emerge under various kinds and degrees of liberalization. In a highly homogeneous country, one could give serious consideration to the specific institutional and constitutional changes that might ultimately produce a political system roughly on the model of the classic two-party parliamentary system—a kind of idealized version of the British system. But in all likelihood the Innovator's country is not sufficiently homogeneous to enable the classic two-party parliamentary model to work. The chances are that his country contains a number of fairly distinctive and potentially antagonistic subcultures—regional, linguistic, religious, racial, ethnic; for high homogeneity is, as we have seen, a rare phenomenon, while subcultural cleavages are relatively commonplace. And wherever there are extensive subcultural cleavages, the classic two-party parliamentary model simply cannot be achieved—witness Canada, South Africa, India, Belgium, the Netherlands, Switzerland, and Lebanon.

The chances are, then, that our citizen will have to keep in view a very different model. It is probably unfortunate, and indeed it may be disastrous, that both the model of assembly government and the classic two-party parliamentary model have been widely regarded as ideal forms of representative democracy, from which all deviations are a sign of defect. For just as the assembly model has been rejected by practically all polyarchies in the twentieth century, so the classic two-party parliamentary model cannot be successfully adopted in countries with subcultural cleavages, that is, in most countries. Yet the prestige of these models is high, and alternative systems that have been developed to cope with the problem of severe subcultural cleavages are little understood, slighted in writings on representative government, and downgraded as second-best substitutes for the real thing. But most countries cannot move toward liberalization, and certainly not toward the degree of liberalization that exists in a polyarchy, except by one of these second-best substitutes that in some countries have contributed to an extraordinary degree of peaceful toleration of diverse and often conflicting subcultures.

Because of the way in which party systems have evolved in the theory and practice of representative democracy, they are often thought of as "natural" institutions that develop spontaneously and faithfully mirror the "natural" cleavages of the society. According to this view of parties, deliberate attempts to relate and control the nature and number of parties in a polyarchy are either doomed to failure or must violate the democratic rules of the game. Neither of these assumptions seems to me to be valid. The first has become increasingly suspect as the relations between various election arrangements and party systems have been carefully explored. The exact nature of these relations is still subject to dispute, but the most systematic analysis to date establishes among other propositions that:

1. All election systems tend to award to larger parties a share of seats in the legislature larger than their share of the votes—and hence to smaller parties a smaller share of seats than votes.
2. The degree of divergence is a function of electoral formula and the size of districts.
3. The maximum divergence results from elections in single-member districts, and the maximum proportionality from P.R. with a large number of seats in each district allocated according to the formula of the "largest remainder." [3]

The party system, then, is not a natural, spontaneous, or inevitable mirroring of social cleavages. It is dependent to some degree on electoral arrangements. And these can be deliberately manipulated in order to maximize or minimize

3. Douglas Rae, *The Political Consequences of Electoral Laws* (New Haven: Yale University Press, 1967), pp. 134–40.

fragmentation. The manipulation of electoral procedure has of course been discredited because governments have sometimes used it to benefit their own party or coalition at the expense of an opposition, but since electoral procedures are one of the few aspects of a political system subject to more or less deliberate alteration, to reject this possibility of social engineering seems to me equivalent to the medical profession refusing to use antibiotics because they have been so widely abused.[4]

Aside from purely partisan manipulation, it is difficult to see why the deliberate attempt to reduce potential fragmentation through electoral engineering is inherently "undemocratic," or, even if it were, undesirable in a liberalizing hegemony. During a century of debate no one has ever satisfactorily demonstrated whether P.R. is more "democratic" than plurality elections in single-member districts or less. The difficulty of any demonstration seems to lie in the fact that all democratic schemes for arriving at a majority vote require formal and informal processes of great complexity for scheduling alternatives and aggregating preferences, and thus finally reaching a decision on a pair of alternatives remaining to policy makers. The institutions in which scheduling and aggregation take place vary in different polyarchies. In any particular country, a two-party system with highly unified parties would require much more aggregation and reconciliation of different interests and preferences to take place within each party than would be the case in a two-party system with heterogeneous parties and shifting legislative coalitions. A two-party system with heterogeneous parties probably would require more aggregation within each party than would a multiparty system, where more aggregation would occur in legislative and cabinet coalitions.

4. A point on which I concur with Giovanni Sartori, "European Political Parties: The Case of Polarized Pluralism," in *Political Parties and Political Development,* ed. Joseph LaPalombara and Myron Weiner (Princeton: Princeton University Press, 1966), pp. 165–66.

Finally, if the country had three or four significant parties more aggregation would have to take place within each party, and correspondingly less in legislative and cabinet coalitions, than if the country had five or six significant parties. It is difficult to see how one of these systems would be more "democratic" than another, unless it insured a more equal weighting of individual preferences in the final choice (including preferences for a satisfactory but not necessarily most preferred outcome). And this has not been demonstrated.

In any case, whether one or the other electoral and party system is more "democratic" is virtually irrelevant to the problem of liberalization of a hegemonic regime. It would be absurd to argue for a strategy of liberalization requiring electoral arrangements and a party system thought to be perfectly democratic if these would lead predictably to high political fragmentation, rapid disillusionment with the game of party politics, and renewed support for stronger hegemonic controls in order to eliminate political fragmentation.

A hegemonic regime taking its first steps toward a plural party system may find it desirable to regulate the number of parties even more directly, by making it difficult—or in the extreme case impossible—to form more than two parties, a government party and an opposition party.

Whether in any given country the number of parties optimal for the expression and aggregation of preferences is two, three, four, or more cannot be answered even approximately without examining the cleavage system of the particular country. Thus a strategy of liberalization might erect barriers to party formation and competition that would effectively limit the number of parties to two, three, four, or conceivably even more. The important point, however, is that in a rational strategy of liberalization the number of parties can and should be regulated. In principle, provided at least two parties exist, to regulate the number of parties is independent of the regulation of freedom of dissent, criticism, and opposition in elec-

tions and legislation. A government might grant the fullest
freedom for dissent, criticism, and opposition in elections
and legislation, and yet restrict the number of competing
parties to two, each with equal opportunities to state its views,
propose candidates, gain votes, and win elections.

Local governments

*Since somewhat autonomous representative institutions
below the national level can provide opportunities for
the opposition to acquire political resources, help to generate cross-cutting cleavages, and facilitate training in
the arts of resolving conflicts and managing representative governments, a strategy of toleration requires a
search for ways of developing subnational representative
governments.*

In a hegemonic regime—particularly, perhaps, in a unified hegemony—it may be prudent to take bigger steps
toward liberalization at lower levels before these are introduced at higher levels, and particularly at the national level.
For example, allowing oppositions to expand their participation in municipal elections may help to socialize both the
opposition and the government. Smaller representative units
provide training in solving concrete, comprehensible problems
for which abstract ideological solutions are less relevant.
Confronting these problems may unite groups that would be
antagonistic in national political life. Moreover, extending
opposition rights and privileges at subordinate levels is likely
to be less threatening to the incumbent national leadership
since it can be treated as a trial; if the trial "fails," the step
can be reversed.

Perhaps the most noteworthy example of subnational
representative governments is Yugoslavia, where not only in
local governments but in the more famous case of workers'
control a very large measure of autonomy has been extended;
and while organized political opposition remains rather re-

stricted in the factory and in the municipality, these units evidently do provide a widely diffused training in the arts of participating in representative institutions, in discussion, debate, conciliation, compromise, concrete analysis, responsibility. In Mexico, the eventual shift from a highly pluralistic hegemony to a polyarchy may well come about slowly and not too painfully as the opposition wins an increasing number of victories at the local level and takes on the always sobering responsibility of governing.

Unless one is prepared to dismiss the experience of polyarchies as irrelevant to the ways in which hegemonies might be liberalized, then one ought not to be overly surprised to realize, as the attentive reader will have done by now, that the main elements in the strategy of liberalization that I have suggested—mutual security among conflicting groups, a strong and vigorous executive dependent on institutions responsive to a variety of interests and demands, an integrating rather than a fragmentary party system, and representative governments at subnational levels—are all familiar aspects of the most durable representative democracies.

APPENDIXES

APPENDIX A

114 Countries Classified According to Eligibility to Participate in Elections and Degree of Opportunity for Public Opposition

Table A-1 displays 114 countries classified according to the opportunity of adult citizens to vote in elections and ranked according to the opportunities available to political oppositions to compete for popular support and public office.

These two "dimensions" correspond approximately to the two dimensions of polyarchy described in chapter 1. The classification of the 114 countries according to eligibility to participate in elections was done by Richard Norling in 1969, but changes since the end of 1968 were not included. The ranking of the countries according to the degree of opportunity for public contestation was done by Mary Frase Williams and Richard Norling. It may be useful to describe the procedures they used.

The Variables

The hunch that underlies an enterprise of this kind is that there may be an underlying, hypothetical continuum that extends from the greatest to the least opportunity for oppositions, as described in chapter 1, and that countries can be

By Robert A. Dahl, Richard Norling, and Mary Frase Williams.

Table A-1. 114 Countries Ranked by Opportunities to Participate
in National Elections and to Oppose the Government, circa 1969

Opportunities for political oppositions: scale types	Elections not held	Percent of adult citizens eligible to vote			Unascertained, uncertain, or transitional[a]	N
		Under 20%	20–90%	Over 90%		
Greatest opportunity 1			Switzerland	Belgium Denmark Finland Luxembourg Netherlands Norway Sweden		8
3[b]			Chile United States	Iceland Israel		4
4				Ireland Italy United Kingdom	Cyprus Dominican Republic	5
5				Australia Austria Canada West German Federal Republic Japan New Zealand Philippines Uruguay		8
6				France Lebanon	Turkey	3
7				India Jamaica Trinidad and Tobago		3
8				Costa Rica	Malaysia	2
9			Ecuador	Colombia Venezuela	Guatemala Honduras	5

Table A-1 (*continued*)

Opportunities for political oppositions: scale types	Elections not held	Percent of adult citizens eligible to vote			Unascertained, uncertain, or transitional[a]	N
		Under 20%	20–90%	Over 90%		
10					Uganda	1
11				(Bolivia)[c] [France][d]		
12					(Libya)[c]	1
13					Morocco	1
14		South Africa			Ceylon Malagasy Republic Mexico	4
15				El Salvador		1
16				Nicaragua		1
17					(Somali Republic)[c]	1
18				Mauritania		1
19			Brazil	Ruwanda		2
20	Peru		Jordan	Paraguay	Iran South Korea Laos Pakistan	7
22[b]	Argentina Burma			Liberia	Ivory Coast	4
23	Indonesia			Algeria Tunisia		3
24				Burundi Cameroun Chad Gabon		4
25	Dahomey		Sudan	Congo (Brazz) Mali Niger Tanzania	Afghanistan	7
26	Central Af. Rep. Ghana Greece		South Vietnam	Ethiopia Guinea Haiti Poland	Cambodia	15

Table A-1 (*continued*)

Opportunities for political oppositions: scale types	Elections not held	Percent of adult citizens eligible to vote			Unascertained, uncertain, or transitional[a]	N
		Under 20%	20–90%	Over 90%		
	Nepal Panama Sierra Leone Taiwan Thailand United Ar. Rep.					
27	Syria			Senegal Soviet Union Spain Yugoslavia	Portugal	6
28	Upper Volta			Czechoslovakia Hungary		3
29				Albania Bulgaria East Germany Mongolia Romania North Vietnam	China North Korea	8
	30 Cuba					
Least opportunity	31 Nigeria Saudi Arabia Togo Yemen					4
Totals	21	1	8	61	23	(114)

[a] Includes countries where a constitutional government or elections have been superseded or nullified at least once since 1960, the constitution has been suspended, a state of siege declared, or massive civil violence has occurred.

[b] No countries were found in scale types 2 and 21.

[c] Countries in parentheses have had a coup d'état, resulting in military rule, since the classification above.

[d] See text for discussion of the case of France.

located along this continuum. This assumption is illustrated
with purely hypothetical countries in figure A-1. The initial
problem, then, is to determine whether it is reasonable to
assume that such a continuum actually exists and whether the
available data will enable one to rank countries along it. In
practice, a scalogram analysis of the kind used to produce
table A-1 requires that both tasks be carried out together.

The first need is to find variables that will accomplish this,
that is, serve as valid indicators of the underlying continuum
—in this case the "degree of opportunity for public contesta-

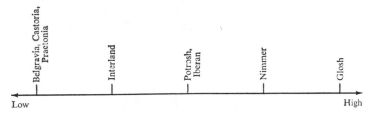

FIGURE A-1. A Hypothetical Continuum of
"Opposition Opportunity"

tion" or political oppositions—and for which adequate data
are available. The solution adopted here was to employ as
indicators of the seven required conditions described in
chapter 1 certain variables from Arthur S. Banks and Robert
B. Textor's *A Cross-Polity Survey,* which sought to classify
115 countries on 57 characteristics as of about 1960–62.[1]

The following required condition:	*Is indicated by the following variables:*
1. Freedom to form and join organizations	Freedom of group opposition [#30][2] Interest articulation by asociational groups [#33]

1. Cambridge: M.I.T. Press, 1963.
2. Number in brackets is the number of the variable in Banks and
Textor.

2. Freedom of expression   Freedom of the press [#13]

3. Right to vote   Representative character of current regime [#28][3]

    Current electoral system [#29]

4. Right of political leaders to compete for support   Interest articulation by political parties [#37]

    Party System: Quantitative [#41]

    Freedom of group opposition [#30]

    Current electoral system [#29]

5. Alternative sources of information   Freedom of group opposition

    Freedom of the press

    Representative character of current regime

    Party system: Quantitative

6. Free and fair elections   Freedom of group opposition

    Freedom of the press

    Representative character of current regimes[3]

    Current electoral systems

    Party system: Quantitative

7. Institutions for making government policies depend on votes and other expressions of preference   Constitutional status of present regime [#26]

    Interest aggregation by legislature [#40]

    Horizontal power distribution [#48]

    Current status of legislature [#50]

Mrs. Williams found that these eleven characteristics did form a satisfactory scale and was able to place 102 countries in 27 scale types. However, because the data in *A Cross-Polity Survey* had been gathered during 1960–62 and resulted in some obvious misclassifications as of 1969, in that year

3. Later abandoned, for reasons described below.

Richard Norling, using the Yale Political Data program and a number of standard sources,[4] attempted to bring the data up to date. He also developed the data for a new variable, the opportunity to participate in national elections, which became the basis for the four-fold classification of countries shown in table A-1. It was then decided to drop, as redundant, one of the eleven variables from the *Cross-Polity Survey* (#28, Representative character of current regime). Hence the scale for opportunities for political oppositions in table A-1 is based on only ten of the eleven variables listed above. The variables are shown in table A-2, with the number and percentage of countries in each category.

Weighting

Since there was no a priori or theoretical reason for weighting the variables unequally or assigning a greater weight to one category than another, the variables were all handled the same way. Since the underlying attribute in which we are interested is the opportunities available to oppositions, the alternatives within each of the ten variables were ordered from the greatest to the least opportunity. The alternative that provides the greatest opportunity was given a score of 1, the next greatest a score of 2, etc.[5] The total score for each country was obtained by summing the scores for the individual criteria for that country.

4. T. E. Smith, *Elections in Developing Countries* (New York: St. Martin's Press, 1960), *Canada Yearbook, Statesman's Yearbook, The New York Times, Christian Science Monitor,* and Carolyn K. Colwell, Foreign Affairs Division, Legislative Reference Service, Library of Congress, "The Independent Nations of Africa: Leaders-Elections-Parties-Population-Electorates," August 8, 1968.
5. For every question a number of countries were coded as unascertained, unascertainable, ambiguous, and irrelevant. These answers were excluded from the analysis and every country that had such answers for more than five of the variables was also excluded from the analysis.

Table A-2. Variables Used as Indicators
of Opportunities for Oppositions

%	N	Var. #[a]	Variable description and categories

13. Degree of freedom of the press

38	40		1. Complete (no censorship or governmental control of either domestic press or foreign correspondents)
18	19		2. Intermittent (occasional or selective censorship of either domestic press or foreign correspondents)
26	27		3. Internally absent (strict domestic censorship. No restraint on foreign newsgathering, or selective cable-head censorship)
18	19		4. Internally and externally absent (strict direct or indirect censorship or control, domestic and foreign)
100%	105		
	2		7. Unascertainable
	7		9. Unascertained

26. Constitutional status of current regime

48	53		1. Constitutional (government conducted with reference to recognized constitutional norms)
34	37		2. Authoritarian (no effective constitutional limitation, or fairly regular recourse to extraconstitutional powers. Arbitrary exercise of power confined largely to the political sector)
18	20		3. Totalitarian (no effective constitutional limitation. Broad exercise of power by the regime in both political and social spheres)
100%	110		
	1		7. Unascertainable
	3		9. Unascertained

29. Current electoral system

44	47		1. Competitive (no party ban, or ban on extremist or extraconstitutional parties only)
4	4		2. Partially competitive (one party with 85 percent or more of legislative seats)
33	35		3. Noncompetitive (single-list voting, or no elected opposition)
19	20		4. No elections (elections not usually held, or suspended by regime in power)
100%	106		
	2		7. Unascertainable
	6		8. Ambiguous

30. Degree of freedom of group opposition

| 40 | 41 | | 1. Autonomous groups free to enter politics and able to oppose government (save for extremist groups, where banned) |

Table A-2 (*continued*)

%	N	Var. #[a]	Variable description and categories
19	19		2. Autonomous groups free to organize in politics, but limited in capacity to oppose government (includes absorption of actual or potential opposition leadership into government)
31	32		3. Autonomous groups tolerated informally and outside politics
10	10		4. No genuinely autonomous groups tolerated
100%	102		
	10		7. Unascertainable
	2		8. Ambiguous
		33.	Interest articulation by associational groups
17	19		1. Significant
12	13		2. Moderate
26	29		3. Limited
45	49		4. Negligible
100%	110		
	1		7. Unascertainable
	3		8. Ambiguous
		37.	Interest articulation by political parties
17	17		1. Significant
22	22		2. Moderate
13	13		3. Limited
48	47		4. Negligible
100%	99		
	10		7. Unascertainable
	5		8. Ambiguous
		40.	Interest aggregation by legislature
12	12		1. Significant
16	16		2. Moderate
13	13		3. Limited
59	59		4. Negligible
100%	100		
	8		7. Unascertainable
	6		8. Ambiguous
		41.	Party system—quantitative
25	25		1. Multiparty (coalition or minority party government normally mandatory if parliamentary system)
12	12		2. Two-party or effectively two-party (reasonable expectation of party rotation)
6	6		3. One-and-a-half-party (opposition significant, but unable to win majority)
14	14		4. One party dominant (opposition, but numerically ineffective at national level. Includes minority par-

Table A-2 (*continued*)

%	N	Var. #[a]	Variable description and categories
			ticipation in government while retaining party identity for electoral purposes)
34	35		5. One party (all others nonexistent, banned, nonparticipant, or adjuncts of dominant party in electoral activity. Includes "National Fronts" and one-party electoral systems)
10	10		6. No parties, or all parties illegal or ineffective
100%	102		
	8		7. Unascertainable
	4		8. Ambiguous
		48.	Horizontal power distribution
29	32		1. Significant (effective allocation of power to functionally autonomous legislative, executive, and judicial organs)
20	23		2. Limited (one branch of government without genuine functional autonomy, or two branches with limited functional autonomy)
51	57		3. Negligible (complete dominance of government by one branch or by extragovernmental agency)
100%	112		
	1		7. Unascertainable
	1		9. Unascertained
		50.	Current status of legislature
26	28		1. Fully effective (performs normal legislative function as reasonably "coequal" branch of national government)
15	16		2. Partially effective (tendency toward domination by executive or otherwise partially limited in effective exercise of legislative function)
22	24		3. Largely ineffective (virtually complete domination by executive or by one-party or dominant party organization)
36	39		4. Wholly ineffective (restricted to consultative or "rubber stamp" legislative function, or no legislature)
100%	107		
	7		7. Unascertainable

Source: Arthur S. Banks and Robert B. Textor, *A Cross-Polity Survey* (Cambridge: M.I.T. Press, 1963), updated to 1968 and recoded.
[a] These numbers are those assigned to the variable by Banks and Textor.

Determining the Scale Types

For each variable, a frequency distribution was obtained (table A-2). You will note that the number of countries that could be classified varied somewhat from one variable to another; consequently the percentages are based on different numbers.

A crucial assumption is that each of the ten variables covers the entire underlying continuum and that this continuum can be divided into various segments that correspond to the categories. On the basis of the information available, it is impossible to determine how the various categories divide the hypothetical continuum into segments. However, we can obtain other information that will serve the same purpose. To do so, we assume that every country is located somewhere along the underlying continuum; that each criterion divides the continuum into segments and the countries into subgroups; and that the frequency distributions reflect the way the questions subdivide the countries.

N variables with a total of m categories will normally cut the underlying continuum into $(m - n + 1)$ segments. With 10 variables subdivided into a total of 40 categories, presumably there are $(40 - 10 + 1) = 31$ scale patterns. The 31 perfect scale types were ultimately reduced to 29 because no countries were found to fit scale types 2 and 21.

Classification of Nonscale Types

Once the perfect scale types have been established, the next step is to assign every subject to a scale type before we can assess how well the data conform to the hypothetical scale. This requires procedures for assigning countries with patterns that represent nonscale types. There are two alternative procedures. One is to assign each country to the perfect scale type that has the same total score. The other alternative is to assign each nonscale type to the type it most closely resembles, that is, to the scale pattern that will minimize the number of errors.[6] Unfortunately the second procedure does

6. An error is said to occur when a country is placed in a category of one of the variables where it would not be predicted to belong simply on the basis of the rank or scale type of the subject.

not yield unambiguous results, since there may be more than one perfect scale type that will result in the same (and minimum) number of errors. If this happens, then auxiliary criteria must be used to assign the subject to one of these types.

Assignment on the basis of total scores is easier and yields unambiguous results, but it is an unsatisfactory procedure for our data since so many of the countries have no information for at least one question. This means that the raw total score cannot be used to assign subjects to scale patterns. Instead the total score must be standardized in some way to take account of the number of criteria that go into making up that score. However, this solution—a standardized total score—proved unsatisfactory for two reasons: (1) the standardized score depended heavily on the identity of the missing question(s) and (2) it resulted in a larger number of scaling errors than the minimum error method. For these reasons, nonscale types were assigned according to the criterion of minimum error.

Accuracy of Fit

The coefficient of reproducibility (Rep) is the criterion commonly used to determine whether the data approximate a perfect scale well enough to treat the data as if it were a perfect scale.

$$Rep = \frac{\text{total number of responses} - \text{number of errors}}{\text{total number of responses}}$$

Thus Rep is the percentage of responses that coincide with the scale pattern to which the subject has been assigned.

The total number of errors under the minimum error method was 180. The value of Rep is therefore 0.829 compared with an expected value of 0.443. While this is somewhat lower than one would like, it suggests that the ten variables form a moderately satisfactory scale.[7]

A Word of Caution by R.A.D.

In considering the rankings, one should remember that many of the variables on which the rankings are based necessarily require decisions based on judgments rather than "hard" data. This is true of the original data from Banks and Textor as well as the revisions and reclassifications made by Richard Norling. Judgments of this kind may be biased by many things, including the simple fact that a great deal more is known about some countries than others. There are several ways of coping with missing data, but no solution is entirely satisfactory.

Whether for reasons of this kind or because of inaedquacies in my choice of the variables, the scalograms resulted in a few anomalies. The most obvious was the location of France, and a brief discussion of the case of France may serve as a useful example and caution on the use of the tables. In both Mrs. Williams' scalogram based on Banks and Textor and in Mr. Norling's revision, France appeared in the same scale pattern as Bolivia. One does not need to be biased in favor of France to conclude that France was badly misplaced. For even before the coup in 1969, Bolivia was hardly a polyarchy, while oppositions in France enjoyed a very high level of opportunity to contest the government. Looking into the details, it turns out that France failed to gain high marks from Banks and Textor on a large proportion of the indicators: #13, Freedom of the Press (intermittent); #37, Interest Articulation by Political Parties (moderate); #41, Party System: Quantitative (one party dominant); #48, Horizontal Power Distribution (limited); and #50, current Status of Legislature (partially effective). It seems clear to me that

7. When Mrs. Williams used all eleven characteristics on 102 countries, the coefficient of reproducibility was 0.881.

standards were applied with considerably more severity to France than to Bolivia and many other countries.

It may be helpful if we look at several of these classifications with the hindsight of 1970. In 1962, Banks and Textor classified France as a country where freedom of the press (#13) was intermittent, along with such countries as Bolivia, Brazil, Burma, Congo, Laos, South Africa, Syria, and Turkey. The higher category, where freedom of the press is "significant," included some 43 countries, among them the Dominican Republic, Panama, and a number of African countries now ruled by a single party. One may well wonder whether freedom of the press in France is not considerably more "significant" and much less "intermittent" than in countries such as these.

Similarly, France was classified as "limited" in "interest aggregation by the legislature" (#40), along with countries such as Bolivia, Brazil, Guatemala, Honduras, Libya, Nicaragua, etc. Finally, with considerable justification as of 1962, France's party system was classified as "one party dominant" along with Bolivia, Mexico, Paraguay, and Vietnam, and others. While tendencies toward one-party dominance doubtless seemed strong in 1962, by 1969 it was becoming clear that France no longer quite fitted the definition of "one party dominant" given by Banks and Textor: "opposition, but numerically ineffective at the national level." Although France may not precisely fit the remaining categories, its party system might be classified with greater justification as "one-and-a-half party," defined as "opposition significant, but unable to win a majority."

Consider what the effects of these changes in classification would be. If France were now classified on the basis of its new total score, it would fall with India, Jamaica, and Trinidad-Tobago. Classified by the minimum error method used in table A-1, it falls in type 6, with Lebanon and Turkey.

Although Mrs. Williams and Mr. Norling were, quite properly, unwilling to substitute their judgment on France for

those of the experts used for *A Cross-Polity Survey,* I am less
reluctant to do so. It is true that once the process of second
guessing the classification begins—except on the basis of actual changes in the political system or the appearance of new
data—it would be hard to know where to stop. And to "ad-
just" all the cases that seem out of line would undermine one's
confidence in the validity of the whole process. Nonetheless,
since France appears to me to be markedly more misclassified
than any other country in Table A-1, it is shown in type 6
and also, in brackets, in type 11. Its dual location will perhaps serve as a visible warning against taking the ranking in
table A-1 as if it had been engraved in stone by the hand of
God. Doubtless there are other errors. Nonetheless, the ranking is, I believe, useful. The time may not be far off when
criteria of the kind used here, or better and more appropriate
criteria, will yield improved rankings that can be an ordinary
part of the current store of information as readily available to
social scientists as data on, say, GNP, which also must be
taken *cum grano salis.* If and when the country profiles discussed in chapter 10 are also available, we shall be in a better
position to test generalizations about the conditions for polyarchy.

APPENDIX B

Contemporary Polyarchies, circa 1969

Using table A-1, it is possible to construct a list of polyarchies as of about 1969. As a cut-off point, I have chosen scale type 8. All countries in column 4 in scale types 1–8 are included, a total of 25 countries. The three special cases are:

1. In Chile, a literacy requirement excluded a substantial percentage of the population until the 1960s. Increasing literacy and perhaps some relaxation in the enforcement of the requirement have led to such a rapid diminution of the unenfranchised minority that Chile may by 1970 have entered the ranks of the fully inclusive polyarchies.
2. Switzerland does not have universal female suffrage in national elections.
3. In the United States, Negroes were systematically deprived of the franchise in much of the South until after the passage of the Civil Rights Act of 1964. (For percentages of whites and blacks registered to vote in Southern states in 1968, see footnote 3, chap. 2.) Although the total percentage of the population excluded was never more than 10% (by 1950 less than 7%), the fact that it was a particular

and sharply deprived minority greatly increased the discriminatory nature of the exclusion. Residency requirements reduced the electorate even further.

The list of contemporary polyarchies in table A-3 is almost identical with the list of 31 "contemporary democratic systems" provided by Rustow (table A-4). Rustow's table includes all countries which at the beginning of 1967 had regimes based on three or more consecutive, popular, and competitive elections. The four discrepancies are italicized. They include Greece, where as Rustow notes constitutional government was overturned by a military dictatorship in April 1967; Mexico and Ceylon, which because of restraints on opportunities for oppositions in the 1960s falls into scale type 14 in table A-1; and Colombia, which I have classified as a near-polyarchy. Moreover, my list (table A-3) includes two countries omitted from Rustow's list (Jamaica and Trinidad-Tobago) because they had not yet held three popular elections since their independence in 1962. Both lists omit several microstates that would doubtless qualify as polyarchies.

The list of near-polyarchies includes four countries in scale types 1–8 that are listed in column 5 because during the 1960s the processes of polyarchy were at some point massively interrupted by civil violence, repression, or military intervention. The list also includes Colombia and Venezuela, where despite sporadic violence the institutions of polyarchy emerged rather fully during the 1960s. Throughout this period Colombia was operating under a constitutional amendment (due to expire in 1975) that imposed limitations on party competition in elections. In all of the near-polyarchies, the emergent institutions of polyarchy were still so fragile that it was uncertain how long they would bear the strains of internal conflict.

Table A-3. Polyarchies and Near-Polyarchies, circa 1969

Fully inclusive polyarchies

1. Australia
2. Austria
3. Belgium
4. Canada
5. Costa Rica
6. Denmark
7. Federal Republic of Germany
8. Finland
9. France
10. Iceland
11. India
12. Ireland
13. Israel
14. Italy
15. Jamaica
16. Japan
17. Lebanon
18. Luxembourg
19. Netherlands
20. New Zealand
21. Norway
22. Philippines
23. Sweden
24. Trinidad and Tobago
25. United Kingdom
26. Uruguay

Special cases: Electoral restrictions

27. Chile
28. Switzerland
29. United States

Near-polyarchies

1. Colombia
2. Cyprus
3. Dominican Republic
4. Malaysia
5. Turkey
6. Venezuela

Table A-4. Contemporary Democratic Systems

Country	Continuous popular elections since
1. United States	1788
2. Norway	1814
3. Belgium	1831
4. United Kingdom	1832
5. Netherlands	1848
6. Switzerland	1848
7. New Zealand	1852
8. Denmark	1855
9. Sweden	1866
10. Canada	1867
11. Iceland	1874
12. Luxembourg	1868
13. Australia	1900
14. Finland	1906
15. *Mexico*	1920
16. Ireland	1921
17. Lebanon	1926
18. *Ceylon*	1931
19. Chile	1932
20. Uruguay	1942
21. Austria	1945
22. France	1946
23. *Greece*	1946
24. Italy	1946
25. Japan	1946
26. Philippines	1946
27. Israel	1949
28. West Germany	1949
29. Costa Rica	1949
30. India	1952
31. *Colombia*	1958

Note: This list is from Dankwart A. Rustow, *A World of Nations: Problems of Political Modernization* (Washington, D.C.: Brookings, 1967), table 5, pp. 290–91. I have included only one of the fourteen columns in his table. Other columns include data on participation, party changes, and constitutional continuity. Countries in italics are omitted from the list of polyarchies in appendix table A-3.

INDEX

Abel, Theodore, quoted, 147, 185, 186
Activists, political (*see* chap. 8): beliefs of, and regime change, 125–29; Great Man and, 126; preference of, for hegemony, 201. *See also* Beliefs, political
Africa: one-party regimes in, as desirable, 30; cleavage and two-party system, 222
Agrarian society: propensity for hegemony, 53–54; and equality, 82–83; effect of industrialization on, 85–86, 92
Algeria, as French failure, 123
Almond, Gabriel A., quoted, 145
American Revolution, impact of, in Europe, 172–73, 209
Amhara. *See* Ethiopia
Argentina: politicized military in, 50; socioeconomic level in, 69; labor force of, in agriculture, 85; failure of party system in, 123; legitimacy of dictatorship in, 130; development of suffrage in, 133–34; failure of polyarchy in, 135–41 passim; political exclusion of immigrants in, 138; mixed profile of, 205, 210. *See also* Peron, Peronism

Aristotle: cited, 81; on importance of early training, 167
Armed forces, role of, politicized, 50
Athens (Athenian democracy): agrarian society, 72; inequalities in, 81; as dual polyarchy, 93; importance of early training in, 167; weakened beliefs in, 185; city-state system in, 191
Attenuation, process of, 101–02
Australia: socioeconomic level in 70; as preindustrial polyarchy, 71; literacy and socioeconomic level in, 75
Austria: demise of regime in, 105; *Proporz* in, 118; polyarchy imposed in, 192; polyarchy reestablished in, 200, 211
Authority, beliefs and attitudes, 140–44 passim

Banfield, E. C., quoted, 163–64
Banks, Arthur S., quoted, 109–10
Barber, James D., quoted, 179–80
Belgium: polarization in, 107, 111, 113, 218, 222; polyarchy sustained in, 113; foreign domination not fatal to, 193, 198–